Million Dollar Mistakes

Steering Your Music Career Clear of Lies, Cons, Catastrophes, and Landmines

Million Dollar Mistakes

Steering your Music Career Clear of Lies, Cons, Catastrophes, and Landmines

By Moses Avalon

Backbeat
Books

San Francisco

Published by Backbeat Books
600 Harrison Street, San Francisco, CA 94107
www.backbeatbooks.com
email: books@musicplayer.com

An imprint of the Music Player Network
Publishers of *Guitar Player, Bass Player, Keyboard, EQ*, and other magazines
United Entertainment Media Inc.
A CMP Information company

CMP
United Business Media

Distributed to the book trade in the U.S. and Canada by
Publishers Group West, P.O. Box 8843, Emeryville, CA 94662
Distributed to the music trade in the U.S. and Canada by
Hal Leonard Publishing, P.O. Box 13819, Milwaukee, WI 53213

Text and cover design: Richard Leeds — BigWigDesign.com
Composition: Michael Baughan

Library of Congress Cataloging-in-Publication Data

Avalon, Moses, 1962-
Million dollar mistakes : steering your music career clear of lies, cons,
catastrophes, and landmines / by Moses Avalon.
    p. cm.
ISBN-13: 978-0-87930-827-8
ISBN-10: 0-87930-827-3 (pbk. : alk. paper)
 1. Music—Vocational guidance. I. Title.

ML3795.A92 2005
780.23—dc22

                           2005028836

Printed in the United States of America

01 02 03 04 05   5 4 3 2 1

Selling the Dream

In 1981, a naive singer, acting on advice from his lawyer, sold the rights to two chart-busting songs for about $1,000. The songs, "Girls on Film" and "Rio," kept the group **Duran Duran,** at the top of the charts for 118 weeks. How did the songwriter get so badly duped?

In 1995, a San Francisco entrepreneur proposed something novel to major labels: a "virtual record store" accessible via the Internet. He wanted *no money*, just a license to use their music so he could develop his concept. They tossed him out. Several years later, labels were forced to spend many millions to catch up to the download sales bonanza. How could they be so dumb?

It's been said that the wise man learns from his mistakes. Perhaps. But learning from *other* people's mistakes is far more fun.

There are more than 100 books that claim to teach you how to be successful in the music business. Few of them will live up to their promise. But there is no book like this one. Here the focus is on catastrophes, the things people left *off* their résumés, the *real* secrets of success—which are actually the *hidden failures* and what was learned from them. They're here, taught firsthand by the producers and executives who developed big name acts. Specifically:

Michael Jackson, Christina Aguilera, the **Beatles, Shawn Colvin, Courtney Love, Madonna, Nickelback, Twisted Sister**, **Meredith Brooks, Dead Kennedys, Suzanne Vega, Chaka Khan, Debbie Gibson, Destiny's Child, Jackson Browne, Bob Dylan, Color Me Badd, Michael McDonald, Chick Corea, Stanley Clarke**, the **Go-Go's, Joan Osborne, Kurt Cobain, Paul Stanley, The Captain & Tennille, Jessica Simpson, Aerosmith, Pink, Ricky Martin, Dido, B.B. King**, the **Rolling Stones**, and literally dozens more.[1]

[1] A list of who does the discussing and who they worked with is in the appendix: *Who We Are Hearing From*.

Anyone interested in this business needs to remember this: big record labels, publishing companies, and billion dollar music entities like ASCAP and BMI bolster their image by selling the glamour of the business itself. This attracts new talent and keeps the machinery fed. There is nothing wrong with this per se, but in the process the dark side is often swept under a rug—the blunders that can cost careers, mortgages, and fortunes. This info is kept hidden by the insiders. Until today.

In the next 250 pages we'll go behind closed doors of over $1 billion dollars' worth of mistakes made in the modern music industry, as well as some common but lesser-known mistakes that seven out of ten people make when starting out. Some are so sensitive that people like this next anonymous insider, who is a veteran label exec, would only speak off the record:

> *Deep Gloat*: Here's the big secret. These big [record] executives don't know any more than the next guy. **Jessica Simpson** was almost dropped just before she sold five million records. **Ricky Martin**'s label didn't want to spend $15,000 to fix his video, after they already spent over $150,000. So MTV wouldn't play it. How dumb is that? The biggest mistake an artist can make is believing that anyone in a position of *power* really knows anything! The industry right now is in need of repair. It is a great time for somebody new because you don't have to follow the rules of an old, failing system.

Some may ask why I chose to anthologize failure. Here's the reason: being in the entertainment business means putting our livelihoods at risk almost every day, and things don't seem so insane when you realize that successful people, while clawing their way to the top, often made the same mistakes many of us have.

Michelangelo[2] had a unique approach to this same dynamic. He told his students that to correctly carve an angel out of marble you don't try to carve an angel. Instead, you simply chip away everything that is *not* the angel. Likewise, we cannot create a recipe for success—for if it were possible, we would all be baking the same cake and those 100 other books on the music biz would all have the same instructions—but we can create a map that exposes the landmines between you and your objectives. It's then your job to step around them.

In my first book I told you what record companies don't want the public to know about how they operate. In *Million Dollar Mistakes* we're going much deeper. The people I've interviewed (and I) are going to tell what the *entire industry* keeps hidden.

Buckle up!

[2] Michelangelo: Painted the ceiling of the Sistine Chapel in the Vatican. The story goes that the Pope blackmailed him into taking the job; otherwise he would reveal that the artist fancied very young boys.

> Who the Hell Am I?

My complete bio is in the appendix of this book along with the others who have contributed, so I won't take up your time by repeating myself here. I am an ex-record producer/engineer/composer who looked around the music business in the mid-1990s and said, there must be a better way for things to work than this. I quit producing and wrote a tell-all book called *Confessions of a Record Producer: How to Survive the Scams and Shams of the Music Business*. The book's success suggested to me that there was a niche in the business of music for someone who tackles the harder issues that many avoid. I became an artist's rights advocate, lecturer, and pundit.

Despite working with several Grammy Award–winning artists and receiving several platinum records from the RIAA, I am not nor was I ever a producer of magnitude like Quincy Jones or Phil Spector prior to writing *Confessions*. However, the book's candor has inspired many others to speak out about the way things work in the business of music. It's been quoted in legal briefs, in scores of magazines, and by significant artists who have used it as a sounding board for their grievances. Since then more than 30 books with similar themes have been published. Clearly there is a need for such a point of view in print.

In 2003 the Senate Judiciary Subcommittee in Sacramento, California, formed a special tribunal to investigate recording industry practices. I was consulted and gave advice for this panel. This led to a now famous hearing on the issues and resulted in new legislation that will protect artists' revenue from being taken by their record companies.

This is only the beginning. Things are changing rapidly in this business and I am just thankful to have contributed to this renaissance in a meaningful way. I am also happy to have you as my reader. I thank you in advance for letting me take you on this tour.

> How to Use This Book

If you peruse the table of contents you'll see there are two types of chapters: those that deal with business issues, like contracts and copyrights, and those that deal with more interpersonal issues, like dysfunctional personalities, arrogance, getting fired, and so on. It is important that you understand that although I did my best to arrange the chapters so that the book has a flow to it, the truth is that the chapters can be read in any order you wish.

Likewise, the sections within each chapter can be read in any order. I have tried to group things together by issue. However, if you read the entire book, you'll notice that many issues overlap the book's various themes and sometimes defy categorization.

What I did try to do is make it so that someone with *no music business experience* can appreciate the articles and those who are well versed will not be bored with didactic explanations of the business's rudiments. And this leads me to the footnotes.

A Word About the Footnotes

DON'T SKIP THEM. The footnotes contain some of the most entertaining information in this book. They have mistakes celebrities made, definitions of industry jargon, and also act as cross-referencing tool to other areas of the book that have similar or related information. So check them out. However, be warned: they are not carefully researched "facts." I am not the *New York Times* or *60 Minutes*. (Although these days that is not much of an endorsement.) I don't have a full-time research staff. The footnotes came from personal knowledge, knowledge from the sources I interviewed, and information that is publicly available on the Internet. Read them, and have a good laugh, but don't worship them.

⊝ Disclaimers

First of all, nothing, and I really mean *nothing*, in this book should be taken as legal advice. Even though many comments in here are by extremely knowledgeable and reputable attorneys, one must remember that attorneys also love to hear themselves talk and often talk outside the areas of their expertise when they're feeling loose. I did my best to make them feel so.

Ready? Had enough introduction? Good. Let's enter this crazy world. Turn the page now.

—*Moses Avalon*

TABLE OF CONTENTS

Chapter 3: Arrogance and Logic **55**

Believing your own hype can have some intriguing side effects. Examples and stories about getting cocky and its effects on a career.

Chapter 4: Strictly for D'Cash: Brainwashed by the Business **73**

Examples of what can go wrong and what pitfalls to consider when taking jobs just because they are offering big bucks.

Chapter 5: Friendly Firings **89**

Even though your best friend gives you that big break, he'll likely fire you for the same reason. How nepotism and the old-boy network can work for and against you. How the cliché of assembling a "good team" needs more clarification.

    Publishing is the key to most of the big money in the music business. Scenarios and real-life examples of lost opportunities and blunders caused by a misunderstanding of how publishing works.

    Stories of the tricky balancing act needed when having a family and navigating a career in the music business come together.

    How the value of the Internet evaded the major labels, and the subsequent effect on the business. Speculations and predictions about the job opportunities that will arise out of new paradigms in music sales.

> Preface:
Skating on a Frozen Lake of Lies

How *Mistakes* Was Put Together

"If we don't succeed, we run the risk of failure."
—Dan Quayle

"An honest man is always in trouble."
—Anonymous

I f you're reading this preface, you are in the top 15 percent of all book readers. Most skip past the introductory fluff, unless it's written by someone important, like **Tommy Mottola** or **Richard Nixon**,[1] at least one of whom is dead, I think. But the "important" people I know are too busy to be burdened with this kind of thing. So you're stuck reading a preface written by me, the author. I'm thankful that you're going the extra yard, and I'm going to reward you by revealing a few very cool things that the other 85 percent of this book's readers will never find out.

This brief section has nothing whatsoever to do with actual million dollar mistakes. It's about the difficult process of trying to publish a truth that few want revealed (which could be a mistake in itself). This information serves two audiences: first, other journalists, educators, and future writers who are asking themselves the same question. Second, the reader who wants to dig a bit below the surface of the book's subject and get into the book's "mind": how do you get successful people to share their embarrassing moments?

[1] Tommy Mottola: Third president of Sony Records. Forced to resign in 2003. Richard Nixon: 37th President of the United States. Forced to resign in 1974.

It should first be understood that I didn't set out to write an exposé. I wanted to write something educational and inspirational to future generations in the music business. While most books on the industry center on the nitty-gritty of what to do and not to do, I decided to write a book about hearts and minds. Some laughed at this: "Hearts and minds in the music business!?" Well, call me romantic, but I believe there would far less malfeasance if we were better informed on how human nature manifests in the music space. How will that happen when it seems that no one really wants to talk openly to address the issues? "No one?" you say. Yes, at least not publicly.

There really is no *music business journalism*. Sure, there is "rock 'n' roll" journalism. The kind of thing we saw dramatized in **Cameron Crowe**'s movie, *Almost Famous*. And thanks to the Internet there is now so much of it that this once great cultural pavilion has been diluted by gobs of blogs. But as far as reporters vetting the motivations of music business people as they do in politics or other industries, we are stuck only with marginal coverage, which is, in effect, an unwilling auxiliary to the public relations agenda of record companies and music publishers.[2] Weekly trade magazines like *Billboard* or the *Hollywood Reporter* are far too dependent on advertising dollars and information from the very people reporters wish to vet to be a true critical balcony. Their editors rarely green-light anything harsh, unless it's to kick someone in the teeth when they're already down, as they did **Mike Ovitz**[3] some years back or **Michael Green** when he was forced to resign as CEO of NARAS.[4] And yet, these periodicals are considered the music industry's papers of record.

And what about higher-learning institutions and their accredited music business education programs? Is there such a thing? For years I have taught an exclusive workshop on how things really work in the business of music. It's been very successful among industry pros. But despite state bar recognition and many, many testimonials by veterans and other educators, attempts to franchise it into mainstream college programs have been met with resistance. School administrators are afraid that teaching the truth to students will discourage them. (Yes, they actually said that to my face.) In their mind a bit of reality could lead to lost tuitions.

Instead of teaching young musicians, artists, professionals, and songwriters how to protect their future assets, most music business programs function as primers on things like copyright administration and contracts, subjects one will practically never use because one will be hiring an attorney in all probability for such matters. This is their idea of "education" and they charge a great deal for it. I get a bit ill at the hypocrisy. For an institution to profit off the dreams of young minds but not give them the tools to avoid opportunists is morally repugnant. It only helps fill the coffers of the unscrupulous and perpetuate the industry's problems.[5]

[2] And in the future, companies like Yahoo!, AOL, and Microsoft will have a large influence on the back-door politics of music distribution.

[3] Mike Ovitz: Former head of CAA, the top talent agency in Los Angeles. Credited with reinventing the art of the movie deal and then called the most hated man in Hollywood by the same papers after he was forced to sell his company for far below its book value.

[4] NARAS: National Academy of Recording Arts and Sciences. They own the Grammy Awards. Green multiplied their earnings almost five fold in his tenure. He was forced to resign amidst sexual harassment charges, an odd priority switch for the music business, which tends to be very relaxed about such behavior.

So, if the papers won't investigate and the school won't educate, how will the business ever evolve?

[5] I'd like to acknowledge two exceptions: UCLA on the West Coast and NYU on the East Coast. Both very good programs. There are several others in Canada and the Midwest as well.

And an answer hit me: by the honest reporting and understanding of stories about failure and disgrace. It's really the only way left available to us. Example by failure. Trial by fire. If we are to learn anything and grow as an industry, we must skate over the proverbial lake's thin ice of hype and confront the reality below its frozen surface.

When I had conceptualized this book I thought that surely those who had achieved so much success in their lives could afford to be generous with a sob story or two. It was on this basis that I sold the book to the publisher. I wanted this book to be more than an encyclopedia of everyday goofs. I wanted it to be entertaining, and for that I needed to have a few juicy celebrity bits—because, in our culture, nothing really happens until it happens to someone *famous*.

Two problems with this theory that I discovered, unfortunately, only after I had accepted a generous advance: the challenges that face a tell-all book that *really* tells all are far simpler when you are the only person doing the telling, as I did in my other two books, *Confessions of a Record Producer* and *Secrets of Negotiating a Record Contract*. Getting others to join you is another matter.

Problem number one: trying to get directly to celebrities (even ones I knew well) was a task I initially failed at most of the time. They simply will not talk about "mistakes" without a pod of lawyers and publicists scrutinizing their every word. Eventually, I rationalized that the celebrities and artists themselves were not going to be of great value to the book's mission anyway. Their handlers excel at diverting them from taking responsibility for screw-ups. So effectively, in fact, that few stars believe that they make mistakes until ignominy gives them the benefit of hindsight.

With this reality in place I turned to those in the background: producers, managers, lawyers, executives. The "star-maker machinery" as **Joni Mitchell** once called it. Artists come and go. The machinery stays in place for far longer and gets the benefit of experience.

At first the concept of a book about mistakes was well received by all of them. About half were very forthright and their interviews were a blessing (thank you). But, in general, as I tried to pin several of them down to dates, they suddenly become horribly busy. And of those that did show up for "the talk," many were more interested in talking about *other people's* mistakes. Specifically, mistakes that *other* people made when dealing with *them*.

Problem two: when it came to those whose livelihoods depend on celebrities (that is, managers, producers, agents, label execs), getting them to talk about the mistakes

THE PRE-INTERVIEW FORM

- What would you say is the biggest mistake made by a new person entering the music business as an artist, writer, or producer?
- What would you say is the biggest mistake made by artists, writers, or producers who have been in the business for over five years?
- What would you say is the biggest mistake made by a new person entering the music business as a lawyer, manager, or label/publishing executive?
- What would you say is the biggest mistake made by lawyers, managers, or label/publishing executives who've been in the business for over five years?
- What is your role in the music business: lawyer, producer, singer, musician, songwriter, manager, label owner, other_____?
- What was your biggest learning experience? In other words, what was the worst thing that happened to you where you learned a valuable lesson or that cost you big bucks? (Just a quick paragraph will do as we'll be expanding on this in the interview.) NO NAMES PLEASE. Use "person X" and "person Y," etc.

of others was easy, but getting them talk about themselves required some divine intervention, two deadline extensions, and a few bribes.

With my second deadline only eight months away and not one word written, I decided to get resourceful. Although some might prefer the word "crafty," other writers out there know what I'm referring to. Basically, I needed a clever method to get people to open up.

The Process

I realized that revealing the truth was like peeling an onion. It needs to be done in layers, progressively, starting with easy questions about others at first, then moving into more personal issues. The challenge is to find the right entry point.

On Sunday, February 4, 2004, I punted. I sent an email blast to my rolodex of about 200 music-biz connections with a subject banner that read: "Teach others the real music business." I stressed the future generations and a book where they could learn from the best. I received about 30 replies. These respondents received

THE FIRST INTERVIEW

Subjects were asked the following talking points:

No matter how many music conferences I go to, no matter how many panels I sit on, I continue to hear the same half-baked advice doled out to unsuspecting artists. Here they are:

a) Run your music career like a business.

b) It's a small industry, so be nice to everyone.

c) Your demo should sound radio-ready.

1) Agree or disagree with the following arguments:

a) How can some "experts" suggest that you run your music career "like a serious business, with financial goals" when it's pretty obvious that many of the most successful artists didn't set goals, or run their bands anything like a serious business. Yet, they've become millionaires. What are *they* doing right?

b) It's a "small industry"? There are more than ten national conferences dedicated solely to music, about three times that of any other industry. And these don't include all the smaller local events. There are about 1,000 people at the executive level alone just at major labels. The most successful ones are known for *not* being nice. So, how did they do it? How does a rude dude get to the top if you have to be nice to everyone to get to the top?

c) Your demo should sound "radio-ready"? How can people say that with a straight face when there is a ton of mediocre material on the radio? Are they saying your music should sound as middle-of-the-road as the top 40? Contrary to popular belief, labels really do sign good creative acts, generally. It's through the development process that the act becomes homogenized into what you eventually hear on the radio. But a label doesn't want to sign a band that has already homogenized themselves.

2) You are addressing the graduating class of "Music Business University." What would you like to tell them?

3) What's wrong with this industry?

a "pre-interview form" to prepare them for what was going to be discussed. The ball had begun to roll. (See the sidebar, "The Pre-Interview Form.")

However, only 14 actually filled it out. Taking what the universe was willing to give me at this time, I proceeded to schedule interviews. When I got the subjects on the phone I employed a somewhat more conversational interview than the one I had them prepared for and one that I had hoped would trigger a more visceral response. (See the sidebar, "The First Interview.")

These three talking points (a, b, and c in the sidebar) attacked the three biggest misconceptions about music business that just about everyone has put faith in at one time or another. "a" attacks the relationship between success and luck—why some make it and others don't despite talent and hard work; "b" the idea of who is worth putting up with, since, at some point, we have all pissed off somebody important (to our detriment); and "c" addresses the quality of one's creative work— which is at the heart of every artist's and every professional's deepest fear: Am I good enough?

These questions became the springboard for a release. Personal stories of blunders they made, assumptions they acted upon, and trusts they regretted became accessible. I had hit pay dirt. Over time more responded and several referrals from the original 14 eventually yielded about 50 final subjects. I could sense a sort of catharsis for some in this process: finally a platform to say things they had thought but never expressed.

Some would ask in the middle of the interview, "Is this the kind of stuff you're looking for?" Rather than insist that subjects be "honest," since this is subjective, I would prompt them to give exact examples of things they were referring to, while trying to avoid rhetorical philosophies. I would respond, "As long as you are specific, it is of value." I was Socratic (probably to the point of being rude, in their perception). I made subjects back up their opinions with facts, rarely letting them get away with general statements. Generalities are one of Man's greatest excesses. I wanted real stories, backed up with real names and real facts. And I got them.

Later, however, I paid a price. About a third of the subjects wanted to retract their comments. "Wait till I put it in context," I told them. "If you still want it off the record, I'll take your name off the quote." And, to make matters more irritating, after hundreds of hours of recorded voices, notes, and emails, the project was a massive malted of "reality" that I had to now put into some kind of informative and entertaining structure.

After the first two dozen interviews, I began to notice categories forming with patterns of common mistakes, like a cloud in an intense windstorm starting to

THE SECOND INTERVIEW

1) It doesn't take long to figure out that publishing is the key to most of the big money in the music business. Can you give an example of a lost opportunity born from a misunderstanding of how publishing works?

2) How confusing are some of the contracts in our business? In no other industry do you have the word "notwithstanding" so many times in an agreement. Can you give a real-life example of a lost opportunity or blunder caused by bad lawyering, conflicts of interest, or careless clauses in a contract?

3) It's been said that "It's not called 'show talent' or 'show friends.' It's 'show business.'" Even though your best friend hires you and gives you that big break, he'll fire you for the same reason. Nepotism and the old-boy network can work for and against you. Give me a real-life example of how being a "good friend" of someone can work for or against you.

4) Many people in the biz become overly mercenary in their rise to the top or their sink to the bottom. What are the pitfalls to consider when taking jobs just because they are offering big bucks?

5) Can you give me a story about how using your own money for investing in an artist can be dangerous?

6) Everyone turns down at least one job that they should have taken. Why did you make the wrong choice? Was it mostly because you started believing your own hype? Give an example.

7) When the girlfriend wants to manage the band, this is usually a sign that things are on their way down. However, there are some great exceptions to the rule of "don't eat where you shit." Can you give me a contribution to this common scenario pro or con?

8) Relying on someone's word in the music business can be costly. Was there a time when you didn't see how a misrepresentation was going to hurt you? Or when you did see it coming and did something about it? What can you teach the future generations of the music business about how to tell when someone you trust is not really on your side?

9) Many times a label or producer thinks they are good enough to play Pygmalion. Often they learn the hard lesson that the best swimmers are usually the ones that drown. Was there a situation where you thought you could beat the odds and tried to make a bad artist sound great? What happened?

10) It seems that the practice of not returning a phone call in this business can be as artful as the making of the music. Has there ever been a phone call you didn't return and, if you could go back in time, wish that you had?

11) In your opinion, what happened when the big labels came in contact with the world of high-tech and the Internet? What went wrong? Was it just a clash of personalities? What did you witness, if anything? And how do the big labels plan on gaining back their ground in years to come?

take a compelling shape. Analyzing the answers revealed about ten basic types of mistakes that were common to the business. So I created a different interview template with a dozen questions based on these categories. (See the sidebar, "The Second Interview.") These questions become the basis of actual chapter headings that remain in the book. I went in for a second round of interviews with these questions and for new subjects just skipped right to the Second Interview Form.

When the last of the interviews was completed, I locked myself in a room for about two months. I lived in my bathrobe, had food delivered. I forgot what a razor was, and sometimes a toothbrush as well. My personal assistant—a well-groomed gal from Nashville—is the only person who saw me. I'm sure that during that time I offended her sense of hygiene. I was thankful she stuck it out.

During this time I wrote chapters and sent them to interview subjects, some of whom still wanted to change or retract their quotes. At each turn I had to negotiate, urging them not to withdraw their stories. Some agreed, others did not. When you're reading these stories, take a moment to commend those who followed through. They truly deserve your appreciation. (Their names and credentials are listed in the appendix section, "Who We Are Hearing From.")

When I emerged from my cave, this manuscript was born. I say "born" because a book like this is never fully matured. Even as I sent it to the publisher for approval I was still writing and pursuing several interviews that I thought were key. While this book is finding its market with readers and schools I will be writing it still. I know people will want to respond for the second edition of this book (if there is one). I will be happy to listen and include their testimony. This book I hope will be a *living* document, updated until I can write no more or until the mistakes it reveals fade into irrelevancy.

If that is to happen it will be in the hands of the future of this business. I have done my part. Now you must put me out of business. Please.

—*Moses Avalon*

➤ Three Opinions

"The only one who makes no mistakes is one who never does anything!"
—Theodore Roosevelt

"Creativity is allowing yourself to make mistakes.
Art is knowing which ones to keep."
—Scott Adams, cartoonist (Dilbert)

"Be not ashamed of mistakes and thus make them crimes."
—Confucius

CHAPTER 1

> Everybody Lies

"Man learned to lie about one hour after he learned to talk."
—Unknown

I t's true. Experience tells us that lying seems to be more vital than food to our day-to-day existence. Want proof? Most can go a day without food before they get too weak to function. But try going a full day without telling a single fabrication, exaggeration, embellishment, hyperbole, prevarication, distortion, or "optimistic" estimation. Not as easy. Especially when your boss wants answers and your squeeze wants a commitment. People who tell themselves that they *never* lie are, in most cases, lying to themselves. Everyday survival in the world often depends on being able to tell someone what they are *ready* to hear more so than telling someone what they *need* to hear. Even with the best of intentions, we are telling small fibs here and there to get by. In the music world, where egos are fragile and inflated, this seems triply so. There are a few lies that most everyone tells in response to common scenarios, even if they don't admit that they are lying:

- **"What do you think of my demo?"** Artists will beg for a response to their work. The odds are it's average at best. Never tell someone you think their music is subpar, no matter how much they beg you to be honest. This is right up there with the cliché, "Do I look fat in this dress?" (Guys, you know what

I'm talking about. The answer is *always* no.) If it's bad or average, try to find the one thing in it that you really love. (Hopefully there is one.) And talk about that.

[1] See Chapter 2.

- **"Can you help me (get a deal, job, whatever)?"** Anyone with connections has heard this one, or some version of it, twenty times a month. Saying no, even though you may want to, can close a door, piss them off, and help build the reputation that you're a dick.[1] Don't say no. Divert their attention toward what you *can* help them with.
- **"I can get you a meeting with _____."** The reverse of the above, where the veteran is baiting the newbie. Connections are currency. But there are plenty of times when that currency is used to get something from someone that has nothing to do with music. Sometimes you have no intention of making that meeting. You're thinking of another kind of hookup.
- **"I worked on the ____ record."** Getting top credits is difficult. And we all like to pad our résumé. Even if we only changed the coffee filter in the studio where a hit was recorded, you can be sure it's going to end up on the curriculum vitae. Given enough alcohol and motivation, that coffee-filter changer can morph quickly into "chief equipment tech."

In our society, honesty is usually the booby prize. Think about it—when was the last time someone said, "Let me be honest with you," and it was good news? We tend to incubate the ugly truths for as long as we can get away with it. It's almost a compliment to be lied to if you can track with that stupid logic. And yet in business, relying on the word of a liar (or someone who's just trying to "do the right thing") can be costly. For those with the talent to steer that course, God bless them. For the rest of us, there's some good news at the end of this chapter: a guide to spotting music business liars.

But before you invest in perfecting this skill, you should know it's a power both awesome and horrible. Years ago I discovered several very large studies done on spotting liars. The study outlined many ways to determine not only if a person was lying but even if the liar was unaware of the fact that they are lying. (Mostly out of habit or denial.) The study also went on to say that less than 30 percent of the people in the study could figure out when someone was lying to them. Which means that when about 70 percent of us are being deceived we don't know it.

I made it my business to absorb this study and began applying it to my life. But there was a downside. Most people can quickly sense that I'm on to them (which is probably something I need to work on) and become uncomfortable. Rather than just nod my head, when I know they are lying, I'll tend to challenge them by pointing out the contradictions in their presentation. Nothing irritates a person who's trying to sell you more than pointing out that their patter is stale or has holes in it. We work so long and hard on preparing what Sigmund Freud called our "social face." They walk away saying "that guy's a jerk," without even understanding that the reason they feel that way is because I hate BS and I'd like them to be honest with me.

People will put up with your annoyances if their primary interest is getting something professional out of the relationship. I get invited to dinners, receive gifts and all kinds of perks from clients who probably think I'm a pain in the butt. This may sound like fun for about 30 seconds, but over time it has a rather anti-socializing effect.

If I had the last 20 years to do over again, I would work harder on my intolerance of liars. These days I'm past the point in my career where I need to interact with people who compulsively fib. But you may not be. So pay attention to the coming pages.

❷ Gossip for the Greater Good

The lyrics in the Kinks song go, "Paranoia may destroy ya." The key to defusing it is education and information. The more you know about a subject, the less of a target you will be for people trying to put crap over on you. But you probably know that already if you're reading this. **Jay Jay French**, founding member of the 1980s rock sensation **Twisted Sister**, has sold over 11 million records. He gave me this:

> *Jay Jay French:* I think that when people outside the business start telling you that [the music] business is fucked and you can't explain realistically what goes on, then you open yourself up for the possibility to be influenced by someone who does not know what they are talking about. And if you are overly paranoid, then you will think *everyone* is trying to fuck you.

So now you're in a band that is playing all the bigger stages on your area. You can pack a room with 700 people. Your CD is making digits on iTunes and Yahoo! and a major is talking to you about a deal. What do you think your friends are thinking? And how are they reacting? Some, of course, are well-meaning individuals who want to see you succeed. These people are usually called your parents. Most everyone else wishes they were in your shoes and in many cases they will tell themselves that they are somehow responsible for your success. Maybe they even deserve a slice. They can get one if they stay close. They will look for ways to become "useful" to you. If they can offer little to nothing, there's always the cheap way to get the attention of an insecure artist—feed his ego with compliments and conspiracies.

Jay Jay French: These people are in fact creating bigger problems than they know they are creating. They will create a scenario that makes you feel unsure about where you are. You have to know what's what, because you'll always hear shit from people: every band is always better off than you—no matter what happens or how many records you sell, everything is never as good as somebody else's scenario. If I didn't know why things were the way they were, I could have been swayed in many [incorrect] ways.

Yes. Whispering negative sweet somethings in a rising star's ear has many agendas. Jealousy is only one. Infiltration is another. Trying to get the artist to feel insecure about his management or label so the whisperer can stealthily move in and take over is the most common.

In such situations the clever gossiper will rarely talk directly to the point, but instead will talk about benchmarks of your career, in hopes of tapping into an artist's unrealistic expectations about success. When it works, an artist can be totally brainwashed by the gossiper's BS. He begins walking around thinking that he should have made more money, that his manager sucks, that his label sucks, and that he's entitled to far more than just one platinum record.

2 **James DeYoung:** Styx disbanded and reunited several times from 1989 to 1996. In 1998 they recorded their first new album in nine years, but DeYoung contracted influenza and could not tour. When he tried to rejoin the group about a year later, he was voted out. Despite being pacifists, their hit "Show Me the Way" was used as the first Gulf War anthem. Styx, in Greek mythology, was the river of the dead.

Jay Jay French: I remember meeting **James DeYoung** from **Styx** in 1985 at an Abrams Convention. I had previously read that of all the bands in the United States at that time, **Styx** was the first to have four triple-platinum albums *in a row*. I said to him, "Wow, what an amazing thing." You know how he responded? He said, "We would have had more if we were on a better label." They were on A&M, a *great* label. What many artists don't understand is that your "career album" is like a baseball player's "career year." You're probably not ever going to repeat that. Thinking that you are is the biggest myth you need to let go of.[2]

An old saying goes, show me a person with one hundred million dollars and I will show you a frustrated billionaire. In the next section, we'll hear a theory from an industry veteran who has a name for this phenomenon.

> Doug and His Octopus

Doug Breitbart is one of the key people responsible for **Debbie Gibson**'s rise to fame and an entertainment attorney for over 20 years. He claims that there is an entity that lives in the belly of the vast ocean of music business professionals. The artist is always in or near its clutches. He calls it the octopus.

> *Doug Breitbart:* The dark force is this collection of service providers tied into the senior executives of a major label and to a publisher and a recording studio. It feeds on artists. They don't usually start or create them. When the artist starts to get near a [seven-figure] critical mass it's rare that one part of this "octopus" doesn't come into contact with that artist or project.
>
> *Moses:* Octopus?
>
> *Doug Breitbart:* I will give you the components of the octopus. It is usually a set that involves the record company and the publishing company. It involves the law firm, it involves the accounting firm. It involves the booking agents, it involves the manager.
>
> *Moses:* That's everybody.
>
> *Doug Breitbart:* Correct. It's like, if you want to do a deal with this label or you want to do this kind of business or if you want to do this or that, go to that firm or go to that agent—if you go to one of them, you will end up in the middle of all of them. They can, if allowed, eat you alive. The primary motivation is to feed, and if the artist stumbles or falls or if there is a false step or failure and it turns, they move on to the next. They are predatory. They look for new breaking situations where the representational team is vulnerable for one reason or another.

Doug's grand conspiracy theory may be too broad to make use of without a bit of specificity. I mean, can everyone be in on the joke except the new person? Well, there's an expression known to poker players: If you look around the table and you can't figure out who the sucker is… you're the sucker.

André Fischer's work with the legendary group **Rufus Featuring Chaka Khan** and on **Natalie Cole**'s *Unforgettable* earned seven Grammy awards. Here's his take.

> *André Fischer:* There is a certain kind of person that is to be made from all of this, and that person is a survivor, a survivor that is knowledgeable and has enough information for checks and balances against the people that handle him beyond his particular realm. In other words, the lawyers, the business managers, and all the folks that talk to you.

⊙ Distributor Distortions

We tend to think that the larger an entity is the less likely they are to lie to us. Why would Disney need to lie to little ol' me?

Distributors need product. Investors need to do something with their money. Producers need distributors to sell what they have and money to finance their speculations. Now here's what I call the deadly trio:

1. Investors generally won't write a check without a distributor's letter of intent.
2. Distributors won't give consent until the talent is signed and some tracks are recorded.
3. Talent won't show up to perform tracks unless they see a check.

A three-way standoff persists until someone blinks. Everybody wants commitment from the other person without committing to the situation themselves. It's a breeding ground for prevarication.

Jeff Weber has a discography as long as a list of Pamela Anderson's ex-boyfriends, mostly in the jazz arena, which includes work with **Nancy Wilson, Jackson Browne, Michael McDonald, Chick Corea, Stanley Clarke, Luther Vandross**, and **David Crosby**. He says that in the jazz world a successful project is measured in the tens of thousands of units, unlike pop where it's measured in the millions of units. One thing both genres have in common is the fact that they need consistent and innovative marketing in order to move sales.

> *Jeff Weber:* The marketing and promotion departments of a record label or distributor will tell you a specific thing, and if it does not happen, which it probably won't, you are dropped like a lead enema.

Promotion is the hotbed of generalities. Estimates generally turn out to be optimistic. This is followed by "surprising results" when things fall apart. When they are successful, however, everybody seems to be saying "I knew it."

Reality check: most projects are *not* successful. Marketing and promotion personnel generalize almost out of necessity so that things remain optimistic and momentum is maintained. This is the hotbed of lies and why the profession of PR has a seedy reputation.

Jeff Weber: In my particular case, I had a situation where I produced a record for [a major label] and the president of the label loved it and asked me and the artist to come in to the Los Angeles offices. I proceeded to play the record for the entire marketing and sales staff, at which point we received a standing ovation. The record executive said to me that this was a phenomenally produced record, and that he would have lots of work for me and that he just couldn't wait to get started. I left that room feeling fantastic.

The policy of labels is called "ABC." *Always Be Closing.* Or *Always Be Selling.* Same thing. This doesn't just mean sell to those buying their product, but also to the producers and artists of the record. They will never say "We think this sucks, we're canning it" to your face. Instead they will throw a big party with lots of fanfare and compliments. Often it's actually a funeral, but you won't know that until after the coffin is in the ground.

Jeff Weber: Absolutely nothing happened with that record. Repeated phone calls to record executives never were returned. It became a joke.

Moses: Did you ever find out why?

Jeff Weber: No, I never did, but the record was nominated for a Grammy.

My personal philosophy is this: In the music business, if they hate it, they tell you, "It's great." If they love it, they pay you to "make it better."

Jeff Weber: Soon after, the then president of [the major record label] and I ran into each other. He said, "Jeff, I have some work for you. I want you to do some stuff for me." I said, "Great." He said, "I am going to give you my *personal, private number.*" He said, "Be very, very careful and don't give this out." So, I called him and it turned out that it was just the main switchboard at the record company.

OPM

Other People's Money. It's essential to be able to acquire some if you're going to produce. In trying to close a deal with people who have promised you money, you will encounter some of the most prolific and least creative lying ever. "I really want to follow through and give you that $100,000, but I had some unexpected expenses come up." This is the investor equivalent of "my dog ate my homework." No one who had $100,000 to invest in something as high-risk as the music business suddenly finds out he had "expenses." (Unless it's a leg-breaking bookie. Which is entirely possible.)

Jeff Weber: The music business attracts the best and the worst in people because of the possible liquidity that it offers over a seemingly short period of time. It happens constantly where someone comes to you bright-eyed and bushy-tailed and says, "I have the funding to make this product happen and I think we can do a great job with this. We want you to work with this girl and we have the songs." You can bet like clockwork that while they may have the best of intentions, the money isn't there, the songs aren't there, the timing isn't there, and the studio isn't like they say it is. Whatever they say, my biggest rule now is that everyone lies. If you approach the music business with that point of view, you've protected yourself from getting too emotionally involved.

Early in my career, I fell in love with a group and asked if I could produce their record. They said yeah, sure. I had to raise money, naturally, so I came up with an idea. Pre-sales.[3] This was at the time in my career when I was an idealistic audiophile producer, which meant every stage of the recording process had to be at the highest state-of-the-art quality that it could ever be. I then went to a distributor of audiophile records in San Francisco. They listened to the demo and said they would [pre-purchase] $20,000 worth of the finished records and they gave me a signed piece of paper indicating such. And then the head of the company said privately, "Since I love this band, why don't I put in half the money for the recording as well?"

Moses: The CEO of the distributor says that? So the distributor wants to invest *and* be an owner in the master itself, not just making money on the sales of units? And they agree to purchase 5,000 units at four dollars apiece as a pre-sale?

Jeff Weber: Yes. I thought, wow, this is a no-lose situation. The owner of the company decided to put in $10,000 of his own money to cover half the production costs. Instead of having to raise $20,000 I now only had to raise ten.

Moses: So you should have thirty grand in your pocket, on paper at least.

Jeff Weber: On paper, because my arrangement with him was for him to pay me for the 5,000 units once I turned in the finished product. I know there are no sure things, but this looked about as sure as you could get. So I went to my parents (very early on in my career) and I told them the good news, and I said, "I need you to give me $10,000 so I can make this record." My parents looked at me and said, "Do you think we are nuts?" But they said they would help me get a loan from a bank, which was even worse. I got the $10,000 from the bank, and with the $10,000 from the owner of the distribution company, I made the record and turned it in. He then said, "My priorities have changed—I don't want to distribute this title." I said, "You're going to lose $10,000." He didn't care. I had to go back to my parents and tell them that I didn't get the rest of the money. It was a horrible les-

[3] Pre-sales have been a consistent part of the business models of films for years prior to this incident. But it had not been done with records due to the fact that records are generally sold as "consignment" items. In the future, with the advent of Internet-based subscription models for distribution, it will not likely be done at all.

son for me. At that time I was just a neophyte and I learned the hard way that you never, under any circumstances, no matter how much of a sure thing you think it is, you *never*, ever put your own money into any of your own productions.

Ferreting Out the Distributor's BS

Joey Akles is presently the co-producer and co-leader of the avant-garde musical act **DJ Monkey**. He has played many parts in the music business, from label executive to vocalist to band manager and hit writer for groups like **the Plimsouls** and the **Goo Goo Dolls**. His experience with distributors qualifies him to give us this unique test for a distributor's likelihood for prevarication.

Joey Akles: The litmus test for me [with a distributor] is this: if you were in their position would you do what they are saying they will do? Would it be good business? Would you distribute your band without any track record? If it's a manager giving you a pitch to sign with him, ask yourself, would you hire yourself as the manager?

Moses: The problem with that is that ego gets involved.

Joey Akles: You have to let go of your ego.

Moses: Easier said than done. To most people it will always make sense to you to believe the lie you're being told. You can rationalize that you're not being lied to because you really *are* that great.

Joey Akles: No matter how great you are, no distributor is picking you up if you're an independent act. They may pick you up as a record company [with a catalog or potential catalog] but not as a distribution for your indie band. No distributor is going to pick up a one-act label no matter how good.

Moses: Because?

Joey Akles: You don't have the money and the firepower to support that distributor's sales, no matter how good you are. You still have to pay for retail promotion, radio promotion, video, touring. It's expensive. Unless you can prove a track record of having done the business side as an indie label, the distributor is not even interested if you are great. If you're an indie and they say "no problem, we'll take you," they will take the CDs and throw them in the warehouse.

It's important to distinguish between an indie act, like the ones that Joey is referring to, and indie labels, who frequently get distribution deals with majors. Much confusion comes from the fact that the big distributors have names that are very much like the major labels (Sony, EMI, and so on), so many people think that a distributor and a label are the same thing. They are not. The Internet age has given birth to several smaller companies that prey on the types of indie artists Joey is talking about. They advertise that they reject no indie artist as long as you're willing to pay for any combination of these several things: a setup fee, restocking charges, or a Web site. There are myriad angles for disguising the fact that they are sponging off an artist's desperation to get distribution, and nickel-and-diming him into a deficit position. Many of these companies call themselves distributors, but they are not. Mostly they are e-tailers (online retailers).[4]

[4] See *Confessions of a Record Producer,* third edition, for more on this, or Chapter 9 in this book.

⊗ Lies Engineers Tell

An old record industry joke goes, "How many recording engineers does it take to change a light bulb?" Answer, "Does it have to be a light bulb?"

Producers and artists have requests. The audio engineer's job is to fulfill them. But many times the engineer may not think highly of the producer's request. Yet he cannot assert this. Saying "no" closes a door. (See Chapter 2 "Neither Commit nor Offend.") Saying "maybe" or throwing the request back at the producer (in the form of a question, like the joke above) gives hope, gives the impression that you are part of the team and racks up many billable hours.

> *André Fischer:* The reason today why I engineer as well as produce is that when I was younger, starting out with Rufus, engineers lied to us.

But many times engineers are forced to lie as a byproduct of dealing with inane requests made by those with intense egos, under very limited budgets and time constraints. Now it's important to understand that I'm generalizing here. Not all engineers are lying in these ways. Just the ones who are working for *you.* What shape do those lies take? Let's see.

The OIC Button

How many times have you seen an engineer search the sea of knobs to find the "right one"? If they're real good they can get everyone in the room searching for what I call the "OIC button." Why? After several minutes the engineer will exclaim, "Oh, I see!" A button suddenly comes into view that was there all along.

Sometimes the OIC is a patch-cable or a switch on a mike. Anything that is hiding in plain sight qualifies. The truth is, an engineer has to keep track of so many things that it's easy to overlook the obvious. Regardless, nothing makes him look like an ass more than the OIC phenomenon. World record for this, according to one subject I interviewed, was three hours, twenty-six minutes. In this case, all sound had ceased to come out of the console. In the end the OIC was the master mute button located front and center over the main fader. Cost for this episode: $2,500—$350 an hour for the studio and $125 for both the engineer and his assistant, $500 for the musicians, lunch, and some extras.

You Can't Ever Get What You Want

Studio work is both exciting and frustrating. You have a sound in mind, but getting it (especially on a budget) can sometimes seem unattainable. At times like this, do we place undue faith and expectations on the engineer? Do we expect him to do on a $500-a-song budget what labels do for $5000 a song? Here's an amusing point/counterpoint between **André Fischer** and **Matt Forger**, a veteran engineer who's worked with high-profile clients like **Michael Jackson** and **New Edition.**

André Fischer: I would say, "I am trying to get the sound I heard on this record," and they say, "Oh, no, we can't do that, that must be something that some guy had a machine for." So, when they go on a break I stay in the studio and mess with dials and figure it out. I play with the knobs till I get a sound I like. Of course when [the engineer] walks back in the room they say, "Oh, that machine is askew, you got this turned too far to the right, there is too much gain...." The point is, I had to take a chance to go farther than what someone told me was possible.

Matt Forger: There have been a couple times when a client wanted something that was just flat-out ridiculous. Y'know, a little information is dangerous, and sometimes people say, "I want to do it this way, I've always done it this way," and you know it's not helping the situation. You have to convince them that you understand what they are asking for, but that it's not really the best thing in this situation. An example: Working with **Chuck Mangione** it was difficult to get the exact sound quality he was looking for. When he said, "I want the mix to sound like this cassette," he had the engineer run the mix through the cassette machine to the 2-track. Along that same theme, a lot of times these little cassette/CD boomboxes have these little buttons on them. They have one for bass boost, they have one for expanding the dynamic range. Someone will run one of their rough mixes through one of these and say, "It sounds so much better on my boombox." You have to convince the client that it's not going to be best for your mix when it gets mastered and released on a CD.

[5] **Jimi Hendrix (1942–70):** Formed the still classic Jimi Hendrix Experience, whose hits included: *Purple Haze, Are You Experienced?,* and *Electric Ladyland.* He died of a drug overdose in 1970. After an estate battle that lasted over a quarter of a century, his father finally got the rights to it in 1995.

[6] **Record Plant:** Since 1968, many of the top musical acts recorded their albums in this classic studio. The studio went bankrupt in 1991.

André Fischer: I wound up having to learn more because I had the feeling that the engineer wasn't doing his best for us. For example, listening to a **Jimi Hendrix**[5] album and wondering how they were getting that great feedback. When two or three engineers in Los Angeles at the **Record Plant**[6] couldn't tell me, I went and found Jimi's producer. I found the engineer. I talked to the people that worked at **Electric Lady** [studio] in New York. I had to do homework. I had to do due diligence.

The Producer's Fader

Not every client can be snowed with a lame excuse. Sometimes a producer will insist on touching the board himself. For him we have the engineer's best friend—the *producer's fader.*

Matt Forger: The producer's fader is a dummy fader (or knob) on the console that is connected to basically nothing and is close to where the producer sits. When the producer says, "You know, in this section right here we need a little more reverb, more EQ, whatever," you play the song and move the "fader" and ask the producer, "Did that work for you? Did that help you?" The producer says, "Yeah, that's exactly the way that I want it."

Moses: The effect is psychological.

Matt Forger: Yes. But if the producer is astute enough he'll say, "No, no, don't give me that fader." The producer will jiggle it violently to make sure that it's doing something real. So, to allow for that, you would give the producer a fader which actually does manipulate *something,* but then you would have another knob on your side which would override the producer's fader.

I have my own story regarding a producer's fader. Once an ad agency wanted a change to a 30-second jingle. The mix consisted of so many tracks that three multitracks were required to hear all the elements. It was a mess.

The agency wanted us to reconstruct the enter mix just so they could change one little thing. On three hours' notice, we didn't even have time to set it up. Instead, we put up the CD of the final mix and then three "dummy" multitracks. They had reels on them, but they were from another project.

When the agency came into the studio, we had several producer's faders set up, supposedly patched into the things they wanted to tweak. Tape reels rolled through the machines. Meters jumped and lights flashed, but the only sound the client heard was the finished 2-track. The ad boys gathered around the producer's fader and tweaked them ever so slightly. After a minute they smiled, satisfied with the "changes."

"Print that," they said enthusiastically. And we did.

> Getting Paid When You've Got No Leverage

An "all-in deal" is one where a label gives a producer the entire budget and the producer satisfies the individual vendors' invoices out of that budget. In other words, he pays the studio, engineer, musicians, and so on out of his pocket—directly. The opposite would be a deal where the vendors each submit an invoice to the record company and the record company pays the vendor directly.

When you're up and coming as a session musician, you are more likely to find yourself hired into an all-in situation. Producers look to cut costs by hiring musicians without union cards or whom they can pay cash. Newbies on the scene are anxious to please and don't ask too many questions. They also don't know what clues to look for to see whether or not they are about to get jacked. Veteran engineer **Francis Buckley** (**Pointer Sisters, Paula Abdul, Alanis Morissette**) tells us this about the engineer's vulnerability to this system.

Francis Buckley: If someone is going to stiff you, there is little you can do about it. In 25 years there have probably been three times I've been stiffed. Only once did I see it coming. The office manager of the studio was on the phone with the record company bitching to them about why he hasn't been paid. I caught up with him afterwards and he was like, "I think this is going to be a trouble session." That is where I learned that you yourself must call the label and get a PO number. That is the only protection you have. If you get a PO, someone somewhere has made a guarantee that a check will get written.

A PO is a *purchase order*. Each project on a major label has one. It's a number that authorizes payment for a project. The PO you should get is not necessarily for your particular service, but just the general PO that is used for that project. But getting it is more like insurance than a guarantee.

Moses: A lot of small labels don't even work with POs. What do you do then?
Francis Buckley: Well, you have to get some form of something from the small

labels. Even if they just *call* it a PO. If you get someone on the phone with some type of guarantee from word of mouth, at least you checked up on it.

Moses: What if it is an "all-in deal" and the producer says he is paying you out of his pocket?

Francis Buckley: Well, then, you have to know the producer. It's really tough. It is hard for somebody new coming into this business. Most of the people I work with are people that I have worked with in the past.

Jeff Weber: If you're good enough, people will pay you to do what you do. If you're not good enough, you shouldn't be doing it anyway.

When You Get Beat, You Stay Beat

Even working for top artists is no guarantee of truth in hiring. In fact, many cases, the bigger the artist, the bigger the lie.

Francis Buckley: It was on a [name withheld] session. [He] came in with **Quincy [Jones]** and was singing on a tune, and he liked the way I was mixing. His wife/girl-friend/manager/company president…you know, everything you could imagine, came in and asked me if I would do some mixing for them and I said sure. There were some things said between Quincy and another person after [the artist] left the room, and Quincy made a remark to me, "If you're going to do business with him then you better keep both hands in your pockets." But I thought, it's [artist's name]. That's when I heard the studio manager on the phone with this girl who was taking care of [the artist's] business, saying that it looks like this is really going to be a "stinker session." Before I went back in I should have gotten on the phone to clear it up, but instead I went back in the studio and finished the mix. The next day I tried to get paid and couldn't find anybody. I haven't talked to anybody in that group since. That mistake cost me about $4,000.

An engineer doesn't have a lot of leverage, even when they have a great reputation. They almost always perform their job before they get paid, and since many projects are financed in iffy ways, they are often scammed out of their fees. This is true even in major-label projects. Many major projects are subcontracted out to smaller production entities, so the engineer is being hired by an entity that in many cases is little more than a DBA.[7]

⊙ Spotting the Liar

A high-profile study recently showed that many of the old cut-and-dried rules for spotting a liar are not really true. If lying is part of one's regular routine, then one will practice to perfection all the symptoms of honesty. The following information is only a brief digest of a larger study, but I've tailored it to the music business to give it some focus.

Eye Contact

"Always look people in the eye," my mother said. However, it's a fallacy that someone is being honest if he can look you in the eye when talking to you. The truth is a bit more complex. Sociopaths are very good at eye contact. In fact, it seems that proficient liars for the most part understand that eye contact is important in order to be believed. Some people are too nervous to make eye contact even when telling the truth (especially if they have a serious drug history). In many cultures, it is considered impolite to look directly in someone's eyes. Context is important.

A&R reps, managers, lawyers, and most corporate executives are great at eye contact. Few would agree that they are bad liars. However, most who can hold a gaze will usually slip up at the very end of a conversation. They will look past you or at your forehead as they end the meeting with the closing line, which is a lie.

Innocent Looks

Studies show that those with a "baby face" tend to be proficient liars when they want to, as we find them easy to believe. A youthful appearance in the music biz is common. Many people look younger than they are, and trade on this fact.[8]

However, though good looks are often thought to be a sign of a suspect person, it turns out this is *not* a given. Many attractive people are too insecure to be good liars. (This doesn't mean that they don't try.) Those that are not tend to rely on their looks as a tool to boost their confidence, confidence being their primary agent of veracity.

Feeling Cocky All Day

Career seminars are rife with advice to job seekers. They stress that you should sit leaning slightly forward to convey confidence. What they don't tell you is that confidence, although taught to be a good attribute, is often met with secret disdain in the music world. Those who have too much are thought arrogant and untrustworthy. They do often get jobs—entry-level jobs. A good liar looking for a middle-management job will be meeting with people higher up on the food chain than a Human Resources person. And so, not wanting to be a threat, a good liar will

[8] One of the most dangerous liars in the music business I ever encountered bore a striking resemblance to the Gerber Baby Food model.

therefore try to look inept or clumsy when necessary to distract you from their ambitions. Until they are in charge. Then the real personality will surface.

If you find yourself dealing with someone who seems to be a charming fool, perform a test by lobbing something to them, like a softball. Test their reflexes. Only a CIA asset could fake slow response time to a surprise attack.

Generalities

Another consistent tool of the liar is generalities. Honest people tend to speak using specifics. Liars are vague. They answer questions indirectly. My favorite is use of the word "basically." Basically means not really and I'm lying through my teeth. There are exceptions, but when used as an adjective, such as "Well, this means basically _____," get out the air freshener.

Pay attention for vagueness next time you're in a business setting. Try to catch yourself lying once in a while. You'll see that we use this technique seamlessly in conversation all the time without realizing it.

> *Liar:* I worked on the _____ record.
> *You:* Really. What did you do?
> *Liar:* I was in on the sessions. Worked with them every day.
> *You:* You wrote the songs?
> *Liar:* I was there when every song was written and was basically working with the producer.
> *You:* So was the cleaning lady. What exactly did you do?
> *Liar:* Tech.
> *You:* Like guitar or drum setups?
> *Liar:* Studio equipment.
> *You:* Changed the coffee, took out the trash?

By now the liar is looking for a way out. Another version:

> *Liar:* I work with _____.
> *You:* Cool. How long?
> *Liar:* Uh, on and off. We hung together like for six months.
> *You:* Cool. Did you work for him or were you his partner?
> *Liar:* Nah, it wasn't like that. We was down together, y'dig? I helped him with the album. Y'dig?
> *You:* Yeah, I dig.

Name-droppers are one of the most common types of liars in the music business. The real insiders rarely drop names. Wannabes will make sure you know everybody they scored drugs for, opened a door for, you name it. Always with vague references and cool street lingo implanted to intimidate and confuse you so that you don't ask too many questions.

Of course, there are exceptions to each and every one of these guidelines. You have to use your judgment as to when it's best to probe for the truth and when it's best to leave it alone. Also note another huge giveaway in the dialog above: *changing from present to past tense*. This is a good giveaway of a person who can't keep the fake facts straight in his head.

Hesitations

It takes the average person about half a second to respond to a question if he doesn't have to think about a clever answer. If he's lying, the brain takes a few extra seconds to scan for inconsistencies in previous given data to make sure he's on track. However, I've known people—often the smarter folks—who are loath to give quick, easy, or general answers. So they take their time answering questions. Then there are the ones who have an instinct for what you want to hear (whether or not it's the truth) and can fire that right back at you. So how can you work with this?

Make a note of how long it takes a person to respond to you in a conversation where you know they are telling the truth. Actually count one-one thousand, two-one thousand, in your head. Eventually, when the lies start to come, that amount of time will extend, maybe only slightly. And here's the up-sell for those who have this technique down. Don't be fooled by the "quasi-answer"—that is, the series of musings uttered by the person before the actual answer comes out. Sometimes people will use an "uh" or "basically" to buy a few extra seconds needed to form their answer. Only the actual answer is what counts when timing responses.

In this business we may have to adapt this theory as many have been affected by drugs. Pot and booze tend to slow down everything. Coke, on the other hand, could mask a slow thinker and instill false confidence.

Manners

We tend to trust those who use good manners. Liars know this. They will apologize quickly to defuse mistrust, say please and thank you a bit more than what is socially normal for the group.

People in the music business, however, seem to have an inherent mistrust of those who have perfected society's standards for being polite. You'll notice successful people who use an inordinate amount of colorful language, inappropriate comments regarding women, and references to body functions as part of everyday conversation.

An Irish friend of mine says he doesn't trust people who don't drink. I know many religious people who favor doing business with people in their congregation. In the music space it seems that this philosophy is converted to the items above: We trust those who are rude. Therefore, people who talk "straight" are thought to be something on the order of a narc.

Liars in the music space find this easy to capitalize on since they had trouble talking straight in the first place. Music is a far easier area for them to freely operate. Thus the business tends to attract many liars.

As a test, try rejecting a shallow apology when you suspect a liar. These are apologies that are usually a bit off-topic, like, "I'm sorry *if* your feelings were hurt." Never about what they might have actually done. Music biz liars subconsciously try to avoid responsibility. The quasi-apology mimics actual remorse without committing to it mentally. If you reject their apology and ask for them to own up, they will usually respond with something like, "Well, let's just agree to disagree," or some faux-diplomatic utterance designed to dismiss you. If they were lying and the apology was a mere tool to defuse your suspicion, they will not make the connection to what they did wrong, since they probably think you are a sucker in the first place.

Geza X cut his producing teeth on mariachi, funk, gospel, and disco. Although his legendary work with groups like **Germs, Black Flag, Dead Kennedys, Redd Kross**, and **Josey Cotton** helped create the face of American punk, he is best known for his production of **Meredith Brooks**'s mega-hit "Bitch," which stayed at No. 2 for an astounding six weeks, prompting *Billboard* to list him as one of 1997's top producers.

> *Geza X:* As a basic philosophy, kissing ass is bad. If you are openly kissing ass, people get grossed out. That can alienate people because you are just too nice and it seems phony. I've had that problem. One of the mistakes that I've made is that I really am that nice. I am not kissing ass; I am just a sweet cat. I would go talk to people and be all good cheer and really enthusiastic, and they would just kind of go, whoa, this guy is a big phony.

Too Close for Comfort

It's a commonly held belief that it's harder to lie to people we are close to. But the same research shows that most of the lies we tell are to the people we see every day—wives, parents, bosses, teachers, and such. A better guideline is that liars find it easier to lie when they think they can get away with it. People they are close to can see their "tells" more easily.

Bottom line: The clichés about liars are meaningless. The examples above are only slightly less so. You want to look for subtle changes in behavior. Does he usually offer you a cigarette when smoking and forgets to this time? Does he usually neglect to offer you a drink but makes a point of it this time? These are "tells" of someone who is trying to get over.

So Who Can You Trust?

I figured, if you want tips on catching a liar, ask a lawyer. It's their stock in trade. **Paul Menes** has been a music lawyer in Los Angeles for many years. He is a frequent speaker and writer on various entertainment matters, with credits including California Lawyers for the Arts, the *Los Angeles Times*, UCLA, *South by Southwest*, and EAT'M, among others, and has been profiled in several editions of *Who's Who in American Law*.

Paul Menes: My first inkling of problems to come occurred during several conversations I had with an artist I was then representing during the record contract negotiations. He went out of his way one too many times to tell me how much he liked me, respected me, and appreciated my hard work, that he and his family were very loyal and looked forward to all of us growing old together in this industry. This kind of unsolicited and repetitive touchy-feeliness is usually a sure sign that exactly the opposite will occur.

Moses: Too much schmaltz[9] as they say in Yiddish.

Paul Menes: Yes.

Moses: I play poker a lot—I look for tics and stuff like that to tell when someone is bluffing. How do you know? What do you look for?

Paul Menes: There are a couple of ways I know. When they state the obvious, such as "You can trust me," or "I would never do such and such." That raises my antenna as high as it goes, even with people I think I know. I also reality check by verifying information periodically through another source just to see if I am being fucked with or the person's perception is bad, or, worse, if I am being lied to. If I am with a team of professionals around an artist and the management tells me something, I may have a chat with somebody at the label or a chat with somebody at the agency to see what their version of this is.

Moses: People who say "you can trust me" you don't trust?

Paul Menes: If you can trust them, they don't need to tell you that.

Moses: What do people who you *can* trust say?

9 Schmaltz: Yiddish. Rendered chicken fat that you spread on bread. In English it means corny.

Paul Menes: Nothing. They don't usually say much of anything, they usually act. I trust people that are one step ahead of me. What I mean by that is, there are certain benchmarks of representing somebody that tend to go on in order. They start out, there is [record company] interest in them, they get signed to a label, maybe they get a publishing deal next, they go out on tour. On the way to those benchmarks you see people working their butts off to accomplish them without telling you they are going to do it or taking a lot of credit for it. That, to me, starts instilling or validating trust. But if they tell me they take credit for them after the fact, that erodes the trust.

Interesting. Over-promising as a "tell." Checking facts as a way of unveiling someone's pathological optimism is a sound policy. But sometimes you have to make a judgment on the spot.

A better technique is what the cops use as an interrogation tool: ask a question you know the answer to and observe the person's body language as they answer. If they tell the truth, make mental notes. Then when the pattern changes during the balance of the conversation, you can label those comments as suspect.

➲ Should You Lie?

So we've learned that lying is epidemic and often necessary. But should you do it? It depends on what kind of person you are. You don't want to get caught in a lie, and if you're not a good liar, you *will* get caught. Here's a few facts about lying and liars.

- Most people think that they are not being lied to. About half the time, they are wrong.
- Most basically honest people are bad liars and will get caught.
- Most people think they are basically honest.
- These same people believe that lying is sometimes necessary.

Conclusion: If you're a good liar, you'll probably get away with it. If you're basically honest, you won't.

Enough about deceit. Next up, we're taking a direct road into the heart of darkness for every pop star. It ranked as the number one reason why mistakes occur. Keep reading.

⊘ You're So Cool

Or, Functioning Within Dysfunction

> *"I don't know the key to success, but the key*
> *to failure is trying to please everybody."*
> **—Bill Cosby**

E go. It's the engine that drives both that which makes artists and moguls great and that which leads to their downfall. In showbiz the ego often manifests as an "attitude" that you're a bit better than the rest of us. You walk between the raindrops rubbing the parabola between bohemia and business, stretching it out in your wake as you snub the glitterati waiting outside the venue for even a glimpse of your greatness. Does it pay off in the long run? It's hard to construct a working policy when successful people in the business say one thing and do another.

When planning this book I first constructed a series of questions for the subjects who consented to be interviewed. One of these was "What is the biggest mistake made by people who've been in the business for over five years?" I wanted to see what happens to people when they achieve some success and start to get lazy. How does that laziness take form? Invariably many people's answers related to times when they just got cocky and started taking their achievements for granted, thinking success was going to last forever.

Jay Jay French: Have you ever watched *MTV Cribs*? Well, I came up with a sequel, *MTV Foreclosures*. A two-year follow-up to the rap artist who was on *MTV Cribs* [two years before]. First, he shows you around his house, his Maserati, and his bling bling. Two years later he's living in a basement apartment in Tampa. They are discussing how he just lost everything because he actually didn't realize that the video that cost a million bucks was being charged to *him* and his record didn't sell the way it was supposed to. He's totally bankrupt. Meantime the problem is compounded when the artist sees their video on MTV and then [goes out and spends money]. They could end up broke.

Often the cars and houses you see in a music video are merely supplied by a production company for the shoot. When the director yells "cut" the models go home and the limo goes back to the rental garage. Not until the artist's second or third album on a major label is there usually the kind of money to sustain that quality of life. Many artists believe their own hype or they feel pressured to be the successful returning son to their 'hood. They get an entourage, and spend, spend, spend. When the second record doesn't do as well, they have an unglamorous adjustment to make.

Jay Jay French: Where is the reality of the business? Yo, MTV, you really want to school the kids, have a real boring one-hour weekly show: "Here's how the music business really functions." And by the way, if you have the smartest manager in the world and he sits down with the band and tells them all this, the musicians, more than likely, won't believe him anyway.

Thanks, Jay Jay. That's why I'm here.

Let's put a microscope on "the cool factor" and see if we can't break it down to specifics, starting by busting open this major myth:

⊘ Be Nice Because It's a Small Business

1 **Music symposiums. CMJ is hosted by the industry tip sheet College Music Journal. SXSW is a clever acronym for South by Southwest, the meeting point of two large US territories.**

It will be noticed that with newcomers, a lack of success often doesn't stop them from assuming the same presumptuous attitude as those who've survived round one of the pop star game. Adopting a posture derived from a commonly used bit of "success training" rhetoric: "Fake it till you make it." As an organic reaction to this, industry symposiums like **SXSW** or **CMJ**[1] employ panelists that dole out conversely infective, half-baked advice. Things like, "It's small business. Be nice and humble to everyone you meet." How could giving such advice be spun as anything but helpful, you might ask? Well, for starters it's so pedantic and without context that it tends to serve no purpose other than to make the speaker sound "informed." When I hear such things I just scratch my head thinking, what the hell are they talking about? It's *not* a small business. **Peter Spellman**, author of *The Self-Promoting Musician*, *The Musician's Internet*, and *Indie Power*, and the head of career development at the **Berklee College of Music**, adds this to the theory:

> *Peter Spellman:* It is not really a small business. I am always amazed to hear about something [going on] and say, holy shit, when did this happen, where was I? There are all these music niches and cool things going on in the corners and margins of things going on that make you realize this is a diffused industry. It's all over the map and all over the spectrum.

There are more than ten national conferences dedicated solely to music. And these don't include all the smaller, local events. There are literally thousands of people at the executive level at major and indie labels. Not to mention DJs, managers, publicists, and so on.

In truth, there are really only two types of people who say things like, "It's a small business." The vast minority of them are in the upper echelon, have survived the five-year benchmark, and so tend to deal with the same people over and over again. The other group, the vast majority who repeat this mantra, want you to think that they are in the first group.

It's not a "nice, humble" industry either. Many of those at the top can be sublimely un-humble.

Just look at some examples of some of the most successful people in the business who are known (or were known) for being anything *but* nice or humble.

Business Side	Artists
Berry Gordy	John Mellencamp
Irving Azoff	Madonna
David Geffen	Bruce Springsteen
Walter Yetnikoff	Prince
Tommy Mottola	David Bowie
Suge Knight	Mick Jagger
Jimmy Iovine	John Lennon
Sean "P. Diddy, Puffy" Combs	Gene Simmons
	Michael Jackson
	Bob Dylan

To assume they only became "edgy" once they got to the top just doesn't jibe with human nature. So, how did they do it? How does a rude dude get to the top if you have to be nice to everyone to get to the top?

Peter Spellman: I think in terms of how you communicate with people, that's just going to be your personality and your style. You are going to build bridges or you're going to burn them. Whoever you are, you've got to just be.

The conundrum: blowing people off to get ahead seems wrong on every gut level of what we've been taught about how to succeed. Yet, in order to support the accuracy of "be humble or you won't make it," you have to explain how all these people made it while being who they are. There must be some finer points to this. **Jay Jay French** brings us enlightenment:

Jay Jay French: This business is controlled by a small group of people that tend to dictate the flow of how things are going. *Their dysfunction is your dysfunction and you need to learn how to function within that dysfunction.*

Functioning within dysfunction. There is our mantra. If we like this paradigm, we can gauge a person's potential success in the record business based on how well one functions within dysfunction. Or, to be more blunt, an equation that looks something like this:

Tolerance of dysfunction or being dysfunctional yourself = Success

Are we through the looking glass yet? No? Let's jump on in and learn about some common (and hilarious) "dysfunctions" in the music space.

❯ Neither Commit nor Offend

Leslie Zigel is a lawyer. One of the best in the music business. For years, he was vice president of Business and Legal Affairs with **BMG**'s Latin American Regional Office and US Latin Operations. Lawyers typically specialize in intimidation. This sometimes means letting the other side sweat it out by not returning their phone calls. Making them rethink their position. But Leslie has a different approach.

Leslie Zigel: I think the biggest mistake that one can make is not returning phone calls and not paying attention to people's feelings. I know this is going to sound touchy feely, but all people want is *respect*. The worst thing that you can do is blow people off, not return phone calls, and not be straight with them.

Moses: Why do you think people are so lazy?

Leslie Zigel: Executives too often are afraid to tell people no.

There is a very real social pathology in entertainment executives. People don't want to commit or offend. To do either is to fail the assignment—to act as though you are progressing toward something when you are actually trying to keep things in a holding pattern long enough for your options to mature. This is why we have the perpetual "Take a message, I'll get back to them" syndrome.

When this happens there's always a hidden agenda, one that you will not likely ever discover. Nor should you really ponder too long, either, because it's likely not anything strategic, but simply a product of the executive's dysfunction. Like being late to meet a beautiful young singer he's trying to date. Or there's a sale on Ferragamos at Bloomingdale's.

One time I was trying to hire a marketing firm to promote an artist. The firm was well overdue for the marketing plan they were supposed to submit. The truth is probably they wanted to pass on the job. But the woman I was dealing with didn't tell me that. Instead her assistant said, "She's going to call you *today*, you're at the top of her list." This went on for weeks. I found another firm, but my curiosity got the better of me. I investigated and found out that the woman I was dealing with (who was recommended by a new acquaintance) was banging her assistant behind her husband's back. When the assistant quit she went into a depression for several weeks. Her business with me became a low priority. Other clients who were embarking on major releases were also caught up in her dysfunction. Press releases went unwritten, interviews unscheduled. She got a new assistant who ended up doing most of the work. Even after I caught her in this dysfunction she played her game perfectly, emailing me with a cockamamie story about a death in her family. (No shame.)

I was not merely being metaphoric a couple of paragraphs back. It *is* a pathology. Using sympathy as an excuse to get out of looking stupid is never beneath those who are its victims. Why not just call and say, "I can't take on your project right now"? Would that save face? No, it would not. The key to the riddle? Behold.

The Client Is the Enemy

Saying no shuts a door. Shutting a door means that at some point you will have to confront this person you slammed, because you will likely encounter them again in the future. "No" creates tension. It creates animosity. It leads to situations where you could be removed from a future situation because "the vibe isn't right" when you are in the same room with this person you dissed.

But saying yes creates potential liability too. The awful, unspoken truth is that the client is usually considered the enemy in many professional situations. Clients have demands. Clients are rarely satisfied, especially in situations of subjective results, like PR, contract negotiations, and record producing. When clients are not happy, the company and jobs are in peril.

So we get the formula that manifests one of the primary dysfunctions in the entertainment business: Never commit, but don't *ever* offend. The technique is employed by very successful people. But the truth is, they are only successful as business persons. As humans, the jury is still out.

John Luongo has been instrumental in mixing and producing songs that have benefited groups from **Aerosmith** to **ZZ Top**, **Jesus Jones**, and **Bobby Brown**. He mixed and broke many hit tracks such as **Don Henley**'s "All She Wants to Do Is Dance" and **Huey Lewis**'s "I Want a New Drug" and "Power of Love," to name a few.

> *John Luongo:* I once did not return a call after meeting with an up-and-coming producer. I met him in my office and loved his material, but as you know things get crazy and you put out the fires that are burning brightest first. That was **Steven Bray,** who was **Madonna**'s old boyfriend and the founder of the **Breakfast Club**. He went on to have a great career. He produced a great Breakfast Club LP and worked on other artists as well. You learn to never put things off and treat everyone the same.

> *Leslie Zigel:* I can give you an example of where saying no bought me business. There was a soundtrack I was working on when I was [a business affairs executive] with BMG and they wanted one of our artists. We were trying very hard to make the deal happen, but at the end of the day the deal went south. I didn't string them along. I was upfront. I made the call with the bad news. Two years later I got a call from [another company], the music supervisor from that failed film soundtrack deal, and he was doing the soundtrack for a cable show called *Resurrection Boulevard* on Showtime.[2] He told the executives in the TV and music departments that the only Latin label to do a soundtrack deal with is **BMG**. They asked why. He said that

2 *Resurrection Boulevard*: A series about a Latin family living in East L.A. Aired on Showtime.

their business affairs executive told them "that of all the business affairs executives I've dealt with you were the most straightforward, you didn't bullshit around. You tried to make the deal happen; it didn't. When it wasn't going to happen, you came back and were a gentleman about it and treated me with respect." That was a reaffirmation of why it was important to return all of your phone calls and treat everyone with respect.... I think the issue of being nice or not nice, polite or not polite is a personal choice, and the karma that one wants to create for themselves. To disprove your theory the one person I would look at is **Bruce Lundvall**.[3] You know how he got **Norah Jones**, right? He returned a call from somebody in the accounting or manufacturing department at **EMI**, who said, "I heard this great artist and I would love for you to hear her." He said, "Bring her in." Norah played the piano in Bruce's office and Bruce said, "Okay, get a lawyer—you've got a deal."

[3] CEO of Blue Note Records.

Fear of Success

Some mental health professionals think that early on in life we develop certain handicaps as an "excuse factory" so that we can continue to fail with impunity. A shy person may actually manifest overly gregarious behavior in an attempt to push people away and fulfill his desire to avoid interaction with people. A fear of intimacy can manifest in many ways. One is promiscuousness to "turn off" appropriate suitors. Seems contradictory, but that's often how the psyche works, in ways that fit into a universe of logic unique to each mind.

SUICIDE MAY BE PAINLESS, BUT IT'S BAD FOR SALES

In 1994, **Kurt Cobain**, lead singer of **Nirvana**, died of a gunshot wound to the head. This started a wave of Nirvana-mania. Suicide or accident? The controversy raced as fast as the media could spin it. Sales climbed and crated a mini-industry. Was his death a contrived sales device? Outrageous. Would a record company stoop so low?

It's a commonly held belief that the best thing an artist can do to launch his immortality is die tragically and prematurely. Is it true? In the late 1960s, a ruse was created to spread a rumor that **Paul McCartney** of the **Beatles** was dead. This turned out to be a false claim designed to do nothing more than boost sales. It was a successful campaign. Renewed interest in the Beatles helped edge their waning popularity back into the number one slot (hedging against, of all groups, the **Monkees**). Is death really good for sales? My interview with **Jim Barber**, who was a senior executive for **Geffen Records**, the company who profited most from Cobain's death, was enlightening. He later managed Kurt Cobain's catalog and is well placed to give us some interesting insight into this question: Can you spin suicide into profits?

Jim Barber: Suicide detracts from the value of the catalog. It hurts merchandise sales. If you're a 14-year-old kid and you bring home a T-shirt with the picture of some rock martyr on it, what is your mom going to say? "Isn't that the guy who offed himself? Take it back to the store." No public figure in [US] pop culture history has ever killed himself. You can rationalize that **Jimi Hendrix** or **James Dean** died in an accident. You don't have to assign them direct responsibility for their deaths.

Moses: **Marilyn Monroe**?

Jim Barber: Accident, overdose.

Moses: **Jeff Buckley, Jr.**?

Jim Barber: Accident.

Moses: You think?

Jim Barber: People who knew him still believe that he was in great shape and about to make the record of his career. Nobody knows how this happened.[4]

Moses: **Sid Vicious**?[5]

Jim Barber: Overdose.

Moses: I thought he stabbed himself.

Jim Barber: You're right, yeah.

Moses: One could argue that these "overdoses" are *all* suicides.

Jim Barber: Of course you could. The myth of **Jim Morrison** dying in a bathtub or **Janis Joplin** OD-ing, they are all really rationalized acts of suicide. People can't deal with the idea of their heroes taking their own life.

[4] Jeff Buckley: A promising singer/songwriter who died in a drowning accident just after the release of his first album.

[5] Sid Vicious: Bass player of the foundational punk band the Sex Pistols. His death is controversial and is dramatized well in the film *Sid & Nancy*.

One of the most prevalent features in the music space is drugs. Don't believe articles that talk about this subject as if it's history. Drugs are everywhere. It's as much a part of the business today as insider trading is to finance.

But an addiction to drugs is not an excuse factory in and of itself. It's the cover for the *real* excuse. **Joey Akles**[6] had a chance to work with one of the biggest female rock sensations of the 1980s—the **Go-Go's**.[7] He gives us a great example of how being a fall-down addict is actually a socially acceptable cover for a real dysfunction—*fear of success.*

> *Joey Akles:* One phone call I should have made and never made was caused not by my ego but by my "illness" at the time. I was just a songwriter, I think it was 1982–83. The week that the Go-Go's were getting ready to make their first real album, they had already released "We Got the Beat." I was really friendly with a couple of them. Now, **Kathy Valentine**[8] had a couple of unfinished songs she wanted to finish with me because she loved my choruses. But I was very "sick" [read: high] and I didn't feel like returning the call, and I never did return her call. She called two or three times that morning saying, "Joey, I really want to finish these songs with you, we are going to New York next week, I know we can finish these songs and get them on the album." I was on a binge. If I would have gotten one song on the album, imagine the money. Even half of a song.[9] For years and years it would be worth money too—it keeps coming in.

It's amazing how easily Akles volunteered this to me. In fact, in my interviews many subjects were not even slightly embarrassed to openly discuss drug use. In this industry it's almost an embarrassment to *not* be indulging. A person refusing to return a phone call and missing out on a golden opportunity because they were hung over or too stoned to remember is the stuff that fills the air at the local Blarney Stone. It's practically a rite of passage. A requisite ticket for admission into the hall of "real music biz professionals." But Akles had a bit more to confess.

> *Joey Akles:* I will be honest with you, the binge had little to do with it. I was frightened. When I saw the video for "We Got the Beat" I predicted that they were going to be big. If I am really being honest it was a lack of self-esteem. I was afraid that [Kathy Valentine] would find me out as a fraud. No matter how many times I had written successful songs I always felt back then that I could never do it again. I think this is the natural insecurity of artists, songwriters, or creators. You always think you can't do it again no matter how good you were before. It wasn't really the

[6] Best known as the co-author of the power pop hit for the Plimsouls and the Goo Goo Dolls, "Million Miles Away."

[7] The Go-Go's: First all-female rock group who played their own instruments. Hits include "Our Lips Are Sealed," "Vacation," and "We Got the Beat."

[8] Kathy Valentine: Bassist for the Go-Go's and writer of several of their better songs. Replaced Margot Olavera.

[9] Half of a song, in those days, on a million-selling album is worth $30,000 in the first year. Residual money would be worth about $150,000 per year for the early years. If it's a mega-hit, add a zero.

dope. I had shown up "sick" plenty of times and did the job, even as a singer. The real truth was I knew those girls and I knew the record was going to be big and I was scared. I knew they were happening, and I was scared they would find me out.

Feelings of being a fake are not uncommon in artists, even ones who have experienced success. Many turn to substances as an agent for their excuse factory. Although I didn't want to dedicate a chapter to drugs as a mistake, done to excess, it's a no-brainer that they surely are.[10]

[10] A bit of irony in Joey's embarrassment about being high in front of the girls: it was revealed in an IRS audit that lead vocalist Belinda Carlisle squandered all her money earned from the Go-Go's, mostly on drugs. She also originally wanted to call the group the Sluts.

❯ I Ain't Puttin' Up with No Crap

Artists are quite sensitive, as anyone who's worked with them can tell you. Even the tougher-looking ones can turn into a prima donna as a way of masking insecurities.

Dysfunction number 235: whining about working conditions.

Many are drawn to the music business based largely on what they think the business is like through dramatizations in movies and TV. The classic misrepresentation is seeing the singer in the studio standing ten feet away from the band as they cut a hit song. The last time this was a reality was before the days of isolation booths—in the early sixties. These days singers are rarely recorded on the same day as the backing track. And this is the most obvious example. See the sidebar for a list of the most common clichés about the music industry as they are dramatized in movies.

The reality is that working conditions are generally far less glorious than Hollywood depicts. You should see some of the bathrooms I've been in in the top studios in New York.

It's easy for an artist to become upset by this. This can work both ways. I've seen many situations where new artists whine about the working conditions and that moment of weakness was costly. Small complaints have a way of maturing into a career burner because you never know how your desire to vent will be used against you by your detractors. Here's a common template. This is a true story. In fact it probably happens about once every day somewhere in the US music business.

- An artist vents about her producer to her manager: "He's pushing me too hard, and I think it sounded fine on the third take." The manager tells the label's A&R exec about it. So the A&R person fires the producer.
- The artist feels a bit shell-shocked by this. The dramatic cause and effect of the situation teaches the artist that she has enormous power. Or so it seems. She laments and tries to make it better by telling the A&R exec that she really

liked working with the producer, she just thought he was being too fussy. But the A&R exec tells her that they can't go backwards and they have someone new for her to work with. He makes it sound like the producer was canned for some other reason that has nothing to do with the artist (handling her). She feels a little better and thinks, "I guess he had it coming."

- The new producer doesn't have the same vibe. He didn't coddle the artist to get this gig. He was brought in to do damage control. He's a cleaner, here to finish this job by any means necessary. His studio also smells like old beer, and people do drugs in the lounge. The prudish artist now wishes the old producer was back with her, but he's not returning her phone calls anymore. She complains again about the new producer to her manager, this time in confidence: "Don't tell anyone this came from me."

TOP FIVE COMPLAINTS ABOUT THE BUSINESS BY PEOPLE IN IT

- It takes too long to get paid, even after you made the money.
- Loyalty is nonexistent. Friends are phony.
- Record company contracts are too restrictive.
- ASCAP's and BMI's payment system is inequitable in many cases, and they take too high a percentage in all cases.
- Ego dominates decisions more than logic or the greater good.

TOP FIVE PRAISES ABOUT THE BUSINESS BY PEOPLE IN IT

- Money is good once you can get to it.
- You get to make a lot of people happy with your product.
- Great perks: tickets, free music, travel, parties, etc.
- People are cool. Morality is relaxed.
- Every day is casual Friday.

- Now the manager is starting to think the artist is a whiner. He wonders how long it will be until she begins complaining about him behind his back. He begins to secretly become less interested in helping her, even though he continues to work for her and, most importantly, he never relays the artist's concerns about the new producer to the A&R exec because he doesn't want to rock the boat. Instead he "forgets" about it.
- Three weeks into the production the situation does not improve, and the artist eventually confronts her manager: "Did you ever tell the A&R guy about the problems I'm having with the new producer?" He confesses that he has not and tells her why. She gets pissed. Now, to her, it seems like *nobody* is listening. She wonders how many other things he (and others) are not doing that they said they would do. Probably many, she thinks.
- With nowhere else to turn, she goes to the A&R exec. She complains about the new producer and her manager. The A&R exec sees his project going to pieces and a pink slip in his near future. He, in turn, starts to distance himself from the impending stink. He tells the new producer, in a private meeting over a drink, that he should just finish the damn thing as fast as possible. The producer gets the message that this project is destined for the reject bin and starts doing less than his best work.
- When the record is done, it's a mess: mediocre performances and half-baked arrangements. The label decides to bag it. The manager quits and the artist is now looking to put together a new team. This will be hard with the manager, two producers, and the A&R exec not singing her praises. She gets a rep that she is "hard to work with" or has a "bad vibe." Her career is basically over and she's only 18.

"All for the loss of one nail," as the saying goes. All because she had a moment of normal weakness and wanted to express her frustration. She didn't think that everyone involved would be so freaking sensitive. She was just venting. Can't they see that?

No, they can't. They see a person who cannot handle herself and feels the need to trash others rather than deal with her problems. That is what people in this business will see eight out of ten times. Few will see their role in the situation or how they could improve upon it by taking a little responsibility.

Lesson to be learned: if you're having problems with a person or situation, fix it yourself. Do not *ever* share it with the other people you are working with. They will become paranoid and begin to secretly dislike you. Share your frustrations with family, *real* friends, or a therapist. Keep the work-loop positive.

WHAT HOLLYWOOD HAS TAUGHT US ABOUT THE MUSIC INDUSTRY

Thank God for those well-paid and detail-oriented Hollywood producers. They love to make movies about the music industry. About three a year grace the screen. Ironically, few of them do well in theaters. Perhaps this is because the world of pop music as depicted on the big screen is so out of touch with reality that even those who are not in the business have a sixth sense that Hollywood's version seen is ridiculous. Here's my top-24 list of things that make me laugh every time I see them dramatized.

Hollywood's Music Business	The Real Music Business
Artists record their albums and sing in the same room and at the same time as the band. (And everybody is in tune.)	Not since 1965. Vocals are almost always recorded in separate sessions. You're lucky if the singer shows up at all for tracking the instruments.
No bar, backstage area, or social situation is too informal for the signing of a binding, long-term recording contract. Lawyers need not be present for these meetings. It's all about trust.	Contracts take months to negotiate. No respectable label would ever let an artist sign a contract without legal representation. It could void the entire deal.
Record executives all have the same interior decorator who lines the back walls of their office with platinum records, shag carpet, and a fully stocked bar.	At big labels, the office of a major-label A&R executive is about 10 by 14 and has little more than a desk (covered with CDs) and a stereo. He gets a window if he's had a good year.

Hit songs are usually recorded in a single take, after which the producer yells, "Cut! That's the one, baby!"

If only it were true. It usually takes many hours and many overdubs. For most of the process the producer is not present. It's done by the engineer as per the producer's instructions. The artist is rarely there for most of the process.

Recording engineers are conscientious nerds who safeguard the gear by prohibiting smoking and drugs in the control room.

Many engineers are chain smokers and are usually good for a lead on great drugs. (Although new laws are making it illegal to smoke in recording studios. We'll see if that has any real impact.)

Even though digital technology has done away with reel-to-reel tape, the best studios have not yielded to the pressure and retain their old multitracks and massive analog mixing consoles.

Studios are getting smaller and smaller. Large consoles exist these days mostly as a status symbol and because they impress clients. Client lounges are also getting smaller and smaller, doubling as vocal booths more often than not.

Albums are recorded and then released a few days later.

They sit on the shelf for months before the marketing department decides whether or not to release them at all.

All recording sessions end at the crack of dawn.

Well, this one may be true.

Artists go from a one-bedroom flat to a mansion shortly after their first album hits the charts.

It takes about two years before royalties are paid from a first hit. During this time artists usually do not quit their day jobs. Some manage to negotiate a "special advance" that pays rent on their current flat.

Every female pop star is an unstable bitch who verbally abuses her staff and clings to her amphetamine-pushing manager like a-long lost father.

Most successful female artists participate significantly in their business matters. They don't have time for drugs, especially if they are mothers, as many of the ones over 27 are.

Recording studios, limo companies, and hotels employ a staff of people to keep potato chips, pretzels, and condom foils from littering their floor.

The only person who cleans the floor at a studio is the intern who is too busy doing errands and making coffee. The floor of a small owner-operated studio is often a science experiment. In hotels the *do not disturb* sign, perpetually in position, keeps maids out for days. Let's face it, cleanliness is just not a priority in this arena.

Drug dealers are down-to-earth philosophers providing an important service that, in a perfect, enlightened world, would really be legal.

They may be on the artist's speed dial, but these days, drug dealers do not socialize with the group. Bad for PR, and insurance companies (who underwrite tours) raise the premiums to very high levels.

Phil Spector: An
amazing producer
who unfortunately
will probably best
be remembered
not for his out-
standing body of
work, but for being
charged with the
murder of a Holly-
wood starlet in
2003. He at first
apologized for the
shooting, calling it
accidental, but
later said she com-
mitted suicide.

[11] Phil Spector: An amazing producer who unfortunately will probably best be remembered not for his outstanding body of work, but for being charged with the murder of a Hollywood starlet in 2003. He at first apologized for the shooting, calling it accidental, but later said she committed suicide.

Every record producer lives in a huge house in Bel Air with a kidney-shaped swimming pool and photos of them partying with **Phil Spector**.[11]

Getting backstage at a concert is as simple as flashing a body part or sweet-talking your way past a 300-pound goon on loan from the Hell's Angels.

Pop stars' girlfriends are hot, bored, bisexual lingerie models who live to do little more than plan their next opportunity to have sex in a truck stop restroom. They also have special mascara that never runs. Even after an all-nighter.

Fall-down-drunk artists who have fits of violent rage are actually just misunderstood poets pushed to work past their limits by mean managers and bastard Jew lawyers.

The backstage area at any rock concert has the best sound mix in the house. Special sensors dim the music to low levels every time people need to talk to one another in normal tones.

I'll concede the part about Phil.

Cash doesn't hurt. This cliché is a leftover from the old days when rockers hung out with bikers. These days the bigger acts hire professional security teams that rival the Secret Service.

I got two words for you: **Sharon Osbourne**. The girls that seem to attract pop stars for long-term relationships tend to be very down-to-earth gals who often take on the menial chores of the star's business. After popping out a couple of kids, few are modeling lingerie.

No. They are just fall-down drunks, but they have a talent that is paying everyone's bills, so we give them more latitude.

If you're hanging out in the wings you're yelling your lungs out and constantly being bumped by roadies and ushered by stagehands. The mix is bad as well.

When concert tickets are sold, the box office makes sure to sell the front five rows to a quota of young girls who promise to remove their tops and paint a phone number across their chest.

A special area around the back of the theater is roped off so that fans can create a gauntlet and attack the band on their way to the tour bus.

Tour buses are pimped-out rides with bathrooms that never fail. When picking out a tour bus, extra sleeping space is allotted for groupies who are inevitably picked up along the way.

Entourages lounge about like window dressing and are incapable of speech.

Every pop star knows that the only way to pay for expensive items, like a Ferrari, is with cash. And the best way to carry around a lot of cash is to put it in your girlfriend's purse or have a minimum wage roadie carry it in a silver briefcase.

Since the 1980s most stages have a row of cops that would arrest anyone who tried this stunt. They might, however, make note of the phone number—for evidence purposes, of course.

Only if the promoter wants a whale of a lawsuit.

Most are so cramped that there is barely room for the act itself. In fact, unless it's a very successful act the "bus" is usually a van.

These days, insurance riders don't permit anyone who is not part of the crew to travel with the group. So pop stars have to find a "job" for their yes-men to perform. (P.S.: Most fights with hotel staff are caused by entitled members of the entourage.)

Ironically, most pop stars I know don't carry any serious cash. Despite their fame they often bum money and offer to pay it back later. If they were to buy a Ferrari it would be purchased by their business manager with a bank transfer.

Every pop star comes from a working-class home where Mom is a simple-minded suburban housewife and Dad just sits in a chair and listens to an old television. Both can't wait for the day when their kid will give up this "music thing" and go back to dental school.	It's amazing how many successful pop stars come from money. After their run, many do retire to a family-owned business—software development, media, entertainment, oil, feminine-hygiene products—or live off their trust fund.
Checking the weather report is never necessary when chartering a small single-engine plane. Airfields will only rent defective planes to pop stars anyway.	I know it seems like this one is a gimme, but the vast majority of acts travel by bus and experience few (or no) tragic incidents on the road.

⊘ I Ain't Paying F'Dat Junk

Money! Yes, another universal yardstick in gauging people's character. Some of us are very generous—often to our detriment. Others hold on to every nickel we make and even the nickels that we haven't made yet. This is the dysfunction that manifests a great deal in the music business: being cheap with money you haven't even made yet. With 40 platinum and 25 gold albums, **André Fischer**, former senior vice president of **MCA/Universal Urban Music Dept.** and vice president of jazz A&R for **Quincy Jones, Qwest/Warner Brothers**, had more to confess about penny-pinching and an artist he signed.

André Fischer: She had a good voice and wanted a record deal very badly. She dropped out of music school in order to hang out with **Phil Ramone**.[12] Then Phil got busy and couldn't finish his project on her. I never found out why. She was angry. I took her on as a manager and had her sing live to [the A&R person]. By the time lunch was over I had her signed. I was able to get her a budget of $400,000 and an advance for publishing as well. It was with Qwest Records before Warner closed it down.[13] I had [a top attorney] but she didn't want to pay for him. She said, "You negotiated most of it, why should I have to pay him that?" I should have taken

12 **Phil Ramone:** One of the most respected record producers in history. A technical innovator, he was one of the first to use fiber optics, digital recording, and telecommunications to produce records. Credits are too numerous to reproduce here.

13 **Qwest was Quincy Jones's imprint label owned by Warner Brothers.**

that as a sign of things to come. The reason why the deal closed is because of him. You know part of these deals are based on your posse. I found a lawyer to negotiate the deal who was the original lawyer that closed the deal between Quincy [Jones] and Warner Brothers. Next, I did all kinds of stuff to set up great gigs for her. But she was real cheap. She tried to get a publicist for $200 a week. I said, it's just not going to work. I had **Melissa Etheridge**'s bass player. I had **Elton John**'s guitar player, **Christina Aguilera**'s drummer, **Fleetwood Mac** and **Stevie Nicks**'s sound guy, **Eddie Coles**. She wouldn't even buy beverages for the musicians and singers for rehearsal. It got that bad. On tour she also wanted people to double up in rooms, and they were already cheap rooms. I thought it was time to part company, but I didn't want her to fail because I still had a vested interest. I had a sunset clause.[14] So, I got **Ashley Ingram**[15] to produce a couple of the songs on the record. And then Qwest shelved the project. Now, in those days if your act gets dropped and you're on a label that is part of a bigger network like Qwest was with Warner, you just walked across the hall to another label in the family. I was getting ready to do that. But before I could get across the hall I found out that she lied about her age; she was closer to 35 than 30. Plus all the other stuff. I said, screw it.

Moses: Is the moral of the story that you have to give to get?

André Fischer: Yeah, amen. You just nailed it! You gotta give to get. I said, "You have to spend some of this advance. It's free money. If the label goes under they're not going to ask for their advance back."

I can't tell you how many times I've seen artists develop an emotional attachment to the advance they get from a label. It's supposed to be spent on building a career, but it often goes to support habits. Artists, in their head, begin spending three times the amount they get. It's important to understand that the advance is for the record and the expenses needed to develop the act—things like musicians, producers, lawyers, and props to the folks who got you to that point.

> I Ain't Giving Consent F'Dat Crap

Being anal retentive with your money is one thing. It may be wrong in certain cases, but we can all relate. But how about being anal retentive with your product—that is, your music and your image? You'd think that after working so hard at becoming famous, artists would be less stingy about who gets to exploit their

[14] **Sunset clause:** A typical manager's provision that allows the manager to earn commissions for a year or two after he is no longer working on behalf of the artist.

[15] **Ashley Ingram:** Best known for his connection to Imagination, a trio from the UK that put a synthesized and often clubby spin on soul groups from the '70s. They had several big hits, including "In the Heat of the Night." The group's success sizzled until their mid-'90s breakup.

[16] Bob Dylan: Born Robert Zimmerman. Was the most rerecorded singer songwriter in history for many years. He is considered a living legend by people born before 1960. His song "The Times They Are A-Changin'" was the launch point of Sixties activism according to some social scientists; however, his career mistakes came in 2004: his antiestablishment image took a bit of bruising when he agreed to act in a Victoria's Secret commercial. (The "legend" looked like a pervert leering at the models in their underwear. Whose brilliant idea was that?)

[17] Prince: Forcing publications to obtain a free license for the symbol if they wished to write about him. The symbol was ⚥ which means androgyny. He's made a few interesting mistakes of his own: believes that Napster may be helping the music industry; after his success developing Sheila E and Vanity he chose Carmen Electra as the next star in his galaxy. His ex-guitarist left

image. But being cheap with one's image can take on some intriguing and self-destructive dysfunctions. Like not allowing the media to exploit you after you begged them to. There are some very famous examples, such as **Dylan**,[16] who would not give interviews for many years. And **Prince**, who, for reasons having nothing to do with cheapness, would not allow journalists to refer to him by name but only the use of a symbol that could not be reproduced by a standard printing procedure.[17] Like all dysfunctions, it's never good for the person manifesting it, but it's hard to see that when they are riding the peak of the temporary crest of the pop music wave.

Leslie Zigel: There are opportunities that one can have that can be lost by being too wrapped up in wanting to have approval over every little thing and micromanaging every single exploitation. You have to look at the forest from the trees and ask, what is the promotional value?

Moses: Can you give us a common example?

Leslie Zigel: If you look at something like the MTV Video Music Awards,[18] MTV requires very broad rights because they transmit these shows to a hundred different territories and they do different versions in different territories. They want to be able to use clips to promote the show on TV various commercials. They creatively grab snippets here and pieces there. [But] I have seen situations where artists' lawyers will prevent this show from using anything but the *entire performance of the song*. They want the whole clip or nothing. These clips can be minutes long. Which means when they run [30-second] commercials for the show in a hundred different countries at numerous different times, that band does *not* get to be in the promos. Literally [missing out] being seen by hundreds of millions of viewers, hundreds of times. Yeah, [the entire clip] will be on the show itself, but as far as promos, they're absent. These opportunities will just be ignored because they put so many restrictions on how their clips can be used. In some cases the bands that [do this] are usually the ones who have the most leverage and have had some success. Has it adversely impacted their career? It is a hard thing to quantify. The only thing that I can say is that too much press, especially to a very targeted music-buying public, can never be a bad thing.

Well, that depends on your perspective. Some bands have been educated through previous cases where the media has perverted their image to suit some cheesy advert. So the rationalization is usually that they want to maintain the integrity of the performance "as is" and they don't want it taken out of context. However, I agree with Leslie's point. You have to know when to give up the ghost.

⊘ Forget D'Fans, It's All About Me

According to an overwhelming number of people I interviewed, a classic mistake made *after* success is obtained (after the five-year mark) is forgetting about your fan base, and the importance of working the fan base. Somebody who doesn't want to do any autograph signing, doesn't want to meet any of their fans, doesn't want to do in-stores. In the 1970s, **David Bowie** made a shocking comment that ended up in the press. He implied that the people who bought his records had bad taste in music, and confessed that he would not buy his own records.[19]

Dysfunction number 437: Thinking that you are indispensable and treating others like they are not.

This is why I looked mostly toward veterans for my interview subjects. New artists generally convince themselves that the reason they are successful is because of their uniqueness. Surely this is an important factor. But it is never the only factor or even the major factor, with rare exceptions. But in their defense, we cannot blame artists for thinking this. Look at this clause:

> "The services of the Artist are unique and extraordinary, and the loss thereof cannot be adequately compensated in damages."

This, or some version of it, appears in *every* major label recording contract. Add to this the hyping that managers give their clients and it's no wonder that artist feels like a superhero. Bulletproof. Invincible. But there is kryptonite for these Supermen: the fickle mood of the fans. Yes, the most fearsome adversary of any successful recording artist is the very thing that launched them to stardom—record buyers. The day they think that the artist has abandoned them, it's over.

Jim Barber was a close advisor of one of the most controversial acts of the new millennium, **Courtney Love**. Courtney has had several cantankerous episodes with fans, once allegedly hitting one with a mike stand. So Jim knows a thing or two about what can happen when an artist doesn't pay attention to what's going on in the audience and how hype can go to the artist's head in destructive ways.[20]

Jim Barber: If you had a hit on your first record you really need to analyze why people responded to your music. Instead, what I see people do over and over again is they write without processing the creative feedback they've gotten from

him to form a brilliant pop group called Wendy and Lisa. Both girls claim he sabotaged their career out of spite.

[18] Even though MTV is a music network, they host their own annual movie awards. Their music awards show is considered by some to be more "successful" than the Grammys and more reflective of the public's real tastes.

[19] He retracted the statement the next day with an apology, citing alcohol as the root. It didn't seem to hurt his career much.

[20] Courtney Love: It was also reported that at the 2004 Grammy Awards she lost her daughter in the crowd.

their audience on the first record. They think because what they had to say the first time was acceptable that it's going to work again. The mistake is not to pay attention to what your audience is telling you.... One thing that really happened a lot in the Sixties that we make fun of now was, when somebody had a hit, the record company and the producer sent them back in the studio and they wrote a song that sort of sounded like the first hit. The way the **Rolling Stones** found their feet was by writing songs that repeated themselves, but evolved. Now, there's sort of the notion that you have to be an artist and you have to do something different. The biggest mistake is not giving the people what they want, and not bothering to take the time to figure out what they want from you. This is where I get into a controversy with some artists. If you expect people to pay you money for your art it's a two-way transaction. Once you are receiving the benefits of people buying your music, you have to understand there is something they are going to want from you.

Moses: How do you explain someone like **Madonna** who continuously reinvents herself over and over again? What is she doing right?

Jim Barber: I think she puts on a different costume, but Madonna is essentially the same. Madonna has had failures when she has tried to reinvent herself in ways that people didn't respond to.

Moses: Like what?

Jim Barber: Erotica. I don't think her audience really liked it. But I am mostly talking about rock bands. In rock especially, understand what your audience wants from you. One thing I never [understand] are bands who go on tour to support their record, and then they go home and don't play any more shows and they write a record in a vacuum. What I have watched happen over and over is that people who have enjoyed some success assume that however they were successful the last time is going to repeat itself. And that every time you start a project you are starting from scratch, so there is no formula. Past performance is no assurance of future success.[21]

21 For more on this subject, see Chapter 10.

> I'm Too Phat F'Dat: When the Only Fan Is Your Label

Losing perspective is not limited only to artists regarding their fans. Producers suffer from myopic dysfunction as well. Producing is not like being an artist. It's like being an artist and manager and record executive all in one. The problems are fourfold, yet many don't employ simple logic: *half of being smart is knowing what you're dumb at.*

CHAPTER 2: YOU'RE SO COOL

When success hits after several years, how do many producers stumble into their career? They forget that they too have fans. Their fans may not know their names the way they do the artists they produce, but they are fans nonetheless. They manifest not as record buyers, but as "potential employers"—the record companies and the new artists who want to hire you. They stalk producers just as a zealous fan would a lead singer. They want "the magic touch" on their recording. They want that same touch you brought to the last artist you worked with, the one that sold a million copies, the one that changed the way a hit record sounded.

New York producer **Steve Addabbo** had a hit record with a fresh sound. He had discovered **Suzanne Vega**, a young singer/songwriter, developed the material, and produced her first and second albums. They struck a hit with the single "Luka,"[22] a song about an abused child. It was all over the radio and Steve was the man of the hour, literally creating the 1980s folk revival and receiving demos and top-dollar offers from every corner of the industry. **Tracy Chapman**, at the time an unknown artist, was one of them. Her next record, "Fast Car," would spawn one of the biggest selling acoustic rock albums of all time. There was only one problem. Steve said no.

Steve Addabbo: I just had a big hit record and I was being fussy at that point. I was in the middle of the whole folk revival. I heard Tracy's demo. The song "[Talkin' 'Bout a] Revolution" just didn't grab me. I passed without even meeting her. Maybe if I would have listened to the demo on another day, I would have liked it, said yes. That's how fleeting these decisions are and I think at that point I needed someone else to say, "You idiot, take that job." I was really not paying attention or not figuring out what this bigger picture was, or what I was getting myself into. I was saying, "I have success, I have money, I can buy a house." That's what I was focusing on. That was a pretty big mistake for me. If I had produced "Fast Car" I'd probably have made over a million bucks. At that point, when you are hot, you should get yourself a *manager*. If I had had a manager he would have told me to follow it through to at least see if we could work together.[23]

Moses: There is an important issue here. A lot of producers make this same mistake. A lot of smart people—and particularly some reading this book, aspiring producers—are wondering if they have what it takes to make it to the top. Does one really need a manager to tell you that you should be thinking about making more money and maximizing your success? Isn't that something that most could figure out for themselves? Why do you think many can't maximize their success on their own?

Steve Addabbo: A lot of creative people are not the best at promoting themselves. We would rather be sitting in the studio working on songs than talking to

[22] Suzanne Vega: Although her debut album with "Small Blue Thing" sold 750,000, it had only one minor hit, "Marlene on the Wall," charting briefly in the UK. Her second album, *Solitude Standing*, with the hit "Luka," sold 3 million copies and reached No. 2 on *Billboard*'s Top 200 Chart. Despite this song launching the "folk revival" it would be her only real hit. Her a cappella song "Tom's Diner" from that same album was later redone as a dance track by Art of Noise and broke the top ten, earning her more royalties than both albums combined.

[23] Her debut album was produced by veteran producer David Kershenbaum. The record was released in the spring of 1988 with a big push by Warner/Elektra. She played at Nelson Mandela's 70th birthday party. The single "Fast Car" began climbing the charts shortly afterward, eventually peaking at number six.

people about what job we should take. I also think that after some small amounts of success, they get comfortable where they are and they think it's going to continue. Never lose the hunger. There were times when I wasn't hungry enough to do some records that had been presented to me. I passed on things that maybe I should have done. What I learned from the Tracy thing is that if a project is presented to you, unless you really hate it, you should do it.

⊘ Should You Run Your Band/ Act Like a Serious Business?

Since we're talking about making rational business decisions in an environment that often is irrational, let's tackle this controversy. Too often I hear the advice given to students that you should run your music career "like a serious business, with financial goals." I know educators out there are going to think I'm mad for giving this next bit of counterintuitive theory, but I hope they'll hear me (as well as some of the guests for this section) out before they judge.

First, it's pretty obvious that many of the most successful artists or producers didn't set goals or run their bands *anything* like a serious business. They play money-losing gigs, sign debt-building record deals, and keep playing music long after a balance sheet tells them it's not profitable. Yet they become millionaires. What are they doing right?

The confusion comes in understanding exactly what the word "business" means. In the real world—that is, the world outside of the music business—business is a strict formula:

$$buy - exploit - sell$$

You see something. You assess its value. You buy it. Exploit it to a market and then sell it for a profit. There are four key components to business:

- Market comparatives (who is your competition?)
- Projections of profit and loss (what can I make and what do I have to risk?)
- Capital (where can I get the money and how do I pay it back?)
- Exit strategy (getting out while the getting is good)

The music business from the point of view of the creative side has none of these.

Instead it has:

Ignorance of competition	What musician starting out ever said, "Let me survey how many guitar players there are in the current region to see what my chances are of making a living"?
A disregard for profits or losses	What successful musician ever said, "I had two bad years in a row, I'll quit now and go work on Wall Street"?
No exit strategy	I don't know too many successful players in this business who said, "Now that I made it, I want out." Some do, but it's very rare. Many have left the business because they had families and wanted a more stable life. That's something else entirely.

Conclusion: The music business is not a business in the traditional sense of the word. Trying to use standard business acumen is a formula for failure. Rather, it's something we do because we love music. It's a business of passion. You don't choose it. It chooses you. It's an obsession. To put it more bluntly, it's an addiction. Shrinks, I'm sure, will one day create a new disorder centered around the business. EIAD, they'll call it: Entertainment Industry Addiction Disorder. Symptoms are people who can't quit even though good sense tells them to. I am afflicted, as I am guessing many of you are too.

Jim Barber: I totally agree. I'll take it a step further. I think running a record company like a business is no good. What has happened in the last decade now is that the music business has been forced to adapt and be run by a model of quarterly projections and making your numbers, and it has really destroyed the creative process of making music. More than any other single thing that has happened, that's what has destroyed the music business: the attempt to turn the music business into a Wharton Business School.

One may ask, what business school did Barber, a former Geffen VP of A&R, attend to have such a radical opinion?

Jim Barber: Harvard. The reason a guy like me, who went to Harvard College,[24] got attracted to the music business in the first place was because it was as far away as you can get from all of this corporate stuff that my friends were going to do after college. The music business didn't make any sense. It was absurd. It was a big sandbox where people did irrational things and wonderful accidents happened.

There's a lot of interesting stuff in there to chew on. Do the labels set much of an example when it comes to using the basic formula of buy-exploit-sell in their operations? We saw how dragging their feet hurt them in the online business. Did that experience teach them to think outside of the box?

As recently as January 2005 I asked one marketing executive at Warner Brothers if they were thinking about cutting back on the CD format (since nobody wanted to pay $15 for them) and begin issuing DVDs with the full album plus added visual content. People seem okay with paying $15 for a DVD, and it would help rehabilitate the visual identify of the artist that is eroding due to the way records are sold now. Plus, they would preserve the album format and it still only costs about $1 to manufacture. He said bluntly, "No, we're not in the DVD business."[25]

Hmmm. This is the type of mentality a person entering the business is going to be dealing with. It's a tough one. It used to be a young business that rewarded innovation. Now I'm not sure what is being rewarded. The people running it are far older than ever before and have far more formal education than ever before. Is this giving them tunnel vision?

Jim Barber: If I was the president of a label, my whole idea would be keep your overhead relatively low. If you were making projections for Seagram[26] on what the next **Counting Crows** record was going to sell, even though the last one had sold 6 million copies, do you know what I would project? 750,000. Seriously. The way the music business should have been run, once corporations got involved—all of the projections in all of the financing and all of the business should have been based on worst-case scenarios. Then when you have a hit, it rains money, you have a big profit, and you reinvest it. You have to run the music business assuming that the next **Britney Spears** record is going to do half what the previous one did.

I believe that tomorrow's executive will need to embrace any new idea that can put their product in the face of the public. Fighting the digital future is a losing game. The job of those who hate the concept is not to rebel against the overwhelming direction the tide is taking, but to fight to maintain the integrity of the music through this transition, so that tomorrow's industry will have a product that is worth being nostalgic about.

Bottom line: Leave accounting to the accountant, law to the lawyers. Follow your heart and create, create, create. If you're good, people will notice. That's your business. Being really, really f-ing good. **Jay Frank**, VP of Label Relations for the world's biggest music subscription service, Yahoo!, adds this:

> *Jay Frank:* I believe that in order to make more money, you make more copyrights. If you have more diverse widgets to sell, hopefully you can sell more widgets. Record companies have forgotten this in the world of quarterly reports. Artists should be releasing a music product yearly at minimum to reflect both their art as well as developing *new* copyrights. In the time that an **Elton John** or **Stevie Wonder** would release three or four albums, artists are now releasing one record, two if they're lucky. How can this possibly be good?

Radio Ready: Should I Spend the Money?

"Your demo should sound radio ready." I'm sure you've heard that one at many conferences. Since this section deals with running a band/act like a business, it stands to reason that when spending what little resources you may have to launch your career, this question will come up. Many newcomers to this game spend gobs of money on top audio quality only to later regret trying to make their demo sound "radio ready." It's all part of appearing cool. But think for a second who you're actually going to impress by doing this. I've been on the other end of this process—believe me, the music that gets distribution on majors has little to do with what is "radio ready." It shouldn't be the goal of an emerging artist.

People who offer this advice are looking for reasons to reject you. They themselves lack the talent to hear past a low-budget production and see the talent in the center of it. Their handicap becomes your handicap. At the heart of what they are saying might be some good intentions. Many A&R people can't hear a great talent through a cheap production, so telling you to make something sound "radio ready" is relatively safe advice. Is it complete or practical advice? Is spending money to create a radio sound a good investment? Consider this:

- **Problem:** There is a 15-month lag time from the time you get signed to a major label to the time the record will be released. If your "radio ready" demo sounds hip today, by the time it's released it will sound old. You can try to predict the future when making a demo, but it's very hard, even for professional producers. Just look at the track record of the majors. They claim a 5 percent success. The odds of hitting the niche are about 20:1 even with all the resources that major labels have at their fingertips.

- **Solution:** Record from the heart. Don't worry about what radio wants. If you see your whole career in terms of whether you have a hit or not, you're not an artist anymore. The goal now for the artist is not to make records sound "radio ready," but to make records that will change the way the radio sounds.

Jim Barber: If we were having this conversation ten years ago, I might have disagreed with you. Now, I think it is *impossible* to make your demo sound radio ready. For a simple reason: the way record companies now make records sound radio ready is by hiring the same handful of mix engineers to provide predetermined sets and sounds. So don't try to make your demo radio ready, it is a fool's game from jump street. It is impossible and [I've] been through it with *America's Sweetheart*,[27] which was completely obliterated by this mentality. It's still a good record but in no way resembles the record that we made.

[27] *America's Sweetheart*: Courtney Love's first solo record.

Michael Ross[28]: There is a fine line between being radio friendly and sounding like everything else on the radio. If you come up with a new sound that people think will work on the radio, you've done it right. If they say you sound like six other bands I've just heard, then you did it wrong. It is such a fine line. They have to say, "It's kind of a mix between this and that, but it has so-and-so's edge to it." If they just say you sound like **Norah Jones**, well, we already got her, too bad, you blew it.

[28] Michael Ross: Engineer/Producer, Christina Aguilera.

Bobby Borg[29]: Screw radio and their formats and politics altogether and build a base exclusively through live performance and touring. **Anthrax** basically did it this way. So did **Fugazi**. So can you.

[29] Drummer for Warrant and music-business educator.

And finally, here's my two cents. Get the "all majors suck" attitude off your repertoire of gripes. Contrary to popular belief, labels really do sign good creative acts—generally. It's through the development process that some acts become homogenized into what you eventually hear on the radio, but this is rarely intentional. No label wants to release a boring or hackneyed artist. You can bet that they don't want to sign a band that has already homogenized themselves.

> Lies that Tell the Truth and Accepted Levels of Theft

Someone once defined art as a lie that tells the truth. Do you think they had in mind the sort of pathological optimism (or misrepresentation) that manifests in the music industry?

I doubt it. Many whom I council in my consultation practice and many who ask questions when I lecture at schools are always promoting as an asset of their employability (or probability of success) that they are honest to a fault. They seem determined not to follow in the conniving methods talked about in some of the stories in this book. It hurts me to tell them that honesty is rarely rewarded in this area.

In **Fred Goodman**'s excellent book, *Mansion on the Hill*, super-manager and label owner **Irving Azoff**, who worked for **David Geffen**, was quoted as saying, "[Geffen] in his mind creates things, and they become facts regardless of what happened." Azoff, no stranger himself to spinning yarns, also recalls one of Geffen's mottos that he has repeated in interviews over the years, that his greatest business lesson came from his mother, who said to always tell the truth. Geffen, often thought of as the father of the modern music business, dropped out of college and claimed falsely to have graduated from UCLA.[30]

In a business where you will often hear people musing about doing the right thing, it seems that what the right thing is is highly subjective. Grammy-winning engineer/producer **Francis Buckley** has been making records for over 20 years. His experience ranges from the groundbreaking punk act **Black Flag**'s first album *Damaged* in 1980 to winning the Engineering Grammy Award in 1996 for *Q's Jook Joint* with **Quincy Jones**. He tells us of this common scenario:

> *Francis Buckley:* Here is a sneaky underhanded trick to watch out for. The guy says to you, this is a good money gig, I got $5,000 to do this gig. Or he would call and say, this is a low-money gig. But it was always cool 'cause he always told me [exactly how much it was going to be]. There was money or there wasn't money. It was what it was. Then one day I found out that what he was doing was telling people he got five when he actually got seven. He was skimming all of this money off the top of everyone's paycheck.

[30] David Geffen: Allegedly, he did this to get a job in the William Morris Agency's mail room. (He also claimed to be mega-producer Phil Spector's cousin when actually Phil Spector's sister-in-law was dating his brother.) He is an avid supporter of self-help groups like EST (Landmark Forum). Reference: *Mansion on the Hill*, p. 116.

[31] **All-in:** Jargon for a budget where the producer receives all the money for the project from the artist or label and then pays out the individual vendors (studio, musicians, etc.). The opposite would be a budget where the producer is another vendor, like the studio, musicians, etc., who each submit invoices to the label, which then pays everyone individually. All-in budgets are preferred by producers in most situations. For more, see *Confessions of a Record Producer.*

Moses: How was he skimming money off of your paycheck if you are invoicing the record company?

Francis Buckley: These are *all-in*[31] budgets. Now, this is somebody that is a buddy. If you tell me, I got $7,000, but I want you to kick me back $2,000, then I am like, hey man, I am making $5,000, and I would work for you forever!

Moses: So what is the difference?

Francis Buckley: The difference is that it was just sneaky and underhanded from somebody that was telling me what a "bro" he was.

Record producers will try to skim money off budgets every chance they get. Is this really stealing? This next interview subject decided to go off the record. He didn't know that I had done a bit of research on him prior to the interview about how he got his break, who stole from him, and who he has in turn stolen from.

Artist: Yes, [it's stealing] because it's coming out of the artist's advance. The artist has to pay it back out of royalties. So, yes, it's stealing.

Moses: But it's not money the artist will ever actually get to put in his pocket.

Artist: Irrelevant. The artist has to pay it back.

Moses: When you hire a plumber to fix your plumbing and he gives you a quote, you hire him based on that quote. If it costs him less, he keeps the surplus. That's his reward for being a good businessperson. You would call that stealing?

Artist: Yes, because if he knew that it was going to cost him less then he should have bid less.

Moses: But if he didn't know it when he bid, then is it okay to keep the difference?

Artist: No. He should give it to the artist so the artist can have some money to live off of.

Moses: Interesting. Now let me ask you this. Most producers I know do lockouts, but they never use all 24 hours in a day. Usually they work for several hours, 8 or 10 hours a day on the project that the label is paying for. Then in the wee hours they will work on their back-pocket project. Is that how you were developed?

Artist: Yes. These days labels don't invest in artist development. The producers do it all. Producers sign singers to production deals and then bring finished masters to the label.[32]

Moses: And in order to do this they "steal" studio time from projects that are financed by majors.

Artist: Yes.

[32] This is mostly a formula for R&B development, because producers in this arena tend to contribute greatly to the material itself. In rock, signing an entire band that writes its own songs to a production deal is rare. Usually the producer develops them as a joint venture; however, this may be changing.

Moses: And that's stealing?

Artist: Yes.

Moses: Even though the time is going to cost the artist who's signed to the label the same amount no matter if the producer uses all 24 hours of his lockout time or only 10 to 12.

Artist: Yes, because he's developing artist B on artist A's time and money. Artist A doesn't get a piece of the success of artist B if it blows up.

Moses: Weren't you developed in this same way, as part of a production deal?

Artist: [Name withheld] signed us. He was working with [name withheld] on Warner Brothers at the time. That album had a huge budget because her first album did like 5 million units.

Moses: And in this case the producer was also using his own studio?

Artist: Yes.

Moses: So then you're saying that you participated in stealing time from that Warner artist?

Artist: I didn't steal the time, the producer did.

Moses: But you didn't object? You knew and you didn't object.

Artist: At the time I was very naive about how this kickback tradition worked.

Moses: When you found out, did you give the money back to [the Warner artist]?

Artist: [long pause] No. I guess... I guess you don't think of things like that. You figure she made millions, she doesn't need the $100,000 or so that my producer stole from her to develop me. She's doing okay.

Moses: Sounds like the same rationalization students use to steal music on the Internet.

Artist: It is. Man, you're tough. You think I should give the money back?

Moses: It doesn't matter what I think. What do you think you should do? Didn't you just say that the producer is stealing because artist B is not going to get any scratch from artist A if it blows up? Why should it be any different just because artist A is already famous?

Artist: It shouldn't. But this goes on all the time. It's just the way it's done.

Moses: Frankly, I've been that producer "stealing time" from artist A to develop artist B. And I learned that trick from engineering for producers when I was coming up. Every producer does it and I can't find a single incident where the up-and-coming artist being developed said, "Wait a minute, who's paying for this time, because I don't want to be involved in stealing from another artist." Most were happy they were being given a chance at all.

Artist: You're right. What can I say. We're all stealing from each other.

So if everyone's doing it, is it stealing? That is the philosophical question.

Instead of trying to label the morality of this common practice and create arbitrary boundaries for "right" and "wrong," I have coined an industry expression I call the ALT: the Accepted Level of Theft. It's a private threshold where only the parties involved know what is a reasonable amount of graft. Producers "steal" from artist and labels. Labels "steal" from artists. Managers "steal" from artists. Promoters "steal" from managers. Everybody takes a little off the top. How much is too much? Only those involved have an idea. There is no standard.

I know of more than one situation where an artist sued their producer after finding out that the producer "stole" money for the budget. What is one hoping to accomplish with these cases? In more than one of them the album was a hit. So why sue a producer for "stealing" $100,000 when he delivered an album that earned you millions, especially when the dynamic mentioned above is in play—where the producer developed the artist on the back of another artist's budget?

❯ Conclusion

Jay Jay French: Don't be so arrogant to think that it's going to last. It doesn't. Nobody is big forever. Even **John Lennon**, as big as he was, after the **Beatles** went without a record deal for some time.[33]

Immortality. It's the word that has escaped use in this chapter. People think that their success is impervious. Most artists' careers peak in the fifth year in the music space and then income streams rapidly decline after that. The artists who outlast those odds, with rare exception, have all laterally integrated their music into other things: movies, merchandise, clothing lines, and so on. The moral: Plan for the future, don't whine about the present. If you're at a point where you can spend significant time playing music, you're already doing better than 90 percent of the world's population. Consider using your music career as a stepping stone toward other things. Have those goals firmly in mind. Don't be cheap. Take the high road with disputes and be generous with your product in the beginning. Understand your "formula" for why people like *your* work. They chose to be *your* fans above thousands of others for a reason. Learn that reason. And as for being a kiss-ass to everyone out of fear, I'll let **Jim Barber**, a professional anti-ass-kisser, get the last word on this.

[33] Until David Geffen signed him to his label. This led to *Double Fantasy*, one of Lennon and Geffen's biggest sellers. Unfortunately, its success has been linked to Lennon's death, rightfully or not. Lennon's mistakes are not incidental either: allowing his second wife, Yoko Ono, to engineer the breakup of the most influential pop music force in history, the Beatles. In his will, he left his son from his first marriage, Julian Lennon, with nothing. On a weird note: he was the first to use the word "nigger" in a mainstream song ("Woman Is the Nigger of the World"), and it is rumored that he was the only rock star to have been assassinated by the US government, for fear his antiestablishment agenda would permeate his comeback.

Jim Barber: You should not worry about being nice to everyone. It's not like all these senior management people from the record industry have a barbecue together every Memorial Day and July fourth. They don't talk to each other. You piss off **Clive Davis** and you can make a deal with **Jimmy Iovine** tomorrow. So this idea that you should be nice to [everyone]… no! But you should be loyal to people that deserve your loyalty.

Nice one, Jim.

Next, we'll look at the ultimate manifestations of the "too cool for school" vibe: when thinking you're "all that" changes you into someone you can't stand. Take a look.

CHAPTER 3

Arrogance and Logic

"A positive attitude may not solve all your problems, but it will annoy enough people to make it worth the effort."

—Herm Albright (1876–1944)

The stereotype of the arrogant pop star is so stale that I don't even laugh anymore when it's lampooned on *South Park*. It's become an accepted part of our culture, just like the dumb hick, the snooty Englishman, and the crooked politician. Wax figures in our mind's museum of the mundane.

In our heart we know stereotypes are just that—generalizations about people we don't really know. Most people, when pressed, will admit that hicks are not dumb, the English can be warm, and politicians can be honest. But what about the arrogant pop star? Boy, that's a tough one. Every time you see one on TV they sure do seem to be putting their foot in their mouth. When they try to get political I can't watch. When it's a client or friend of mine I want to hide my head in an old box of Cream LPs. It can get very entertaining as some stretch facts to conform to their often emotion-inspired points of view on world affairs. Shortsightedness also seems to live in this neighborhood. A recent example is **Lars Ulrich**,[1] drummer of the very popular group **Metallica**,[2] who thought it would be a good idea to act as a spokesperson for the RIAA's lawsuits against fans who were downloading their

[1] Ulrich: A friend originally came up with the name Metallica for a heavy metal fanzine. Ulrich rejected it and then used it for the name of his band.

[2] **Metallica: Their litigation C/V is extensive. They sued their record company, Elektra, for severance. In 2000, they sued Victoria's Secret for using the name Metallica for a shade of lipstick, and the same year filed a copyright infringement and racketeering lawsuit against Napster, Yale University, the University of Southern California, and Indiana University.**

[3] **Napster has now been legalized.**

music from the illegal peer-to-peer network Napster. Despite Lars's obvious intelligence, passion, and desire to do the right thing, watching him testify in front of the California Supreme Court was surely a low point in dissolving the arrogant-rock-star stereotype. While his point may have been a valid one, its finer points were probably lost on the average viewer, who undoubtedly just saw a millionaire whining about losing theoretical pennies.

But hey, isn't this why we love them? Isn't this why we buy their records? They're rebels. Isn't part of their job to be defiant to the point of stupidity? Sure. It's practically in the job description. Up-and-coming musicians fueled by the bravado of their role models emulate this behavior, thinking that it's expected of them.

In the survey done for this book, every person was asked what they felt was the number-one mistake made by artists entering the business. The most common answer, by an overwhelming majority, was some version of this comment by stellar painter, friend, Burning Man advocate, and platinum punk producer **Geza X**: "Thinking that the hype in *Rolling Stone* or on MTV is really the way artists behave, record, and perform, thereby sabotaging interviews and recording sessions. Artists, especially up-and-coming ones, are *not* in charge of anything."

But saying things like "don't be arrogant" can be too general and therefore too useless a piece of advice. I have found that sometimes arrogance is necessary in order to be persuasive. Arrogance might actually be too *passive* a word for what sometimes takes place in the music space.

Geza X: My philosophy is that you have to absolutely scare the shit out of an A&R person to get signed. That means he has to be in fear of losing his cushy job. He has to say to himself, "Oh my God, if word gets out that I passed on this and somebody else picks it up and it's a big hit, then I am going to double-lose my job and I am going to look like a joker."

The music business, like other businesses, operates out of fear rather than greed. Arrogance can be very fear inspiring. And it can affect our ability to think logically—something that apparently is needed in order to get someone unstuck if they have a decision-making disorder. So I guess what we have in this chapter are not anti-arrogance stories but a few lessons about "arrogance management," or lack thereof, and when to apply the pressure and when to know you have a weak hand and shut the hell up.

⊙ When Dating Your Label, Don't Give It Up Too Soon

In the spike-through-your-head world of punk there are no fancy tour buses stocked with Campari. The punks have embraced the "bad boy" image of rock while doubling the energy put into the music. However, despite their differences in musical style, the same human emotions come into play. Fueled by the punk image, young punk bands sometimes forget that when applying for a contract with a large conglomerate, like a major label, they need to learn to keep their elbows off the table while throwing up.

Our source for this story wants to remain anonymous, so we'll just call him the "NY Manager." He put his heart and soul into getting a band called **Postmen Apostles**[4] signed to one of the biggest labels of the day and with the top A&R man at the time. In the end all he had to show for his trouble was an empty aspirin bottle. His mistake: letting the label really get to know the artist. I call this Coyote Ugly Syndrome.

> [4] Postmen Apostles: A fictitious name. Real name withheld.

NY Manager: Talk about thinking you're talented and can do anything, you should have heard these guys [brag about themselves]. They got a tremendous offer [from Capitol], and it took about two months to negotiate the deal. One week before the signing, we had a meeting at the label, with the head of A&R. We'll call him Tim. This was the key moment. They came in and put their feet up on the desk, threw soda on the floor, and were just disgusting. Then, when Tim said, "I have some opinions about what songs should be on this album," they began making fun of him and his haircut, and [the lead singer] said "No, we will tell you what songs will be on the album." Though Tim laughed along with the guys, I saw in his eyes and in his face, "I am *not* risking my career signing these guys." I read people reasonably well—I could see he was not following through. That was on a Wednesday or Thursday; suddenly my lawyer couldn't reach their lawyer on Friday or Monday morning. Tuesday we were supposed to show up and sign the contract, and with the band on the way to the office, my lawyer told me Capitol dropped the deal.

Moses: So it's a Coyote Ugly scenario? You wake up the next morning and you realize your date is not what you thought the night before.

NY Manager: Yes, that's what happened. [The label] realized the band was very difficult. The band thought they were God's gift and said so on a regular basis. They took themselves and their artistic privilege too seriously, all of that punk imagery. They were nasty to everyone and especially to Tim.

Moses: Playing devil's advocate for a moment, isn't that what's expected of them? Shouldn't they be aloof to the label?

NY Manager: No, aloof is different. Aloof, yes, punky, no.

Moses: Isn't the distinction so slight that it's asking an awful lot from an inexperienced band?

NY Manager: Yeah it is, that's why it is my fault.

Moses: So, punks shouldn't be punky? That's the message? Isn't it why we are attracted to punk music and these people in the first place?

NY Manager: Yes, it is. It is absolutely a high-wire act. Of course in our industry one must recognize that there will always be some tension between image and reality. You need to walk the high wire, but you have to be careful where you step. You don't want the A&R guy to think he's going to get screwed by the band, that the band is not going to do what he needs. Yet, the A&R department has to be able to say, "This is the real deal. They really are fucked up, they are nasty, they don't have to put up with any shit." But on the other hand, "They love *me* [the label], they trust and understand *me*." Also, you can't let them know that you are not interested in what they have to say about your record in the end. The band has to be a *player*. Like a guy that is dating every girl in town, but every girl thinks she is the only one he's dating. Everybody wants to see themselves as a contributor. I lost control of the business situation and allowed the Apostles to act as if they were already box office. They became too great a risk in the eyes of the label people. In blame myself. The way the band acted suggested that my management might be incapable controlling them. Successful managers have a strong sense of self, and don't let the band's hyperbole swallow them.

In my workshops I teach that a deal memo is not a contract. It's more of an ad for a contract. You sign it and almost immediately the label starts carting you around to parties at modeling agencies and has you making demos in class-A studios, with top-level producers, and it can take ten months to negotiate the final contract. During this time you are one of the family. They use this strategy because it's very hard for the band to back down after all this consideration. Simultaneously, the label gets a lot of exposure to the act that they didn't have when just seeing them at a club once in a while. In the NY Manager's "Coyote Ugly" case it proved disastrous.

NY Manager: The mistake I learned is that you should never let the label get too close to the act before committing to them. Keep some distance until the money crosses hands and the paper is signed. Never let them take you anywhere or do *anything* for you. Continue running your own show. When they invite you to A&R meetings about what songs are going to be on the album, say, "Not until we finish the deal. We hate to be that way, but I can't let my act do that right now. We need to finish the deal." There is a nicer way to do that—put the band on the road and make them inaccessible.

The subject pauses and laments his own failure here:

> *NY Manager:* I made some tremendous mistakes with the Apostles. I thought that my talent, my knowledge of the industry, would allow me to overcome the dumb luck and the power issues in the industry. It is a business, and big money controls it more than talent does, and management must therefore be a money/power game—it is not a talent game. I didn't have a lot of money and power then. But I could tell good stories—which is the other half of what management is about.

Bottom line, artists: save your arrogance for the music video. What punk rockers don't want their fans to know is that when they are in the label's office, it's "thank you" and "yes, Mr. Record Exec."

◉ Record Companies Never Forget Their Problem Children

Fame and the Forgotten Star: Irene Cara's Story

Few professional flameouts compare to the story of **Irene Cara**, Grammy-winning singer, a bright talent who landed the starring role in one of the 1980s' biggest trend-setting films, *Fame.* Things got better and then things could not have gotten worse. "How can you have the number one song of the year in 1983 and then never have a hit again? That is crazy," says one of our sources for this story. "Everyone expected her to be the next **Madonna** or **Cher**. Of course, even though she was one of **David Geffen**'s first acts, it never happened."[5]

This segment is told from an amalgam of anonymous sources, including a former label attorney and former manager. I've grouped them together to make reading simpler and called all the sources "The Insider."

[5] Another source claimed to have been in the room when Cara co-wrote lyrics for a song on the *Fame* soundtrack. Another project that she has never received credit or royalties for that could have added to her attitude.

The Insider: [Irene Cara] had a really big head back then in the early eighties. According to her, both she and Geffen shared the same [male] lover for a while. He got jealous or she got jealous, and David Geffen is David Geffen. They actually got in arguments over it and Geffen pretty much blackballed her in the industry. That is her version of what happened. That sounds like it could be true. There were lawsuits too. She sued for not getting promoted and for getting dropped, and I guess she apparently co-wrote the theme from *Flashdance*, but for years they didn't give her songwriting credits. "Flashdance" was a number one song for like ten weeks, and she was one of the first biracial female stars to carry a major movie, *Fame*. She won a Grammy in 1984 and the American Music Award the year before that.

No matter how many awards you've won, a common misconception about major-label deals is that no recording contract guarantees that a label *has* to release or promote an artist. Can you imagine if they did? Artists would not work to deliver the best album they could, and labels would be forced to invest millions to promote a master they didn't believe in. Cara would have accomplished little by suing for "non-promotion" or being dropped.

The Insider: She said David Geffen was behind it all but I don't know. [The *Flashdance* credit] eventually was corrected to where now it does say that she is the co-writer. You have to play ball in this industry and you have to be a team player. I don't think she was. [An agent] said that he remembered her at the wrap party for the movie *Fame*, that she seemed [not herself] and upset with the producers for "cutting out most of her scenes." Meanwhile she was the lead in the movie, you understand? She said they did it because she looked black and that the business is run by white Jews. Which at the time was an interesting observation, because the producers of *Fame* were not Jewish, I don't think. She badmouthed a lot of people and blamed them for her career demise. How can you have the number one song of the year in 1983 with two movies that are massive, *Fame* and *Flashdance*, and then never have a hit again?

Moses: Actually, it happens quite a bit. You have a lot of artists that have one or two big hits and then they disappear; it's not that unusual.

The Insider: Irene is a really sweet girl. Now she is doing the oldies circuit and she had some success in Europe. She did a duet with some artist on Universal. She also did one of those celebrity wrestling or boxing things. Have you ever seen where they bring older celebrities out to box?

Moses: I really haven't had time to set my TiVo for that yet.

The Insider: She did one of those a couple of years ago. She does things like that just to get by.

Just to get by.

Moral here: Everybody has issues. Recognize them and get help if you need it. Paranoia will get you nowhere. On the other hand, paranoid people still can have real enemies. I guess a better moral is don't share lovers with the most powerful person in your life—the president of your label.

The Sara B Story

And what if you're not paranoid? What do you do if you're a female artist and the president of the label actually does make lewd, sexist comments about you and your music? How do you react when this person has so much control over your career? One thing you should not do is believe that you're irreplaceable just because articles in fanzines say you're the hot new thing. Remember, the record company planted those stories in those fanzines.

Sara B, a 1980s pop sensation, had it all: a successful record right out of the box and an offer to do a second record. Yet these days she's not even a footnote on All-Music.com. What happened? As it turns out, it's all about breast size. To protect certain parties some names have been changed.

NY Manager: She was such a natural. Very talented, a great poet, and a very good singer/songwriter. The first album sold many copies and it was made for only fifteen grand—we're not talking about the days of digital. This was still analog. But when she turned in a second album, there was a song on it called "I'm Not Perfect," referring to her body. The president of the company said that he didn't like it. Sara was a hotty and he said, "Nobody wants to hear about a hot woman who says I got one tit bigger than the other." This comment and rejection really hit Sara hard. She wanted to walk. I was telling her, you have a deal here, make the record. She said no and held out.

Moses: **Relativity Records** said make another record and she said no?

NY Manager: Yeah. One of the things that happens when people have success and read their own articles is that they forget that it is a business. Then this new boyfriend told her to lay back for a year and let the label drop you and then she could pursue getting a better deal elsewhere. She bought that. Her manager thought that was ridiculous, but she wouldn't listen to him either. When artists start fucking someone new, that person often becomes the whole world to them. People stop taking you seriously when that happens. Everybody told her to make the second record. She absolutely refused. She said, "I deserve better after being number one on 35 of the 36 modern rock stations." She said, "I can sit out a couple of years if I have to until this contract expires." I felt differently. I thought no one is going to remember her and she is going to lose her publishing deal[6]. It was crazy. A lot of artists take four or five records before they really hit the big one. She got lucky and then said, no, it's not enough money, and the president of that company is a sexist.

[6] Typically publishing deals are valued by the recording contract of the artist. If the artist defaults on delivering a next album, the economics of the publishing deal are often seriously impaired.

In Sara B's case it might have been better to overlook the attitude of the executive, since he was not going to put money in her pocket anyway. The fans were. Don't believe the hype that record companies put out there about you. Remember that it's their story you're buying into, not reality. Choose your battles.

Former Geffen executive **Jim Barber** has this to add:

Jim Barber: The biggest mistake that people make is assuming that their music is going to speak for itself. The music business is not about the manufacturing and selling of music. It is really about networking and connections. I have watched a lot of kids come into the business that wanted to come in on the A&R or the creative end, not understanding that it's the relationship between the record company and the radio stations and the retail outlets that have as much to do with keeping the system running as it does with the records that get made.

⊘ Genre Bias

I have to admit it. I just don't get into country music. I've tried. God knows I've tried. But it just won't stick with me.

Genres. We all have our favorite ones. These are the ones that drew us into a career in music in the first place. I was a rock head in high school. I grew up on things like **Steely Dan**, the **Rolling Stones**, and the **Beatles**. When I entered the music business that's what I imagined myself recording.

[7] KRS-1 (born Kris Parker): The leader of Boogie Down Productions, one of the most influential hardcore hip-hop outfits of the '80s.

Unfortunately, at the time that I was doing my internships the only music that was getting any decent budgets was rap and R&B. I hated rap at the time. I made fun of it in high school and thought that it was not real music. In my twenties I did countless sessions of mixing drum machines and samplers, hating every minute of it.

Then one afternoon I was assisting a session with one of the most talented rappers I have ever had the pleasure of being in the studio with, **KRS-1**.[7] A mid-eighties rapper who put socially conscious raps in his "songs." Okay, they were still sampled off other people's records. (Ironically, some Steely Dan records.) But still, it was starting to sound like music to me. Had the music changed or had my ears?

I developed an appreciation for rap, but not in time to not earn a rep for being a snob about it. For a while this hurt my professional opportunities. And I was not alone. Matt Forger, engineer for Michael Jackson for many years:

> *Matt Forger:* There were a lot of times when I was listening to music and I would think that I was not hearing production value in it, and in retrospect I was wrong.
>
> *Moses:* Were you ever rude to anybody because of it?
>
> *Matt Forger:* It is more like you've picked up this condescending attitude and that is the vibe that you give off. I would sometimes write off someone's efforts and dismiss something. This was a reaction to all of the giant overproduced records of the time because the generation coming up didn't want music that sounded like what their parents were listening to. They wanted the stuff that was really raw. I think when grunge started to come in, there were a lot of rumblings that I heard from musicians upset that this very raw, loose, imperfect music was actually becoming popular.

Whether you're an old rocker who thinks alternative or grunge is too raw, or a rock snob (like I was) who looks down on music made with samplers, it never pays to have an attitude about a genre that you don't immediately get. If it's selling millions of units, somebody's getting it. Your best goal, if you want to succeed in music, is to understand exactly what makes it work, even if you don't like it. In fact—especially if you don't like it. You never know what shore the tide of your career will wash you up on. Genre bias will ultimately pigeonhole you and lead to lost jobs. Expand your palette. In fact, I'm going to go out and buy a **Hank Williams** record right now.

❯ Stupid Names and Trademark Testosterone

I have always disagreed with many attorneys who try to coax a new band, with little going on yet, to spend their hard-earned money on a trademark for the band's name. Attorneys make good arguments designed to stimulate an artist's easily inspired paranoia. "Protect your name, it's the most important thing you have. Imaging getting signed to a major and then they find out that you don't own your name on a national basis. They'll drop you."

Not true. This happens all the time, as we'll learn in a minute.

By just registering your domain name and then advertising your band's appearance in the paper you are establishing a "poor man's trademark." This could cost more in the long run than doing it the "legal way." So then why not follow the lawyer's advice and just do the real one? Well, it's about $800, just to get started, and you don't get any advertising or services for it, other than the registration slip. In fact, something some lawyers will avoid telling you is that you could spend the $800 and have your trademark rejected. However, most importantly, what the lawyer who's advising you to do this will almost always leave out of his presentation is that you can lose your trademark even after you paid the money and received a registration approval.

If another band begins using that same name in another part of the country (or state) and you don't stop them from doing so, you could lose your rights to the name. You've given what lawyers call "tacit approval." Which means that you're okaying it by saying or doing *nothing* about it. How do you stop another group from using your name? You hire a lawyer to send threatening letters at a fee of about $250 an hour (at least).

Therefore, I have always found the advice for a new band to trademark a bit self-serving from the lawyer's point of view. Once a major signs you they will handle any disputes. After all, they are not going to pay advances of upwards of a million dollars and then not settle a dispute over a name that will cost them at best about $25,000.

Right now, attorney **Ben McLane** and I are going to face off in a debate about this issue. Ben is a very experienced attorney who has been presented with platinum and gold record awards for his involvement with the **Dixie Chicks** and **Guns N' Roses.** He makes good arguments and I mean no disrespect by arguing with him. It's designed to show you that there are sometimes no clear answers to these issues, and the Socratic[8] approach is the best way to demonstrate a well-rounded perspective on the subject. Plus, it's more fun to read this way. Enjoy.

[8] Socratic approach: Asking pointed questions designed to challenge the conventional viewpoint. Also known as belligerence to the less enlightened.

Ben McLane: I work with a ton of new, up-and-coming bands, and at least 30 percent of the time we have [trademark] problems with names. Somebody else is using the same or a similar name in a different part of the country. Sometimes maybe they even used it first, and then you have to fight about it and somebody has to give in. It seems like bands can put a little more effort into coming up with a unique name, or researching it more before they start performing or something.

Moses: How is this a career killer?

Ben McLane: If you go to sign a label deal, the label wants to make sure that the name is free and clear before they start pumping money into it. There is a band that I worked with, they got a really big deal with Elektra, but as soon as we got the deal we found out there is at least one other band that had the name and actually has *superior rights.*[9] We had to buy them out, and by the time a major label gets involved, the other band holds you up for more money.

Moses: What does a standard buyout like that go for?

Ben McLane: It depends. There is no standard. If it's an unsigned band it could be just a few hundred or a thousand bucks. If a band gets a major record deal it could be $25,000 or $50,000 or $100,000, maybe even overrides[10] and things like that.

Moses: Do you actually know of situations like that where a newly signed band had to pay $100,000 to get a name?

Ben McLane: Not one that I've been involved with. But just think about it logically. If you are some broke band in Nebraska and you use a name and all of a sudden you see that some band just got a three-million-dollar deal with Epic Records and they stole your name, you have a lot of leverage to get that kind of money.

Moses: I would argue differently. That's why I always ask an interview subject if they know—firsthand—of a circumstance they're talking about because this business is not a logical business, and things you think would be "natural" are not. As I am sure you would agree. Even though the "Nebraska band" might think they have all kinds of leverage, once they call the label attorney and he gets ahold of it, the whole situation changes. Especially if the label has the hots for the band they just signed. Then the label gets on the phone with this Nebraska garage band's attorney (who is practicing out of an office above the 7-11 in God knows where) and says, "You want to piss us off? A major label? Then you go ahead and play hardball right now and your clients will probably never get signed to anybody and we'll never do business with you again. Or do the right thing, give us the name for a few thousand bucks and send us your demos along with it and maybe we can talk about a production deal." In my experience that's the MO of majors. Intimidation. They have the leverage and they use it.

Ben McLane: That's assuming that the [Nebraska] band really feels as though they have a shot at getting signed in the future. There are a lot of bands that are, say, older or just aren't motivated, they know they are never going to have a shot, or their music just doesn't cut it. This is their shot to get as much money as they can.

Moses: I don't know too many artists who are so self-actualized as to say, "Let's be honest with ourselves, our music really isn't that commercial, and we are really kind of long in the tooth. So the big bad label can't intimidate us." Most think they have a real shot. And this might be it.

[9] Superior rights: Fancy legal talk for "they filed the name first and have been actively using it."

[10] Overrides: A profit point on the record or percentage of any income earned by the band.

Ben McLane: In today's music business at the majors, if you are over 25 and you haven't happened yet, your days are really numbered and you are going to be very fortunate if you get something going. If you are 30, forget it.

Moses: That may be true, but most bands—even though they might be 29, 30, or 31—they might think they still have a shot. I can guarantee if you are some 30-year-old rocker and Interscope's lawyer calls you (even if it's to strong-arm you) and says we understand that you [morons] want over $100,000 to release your name for a group we are going to sign with the same name, I don't see the [Nebraska band] standing firm. I see them saying, "Interscope Records is calling us! Yow-ee. Hey, this is our lucky day."

Ben McLane: Maybe, but if I was the no-name band's attorney, I would say hold out for the $100,000 because the chance of you getting a major record deal, even if you were the next Nirvana,[11] is slim; there are no guarantees. They sign so few these days. I would say take the money, get as much money as you can.

[11] Nirvana's first advance was only $25,000. It all went toward the production of the record.

Moses: Yeah, but Interscope's lawyers are saying, "We won't give you $100,000, we will give you $5,000."

Ben McLane: Well, yeah, you are going to end up somewhere in the middle. My experience has been through people I know that have done this. It's anywhere from $5,000 to $25,000 if a band is signed to a major. I am just saying, because those huge deals are so rare anymore, if there was one that came into play and you really had leverage, I don't think it's out of the question for someone to get paid money like $100,000. It has probably happened, I just haven't been involved in it.

Moses: Not only do I doubt that it happens with any degree of regularity that one could call "normal," the reality of that situation is so remote: a garage band, still living hand to mouth off of the money that they are making from their music (assuming that they are actually making money from music and nothing else), if the label said, "You keep your name, we are going to release this as-is anyway, you try to stop us," the garage band wouldn't have the legal wherewithal to fight the label. They won't have the money. They'd lose. And Nebraska's lawyer knows that, if he has a brain in his head. He's gonna say, "Go easy, take whatever they offer," 'cause he knows that his clients don't have the money to fight the big label and he's probably not going to do it on a contingency.

Ben McLane: That's right. At some point you are going to get ground down. But there is somebody out there with some music business experience willing to spend the time on it because he or she is a real pit bull, a new, young attorney that wants to make a name for himself who will do it on contingency.

Moses: And there's a plethora of them in the sticks?

Ben McLane: You can find people out there that want to be in the business, but they are in Detroit or Atlanta or maybe even Kansas City. This is their only entry into the business, to sue some big name, what do they have to lose? They are probably never going to be players anyway, and if they hop in and win a big case all of a sudden they get notoriety. I know there are people out there like that. That is just one example. I could see that happening—you could find a lawyer that would take it on a contingency and hold out for $100,000.

Moses: You think?

Ben McLane: Yep.

Moses: Good luck. What did that band you worked with on Elektra end up paying for their name?

Ben McLane: I think it was like $15,000. Plus a point from the record. That wasn't horrible and I think we were able to get the label to pony up that money too.

> Crowd Pleasers and Literally Killing Off Your Fan Base

In an effort to boost their images, the stars of the music world can often be very shortsighted. Sometimes it can end in tragedy, as with the two cases below involving **Puff Daddy** and **Diana Ross**.

Sean Combs: Ghetto Fabulous

The role model for the term "Ghetto Fabulous," **Sean "Puffy" Combs**'s[12] label **Uptown Records** took rap from an urban folk music to a chic crossover genre in the late 1980s. The price, many thought, was a selling-out of its roots. Puffy got a $55 million advance from **Arista Records** and immediately upgraded the image of his artists, dressing them up in mega bling bling and moving the music more toward R&B pop than the hard-hitting ghetto roots that took rap to the charts in the first place. The following years, while Puffy took Uptown in the R&B direction, rap sales tripled, seeing the largest surge of sales in its history. How could such a marketing "genius" miss such an important trend?

André Fischer: People entering the music business on the business side don't know enough music. They are not involved enough with the creative aspect to

[12] A little known achievement by Combs: he completed the New York Marathon in 4 hours, 14 minutes, and 54 seconds.

13 **Motown:** Label
founded by Berry
Gordy in 1959.
Created a stable of
artists similar to
the old movie-
studio method of
production. A team
would churn out hit
after hit, with the
artist acting as a
mere figurehead.
Unfortunately
many received far
too little compen-
sation for their
efforts. As a result
the names Berry
Gordy and Motown
have remained a
bit tarnished in the
folklore of the
music business.

properly liaison with creative people. They leave that job up to A&R, but A&R is no longer in the same capacity as it was 20 years ago. Nor are the people they hire to be A&R [assistants] qualified as good liaisons between business and art.

Puffy learned well from his mistakes. He became very involved with the music itself from then on. He produced tracks and sat in on mixes. He also controlled the image of most of the artists that he signed. It was the Motown[13] of the 1990s. A factory where one man's vision was the signature.

In 1991, however, his arrogance hit a brick wall in an ugly situation that ended with nine people dead and 29 injured. Combs had planned an all-star exhibition basketball game to raise money for AIDS. However, he sold far more tickets than the school gymnasium could legally handle. On the night of the event the crowd pounded against the front doors, but Puffy refused to open them. Why?

> *Uptown Exec:* The promotion business is all about perception. You want peo-
> ple to see a big crowd outside. Puffy was doing what every promoter did. You let
> a crowd build up outside so that people go, "What's happening in there?" You
> even keep the press outside the rope for a few minutes. Make them get the point
> that this is something real.

14 In 2003, thirteen
years later, Puffy
helped raise $1
million for city
schools and the
Children's Hope
Foundation.

By the time Puffy's staff realized that the situation was critical, several people had already been trampled to death. Puffy had to defend himself in court but was eventually cleared of any criminal charges. The AIDS charity turned out to be fictitious and the money earmarked for donation was never recovered or refunded. Puffy's net worth today is estimated at over $50 million.[14]

15 **Mariah Carey's
deal:** A five-album
deal for
$20,000,000 each.
She did the first
one and was
bought out. The
combined moneys
for both the first
CD and the buyout
was $49,000,000.
The CD sold about
550,000 units, mak-
ing it the most ex-
pensive artist deal
in the history of
pop music.

> *Uptown Exec:* Don't weep for the man. He's bounced back a hundredfold.
> *Moses:* And why? Is his track record all that? Look at the numbers.
> *Uptown Exec:* They're good enough. His money is based mostly on advances
> from the label and his sponsors. Advances are only based on results *in theory.*
> Look at **Michael Jackson** and **Mariah Carey**.[15] Can anyone really tell me that
> their talents, great as they are, are really worth the one billion dollars that labels
> have collectively paid them in advances? It almost seems like in this business you
> fail upwards.

I'm reminded of a story that **Donald Trump** told when I did some work for his company back in 1991.[16] We were standing in his newly purchased hotel, the New

York Plaza, and he was hosting a modeling contest sponsored by Elite Modeling Agency. He said to several of us, "I was walking down the street with **Marla [Maples]**[17] and we passed Trump Tower and there was a homeless man lying in front of it. I said to Marla, 'See that guy? He's worth more than me.' She said, 'How can that be? He's worth zero.' And I said, 'That's right. He's worth zero, I'm worth negative $860 million dollars."

Ha ha, Donald.

A story like that has a tendency to stick with you, especially if you understand what the hell he's talking about. Y'see, anytime a person worth negative $860 million dollars needs a loan, banks will line up to lend it to him. Kind of like if you have a lot of credit card debt it's not hard to get companies to send you a new "pre-approved" card.

> *Uptown Exec:* Puffy has no problem finding people to lend him cash. He prac-
> tically invented the term "bling bling." So no matter what the numbers read, he'll
> always be producing something high-end.

> Information, Education, and Power

I've included this sub-chapter on education because I feel that thinking you're "too cool for school" is the major cause of arrogant screw-ups. In most any business, step one is doing some kind of survey to see what the public is interested in. There is little point in opening up a kosher pizza parlor if no one in the area wants kosher pizza. After you're convinced that you know there is a demand for your idea, you learn about the basic business—how to run a store, leases, and local law. Then you get a loan and you're on your way.

In music, however, these two vital steps are universally ignored. I don't know a single band that said, "Let's survey the public to see if there is a real need for a blend of punk and zydeco." Music is innovation, and innovation cannot be surveyed. It's the element of surprise that makes something hip.

Okay, given that you can't survey the public, you'd think that at least people trying to break in would get to know the tangibles of the business: basic laws that apply, how the business operates, and so on. For example, you can't survey the public to see what they want for their next record, but you can survey record companies. They are far easier to get a feel for since there are only a few of them (35 majors approximately). Yet newbie artists and professionals on the business side will

[16] He's told it to many people and in interviews as well, but the version has changed over the years. This is the way I remember him telling it.

[17] Marla Maples: The Donald's second wife.

avoid learning about the business at all costs. They rely solely on things like MTV as their primary source of information. This is like relying on network news for objective journalism.

> *Geza X:* Everything that goes out of the press and on TV is hype, it's like fronting. It is like an image-making machine that gets a hold of larger artists and manufactures what the public sees: the artist gets screwed up on drugs. They get drunk and trash recording studios because they can afford it.[18] Up-and-coming artists see all of that going on because they read the press. They read *People* magazine, they are checking out some artist's anorexia story. They think this is the code, how they are supposed to behave, and they start behaving like that before anyone even knows who they are. And everybody just goes, ewww!

Taking behavioral cues from the media? Bad idea. Spend a little time on *real* education. And yet, if you added up the sales of all the copies of all the educational books on the music business it would not equal one-tenth of the musicians in the United States, let alone their managers, lawyers, and such. Frequently talent accompanies ego and arrogance. This is a huge barrier against education, the lack of which is a primary barrier against success.

But who can blame artists for feeling this way? Most don't have much more than the gift God has given them. They work at perfecting it, get on stage, and everybody who knows them feeds their ego. Can this be dangerous?

> *Geza X:* It's true that you have to believe in yourself and you have to have enough energy behind what you are doing to survive all of the negatives that you get thrown at you. But too often people think they are going to have the next big hit because there is nothing good on the radio, so the industry must be starving for talent. I used to see people getting off of these buses that arrive in Hollywood every day. They're carrying a guitar case, shuffling up to Capitol Records in bell-bottoms, and I can just imagine that this guy has a bunch of lyrics he wrote in giant letters with a Crayola inside the guitar case, scribbled on a napkin or something like that. And they are like, whooo-weee! As soon as they hear me ... I am gonna walk right up there! Many people find out much later, to their detriment when it's too late, that connections are a very large part of the game. Not talent.

An interesting fact to chew on: major labels receive over three thousand demos a year. They sign about five new acts each year. With that fact more or less well

18 Geza says: "They do this because that is the frustration of realizing how little actual power they have and they have everybody sweet-talking them and telling them how great they are. Pretty soon they are so confused that they don't know what's going on. Their hearts and souls tell them that they are somehow powerless and that there is something large controlling them, but their ego tells them that they're the man and so that creates a lot of violent disruptions in these artists' psyche."

known by the up-and-coming artist, you'd wonder what they must tell themselves to keep the faith. Too often it's a mantra that their job is simply to keep creating and that the business will come to them. Never true. Like all industries, being on the inside means access to information that leads to opportunity. **André Fischer** serves on the advisory committee for the **Arts and Humanities Council** in Washington, DC, and is a multi-platinum producer and musician:

> *André Fischer:* Success is nothing more than the maintenance of new information. A lot of folks are given information or shown things, but they don't take the responsibility to learn it. At that point they definitely do need a surrogate to give them help.

Someone once said, "Success is the application of good intelligence. Those with the best information can make the best decisions and tend to be the most successful." And yet some of the most successful people in the business make bad decisions every day. This is largely in part because they think they can beat the odds. As the saying goes, the best swimmers drown.

⊘ Conclusion

On more occasions than I can count I have been accused of being arrogant. I often ask the accuser exactly what they think "arrogant" means. Most then proceed to give the wrong definition. They tend to define other words like "conceited" and "opinionated" and mix them up with arrogance. Webster says arrogance is "a false sense of pride." I have always responded to these accusers (who I think are confessing far more about their own insecurities than they are exposing mine) that there is nothing false about my sense of pride. It's genuine.

By the common popular definition of arrogance (meaning *opinionated*), just about everyone I know who is good at anything is guilty. It's hard *not* to be arrogant when you want to help people and you're smart enough to be right more than you are wrong. But there are always those who will hate you for being right or for having the courage to express yourself. Ignore them. They are making the mistake of being cowards. They have a rationalization for their behavior: be humble, keep your opinions to yourself. That may be a good way to live a safe life where most people will like you, but few will ever respect you. Especially if you are an artist. Speak your mind, but remember a rule that it took me far too many years to learn: let others be "arrogant" as well. Give them space to be who they are. If you're in their house and they are acting "arrogant," don't try to outpace them. Show respect. And if you meet someone more "arrogant" than you in public, don't engage them. You'll both come off looking like fools.

In the next pages we're going to look into the heart of most people's arrogance. The quest for the almighty buck and how it often strips you of good judgment and fosters ruin. Turn the page.

Strictly for D'Cash

Brainwashed by the Business

> *"Every man thinks God is on his side.*
> *The rich and powerful know he is."*
> — Jean Anouilh, *The Lark*

Money may be the root of all evil, but it is also the path of least resistance. The need to pay bills will always win out over altruism with the generation now coming of age. They see few moral conflicts about selling their services for big bucks. The older generation—the Baby Boomers—don't get this mercenary attitude. Hold out, they would say. Wait for the right opportunity. Often forgetting that they grew up in the most prosperous economic period in the country's history. They didn't have to work as hard to make ends meet and make a decent living by doing something altruistic. Today, you take the gig that pays the most and requires the least amount of work. Period. Instead of "Give peace a chance" we have a new work-ethic mantra: "Work smart, not hard."

Tweeners (people between the Boomers and the Gen Xers, born between 1960ish and 1970ish) have a slightly different philosophy. They tend to be caught between the Boomers' sense of brotherly love (a byproduct of the civil rights movement) and the Gen Xers' disregard for paying their dues (a manifestation of their anger at people in the Boomer generation who had it easy). For Tweeners, taking gigs just for the money is a complex equation.

So depending on the generation, one may find alternative perspectives on this subject. And then there is the trust-fund factor. Not talked about much in the business is the fact that many people starting out in it—particularly on the business side—come from privileged backgrounds. These folk always have more choices than those not in the "lucky sperm club." The better internships are those that pay the least. How can someone who is not being helped out by a relative afford to take them? The better internships lead to the better jobs and opportunities. This is the music business's version of the rich getting richer.

What can go wrong and what pitfalls to consider when taking jobs just because they are offering big bucks are the targets of this mistake, which tracked in at number one on my survey when taken by people on the business side of the industry (see the appendix): taking gigs just for the d'cash.

❯ Knob Turning and Career Burning: The Tough Choices Facing the Recording Engineer

Unlike recording artists or producers, engineers have to be particularly mercenary. Especially since it seems that more and more, everyday technology is turning their profession into little more than waiters with patch cables. Right now we're going to hear from three engineers whose credits range from **Alanis Morissette** to **Michael Jackson** and **Aerosmith**, and see what it's like for them when conflicting job offers come their way.

Jagged Bitter Little Pill

Jagged Little Pill, **Alanis Morissette**'s first US release, was the biggest-selling debut album in US history—a staggering 30 million copies worldwide in the first year. Many journalists felt that were it not for this album the music business that year would have had little to contribute to the world market. If you were a recording engineer or producer and you were offered an opportunity to work on that album, would you take it? Sure you would. It's a dumb question. Well, here's someone who did turn it down.

A Grammy-winning engineer/producer, **Francis Buckley** has been making records for over 20 years. Buckley's contributions as engineer and mixer to such multi-platinum recordings as the **Pointer Sisters**' *Breakout*, **Paula Abdul**'s *Forever Your Girl*, **Wilson Phillips**' *Wilson Phillips*, and many others, have helped to sell over 50 million–plus records worldwide.

In 1981, he moved to **MCA Music Publishing**, beginning a ten-year stand as director of recording services. It was at MCA that he met producer **Glen Ballard**, the producer of *Jagged Little Pill*, with whom he shared a 14-year partnership.

Francis Buckley: There were two versions of *Jagged Little Pill*. [Producer **Glen Ballard**] and I first met Alanis and did a whole bunch of songs with her. The original song of mine that wound up on there was "Perfect."

Moses: So you and Glen did a first version of the record, and that version for whatever reason was rejected?

Francis Buckley: They just continued to write while he was out shopping the deal. I landed on this **Quincy Jones** record, the one that I won the Grammy for. That was supposed to be a short gig. I was going to be on it for only four or five days. I figured I'd be back with Glen after that. Instead, I wound up doing seven and a half months with Quincy. In that seven and a half months Glen and Alanis wrote an entire second album, released it, and it was working its way toward being the third-biggest-selling record of all time.

Moses: Are you bitter?

Francis Buckley: The first 12 years that [Glen and I] had worked together I probably spent more time with him than I did with my wife. Sometimes we would even work New Year's night. When I went off and did Quincy and came back, the Alanis thing was blowing up and suddenly he had a billion people calling his name. He had thousands of offers coming from people all over, he had his own little record company, and he wasn't in the studio as much. The way you pay an engineer is when he is in the studio with you. I do know at the time I was tired of being there. It just got so high-pressure every time, it didn't matter what we were doing, whether it was cutting a demo with some big-name artist or just in there with some unknown songwriter. I remember one day Alanis came to the house, and you would have thought the president of the United States had shown up. So I left. From the point I left he had [a new engineer] who knew how to run the studio.

Moses: Did you ever consider discussing a partnership with him? So that rather than not getting paid for two or three months you were getting a piece of the action?

Francis Buckley: On one project that was very low-budget but turned into a big seller, someone went and asked for a bonus. He was told that "your bonus is you

1 Meaning, try to get
1 percent of the
retail sales price of
the record. Artists
typically receive
9–12 points and
producers 3–5
points.

can put this on your résumé and say you did it." Someone told me one time that I should go after a point.[1] But I thought about it. Add up the albums that you've worked on and see the ones that have really made a lot of money—if you would have gotten a point from them, how much more would you have made? I think that it averages out. There were very few engineers who participated in anything other than getting an hourly fee. If you get your real engineering rate you probably make as much money just working as you would trying to collect royalties.

Probably true, especially when you consider the litigation that inevitably ensues when you try to collect. I've also noticed that while successful engineers rarely live better than successful recording artists and producers, the average mid-level to upper-level engineer lives a bit better than the average mid-level artist or producer.

> *Moses:* So it's okay that you didn't end up working on the third-best-selling album of all time?
>
> *Francis Buckley:* I have an invoice hanging on my wall from that. People think that I have it hanging on the wall so that everybody says, "Oh wow, you worked on Alanis Morissette's record." Well, I don't tell them that that is to remind me not to ever be that stupid again. I should have somehow participated in the company in some way, shape, or form.

Moral of the story: No one has ever bet enough on a winning horse. Also, the human body is cleverly designed so that you can neither kick yourself nor pat yourself on the back too easily. Buckley has the right attitude. Never look back in regret just because you didn't push for more on a deal that blew up—or, as in the next two stories, because you made decisions based on prior commitments or personal standards. If you play the law of averages you'll make about the same, and you'll make more friends in the long run because you will be less demanding.

Jettison Jackson

Matt Forger has worked closely with **Michael Jackson** for over a decade, providing a technical foundation and an environment conducive to the artist's creative needs. Shortly after moving to Los Angeles, Forger secured a staff position at **Westlake Studios**, where he teamed up with producers **Quincy Jones**, **Rod Temperton**, and **Bruce Swedien**, working on albums that included Michael Jackson's *Thriller*.

But can having such a strong tie to one particular client have its drawbacks?

Matt Forger: There was a time when I was literally walking out the front door for my session and the phone rang. The person on the phone was Michael Jackson's assistant, and she said, "We need you in the studio right now." I was a 15-minute drive from my other gig and I couldn't just not show up. I couldn't make a call and say, "I am sorry, I am just not going to show up today because MJ wants me." At a later date I found out that the session with Michael that I turned down was the demo recording for the "We Are the World"[2] project....There is this line between making decisions which are strictly short-term monetary decisions and what are going to be longer-term career-type decisions. I find sometimes that I get boxed in to very strange positions where I find it impossible to uncommit myself when a better or more prestigious thing does come along. There is always that case where you would rather work on something that is more exciting or more high-profile for a cut in pay or take a gig because it pays well but has no mojo [i.e., jingles].

Zadora Schora

John Luongo has done remixes for **Don Henley**, **Patti LaBelle**, **Gladys Knight**, **Dolly Parton**, **John Waite**, and **Cheap Trick**, yet he regrets an opportunity he turned down for, of all people, **Pia Zadora**.[3]

John Luongo: I have a backwards version of the scenario of taking a gig for the money. I turned one down for Pia Zadora for the money and kicked myself. I did not like the track and thought that she couldn't sing very well or with much power.

For those not old enough to remember, Pia was the **Anna Nicole Smith** of the 1970s. She's a great example for this chapter, because her entire career has been a mantra of "strictly for the cash," famous for marrying a mogul strictly for career purposes. He then bankrolled her career and created starring roles for her in movies that unfortunately for her went nowhere. However, it was well known that her husband's inducements to get very talented people to work with her could be quite persuasive.

John Luongo: As I remember, **Jimmy Jam** did the project with another producer and got cars sent to them after they finished. Boy, do I wish I had not been so freakin' picky!

Ironically, Pia went on to have a relatively successful singing career. She made pop and traditional vocal albums in the '80s, scoring a Grammy nomination in

[2] "We Are the World": Written by Quincy Jones and Michael Jackson, was originally recorded in 1985 and featured many of the most famous pop singers and performers of the time. The project raised about $60 million for famine relief to Africa and was the trendsetter for a string of aid projects, such as Farm Aid, Live Aid, Hands Across America, and the nauseatingly pretentious "Do They Know It's Christmas" that permeated the 1980s. Although no conclusive study was ever published, it has been alleged that much of the money for these follow-up events after "We Are the World" went into the pockets of the promoters. The artists probably had no idea.

[3] Born Pia Alfreda Schipani. Biggest boner: She bought the Pickfair mansion in 1988 only to have it demolished. The outside gate with the letter P is all that remains of the original home. Zadora is her mother's maiden name.

1982 with "Rock It Out." Her biggest hit in the US was 1983's "The Clapping Song." In 1984, she scored a worldwide hit with "When the Rain Begins to Fall," a duet with **Jermaine Jackson**. Between her and her beau, maybe it wasn't *true* love. But who can say what is?

⊘ Taking a Big Salary for a Small Job

The business changes so quickly. Trends in musical styles, video productions, business administration styles, even contract negotiations have an ebb and flow to them. If you're a lawyer representing an artist negotiating a deal with a major and you're pressing last year's point—like Internet rights—when this year's point is royalties for music videos, you seem like the lawyer who is wearing last year's suit. This former label exec, who has managed some top acts, would only talk to me anonymously about what it's like to work at the same job or with the same company over the course of time.

> *Moses:* If you were mentoring someone and they asked how long they should stay at this job, what would you tell them?
>
> *Former Label Exec:* Don't fall into a routine. Don't stay too long in one place. If it's not your company, remember that. You have to be passionate about what you do. It's the music that matters, not you and your ego and all the other bullshit.

Moving to a new location has advantages and disadvantages. As the newbie you get a lot of attention combined with lowered expectations (depending on your reputation). People initially love and hate you simultaneously. This kind of controversy is always a good thing. You're the new kid. In a year or two you're the person sitting around who either hasn't done much or changed much, or has left gracefully. Is this a realistic expectation? No, but it's human nature.

People secretly want great things from new people You'll get favors that the old guy can't get because people still in their jobs want to earn "favor currency" with you.

However, the downside is daunting. If you don't perform out of the box, then your currency dies fast. It's for this reason that A&R people new on post are loath to sign any acts, no matter how great they think they are. And if they're taking over someone else's signing, they are even less interested in doing anything for that act. It has no upside for them.

So now you have to figure out how to justify your six-figure salary without actually disappointing anyone. I know A&R people who say the key to keeping your job is to never sign anyone. Ironic. This kind of thing goes on at every level of employment. Even CEO.

> *Former Label Exec:* [The president of the major label I worked at] pit everybody against each other. He spent hundreds of millions of dollars, and he's a moron. I don't care how successful he is at making records. He doesn't know how to run a company.
>
> *Moses:* So, what did you learn from that experience? What can you teach others?
>
> *Former Label Exec:* Just trust yourself, believe in yourself. That's really what it comes down to. And get out while you're on top. That's really it.

Obviously one should not stay at a post to the point where hostilities boil over. But all this begs the question…

> *Moses:* How long is too long?
>
> *Former Label Exec:* Five or six years.
>
> *Moses:* What happens after that?
>
> *Former Label Exec:* You get burnt out; you have to go somewhere where you are moving forward and upward. You have to be excited about what you are doing, or else it doesn't matter. I had to leave [my label]. I was there too long—eleven and a half years. I had to have my own life. I didn't want to be asked, "Where are you? Exactly where?" like a little f-ing child. No one needs that. No one wants to have to report in. That happened because I stayed too long through too many regimes.

❯ Pitfalls of Big Advances

Every band and artist wants one: a huge advance, one so big that it's not just screw-you money, but screw-everybody money. However, many experts in the business are quick to point out that taking such an offer can lead to disaster. It means that the record company's investment in you is so large that they might not renew your contract if you only do marginal sales on your first release. This creates a common strategy of bands taking lower advances so that there is not as much pressure on them early in their careers. Others believe this way of thinking is ridiculous. Let's hear both sides.

In a speech that he's given on more than one occasion, industry mega-mogul **Alan Grubman**, lawyer to the stars, has said, "If my client gets royalties, I haven't done my job."

It will probably be his epitaph. In the years since the publication of my first book, *Confessions of a Record Producer*, the focus on artists being victimized by record company accounting practices has been the catalyst for new ways that regulate how they get paid. Alan Grubman, as history has cast him, is one of the architects of the old system. Many feel that his business strategies, often layered with conflicts of interest, are the cause of many artists not receiving their due. All the while he represents them in the negotiation with major labels, he also represents those same labels in other matters that concern those same artists.

Grubman, in his keynote speech to a room filled with industry executives and artists, laid out a rationalization for his strategy. The logic: since the methodology of calculating royalties is so complex, such as to make it virtually impossible for an artist to receive any royalties, one may as well take as large an advance as the label is willing to offer. So, his comment above sort of makes sense in this bizarre universe. If I told you I was going to loan you money to start your business, and I was going to take all the money the business brought in and wouldn't pay you your share until you paid back the total amount of $10,000, then you'd probably start thinking, well, maybe then I should ask for $20,000.

Unfortunately the logic doesn't hold up, in the opinions of some other attorneys. **Paul Menes**, who has been profiled in several editions of *Who's Who in American Law*, is one of them.

> *Paul Menes:* I agree with [Grubman] to a point. The point that I don't agree with is at the beginning [of the artist's career]. Unless there is some huge bidding war and everybody thinks this artist is the hottest thing since sliced bread, then yes. And if the artist becomes successful and you have the leverage, then I think you go with that philosophy because at that point you want to be able to give your artist the luxury of not having to worry so much about the accuracy of royalty statements and everything else. But generally, I don't think that starting out this way is a good idea, because until the artist has a proven track record they are setting the stage for a very short career. If they are just doing this to cash out as soon as they can, great. I can think of a lot of artists that have done that. **Kingdom Come** was one, if I am not mistaken. There was a huge buzz and they signed a huge advance and nothing happened.

Moses: The only downside to taking the huge advance is if you don't sell a lot of records, right? Well, how many artists think that they aren't going to sell a lot of records?

Paul Menes: None of them. They all think they are going to be huge.

Moses: How are you going to convince your client that they should take a smaller advance based on your logic?

Paul Menes: Because if he takes a smaller advance he will be on the label longer, which means the odds of him selling a lot of records goes up by the number of albums he'll get to release. If he takes a huge advance and releases one record, maybe he does okay, maybe he doesn't do okay—he's not going to get a second chance if he owes the label too much money. If he takes a smaller advance, chances are they will exercise the option for the second record and maybe a third.

Moses: Most managers and a lot of lawyers I know would absolutely disagree with that advice. They would say no, make the label pay, make them spend the money, because if they've invested a million dollars in this artist they will work harder to get it back.

Paul Menes: Not true. The label is a business. They might as well be selling bathroom scales, really. They have a business plan, they have a profit/loss statement. They have quarterly sales or income figures to hit. They expect to make a certain amount of money, but they expect to lose a certain amount of money. The risk involved in paying a huge advance to an artist is part of the yearly plan, I guess. They know that X number of artists are going to sell and Y number of artists are not. They understand that some of that money is just going to get flushed down the toilet, but hopefully get made up by the one artist that becomes a superstar. I think it has been proven time and again that just because a label pays a lot of money upfront for an artist, it doesn't mean they are going to stick with the artist or the record. There is a point where it is going to be gone. I have had several artists where that has happened. All good intentions. The label spent a fortune and the band worked their ass off, but there was so much money spent by the label, both in advance and promotions, that the decision was made not to do a second or third record.[4] These days, the labels are more concerned how money is spent and much more likely to stick with an artist if, when they look at those quarterly numbers, the artist is closer to recouping than if they would have paid a whole shitload of money upfront.

[4] See the saga of the Tuesdays in Chapter 6's section called "Norwegian Would."

Just so it doesn't seem like I'm endorsing one viewpoint over another, here's **Mark Avsec**, a songwriter turned music lawyer. He's written more than 300 songs and produced more than 25 sound recordings for, among other artists, **Bon Jovi** ("She Don't Know Me"), **Donnie Iris** ("Ah! Leah!" and "Love Is Like a Rock"), and **Wild Cherry** ("Play That Funky Music, White Boy"). He has a different perspective.

Mark Avsec: As a lawyer representing an artist I want to get the label vested. I think the more money labels put into acts the harder they will work to get that money back.

You'd think. The next story shows how a major label can put $500,000 into a new act and then toss it aside like yesterday's garbage. And why? Read on in this next section appropriately called...

◯ Label Droppings

Ever wonder, when the big labels take a dump, who cleans it up? For those who are sucked into the concept of big-label security, here's few cautionary items that need to be considered.

Truth Seeker

Most artists I know dream of a day when a major label signs them. Imagine you are an L.A. rock band, playing local gigs, still working your day jobs. Now a small indie signs you. They have so-so distribution, but the advance is serious enough that you give them a shot. Then a year into the contract they come to you and say they have sold you to a major label. Immediately you start seeing limos in your near future. Do you think you would have the foresight and guts to say, "No, I'm going to fold this hand"?

In the case of **Truth Seeker**, they got a deal on an indie label called Milestone [name changed] and then the mega-major label Pacific Records[5] bought out the Milestone contract for twice what the label had spent on developing the band. It seems like everybody was going to win on this one. Milestone spent less than a quarter-million developing the act. Pacific was willing to give them about $500,000 and the promise of all the major-label trimmings: radio play, national exposure, and a video. It was paradise. Until it all went wrong. **John Brodey**, former general manager of Milestone, tells us the story.

[5] Pacific Records: This is the fictitious name I often use to refer to a major that I don't want to name. No significance should be made or parallel drawn to any other major label named after a different ocean.

John Brodey: This band had real radio potential, but Milestone was not in the position to take that the whole way.

No independent label has the money (with rare exception) to pay for mainstream radio promotion. Costs range upwards of $250,000 per single. An MTV video can cost anywhere from $50,000 to $500,000. Getting on MTV can cost about $150,000 in fees. All in all, it adds up to far more than Milestone had in their kitty. They spent about $150,000 on this band's recordings. In these cases when a real contender emerges from the smaller labels, majors step in to take the act national. Pacific offered to buy the contract for $300,000.

John Brodey: It ended up being closer to five [hundred thousand] plus an override. Initially they wanted to buy the band and take it over. Obviously we wanted to maintain some type of interest both artistically and financially over the long haul. More than just an override, the deal took the form of a *joint venture.*[6] We managed to hammer something out that was certainly not conventional and certainly not [Pacific's] first choice.

Moses: Did you need the band's approval to make this deal?

John Brodey: We didn't need the band's approval. It seemed like a reasonable thing to do. They got a chunk of the money. I don't remember exactly how much, but I think they had got about half.

Moses: Had anybody discussed the possibility with the band that this could be a disaster?

John Brodey: Absolutely. I told them, this doesn't mean that all of our problems are over. It's a gamble and there is definitely a downside. These things have an insidious way of blowing up in one's face.

Moses: Pacific then records a couple more songs and adds them to the already finished album. I heard them; they sounded like hits to me. Was it Pacific's call to stop the promotion of the record?

John Brodey: Yes, it was Pacific Records' call, and it was at that point where their A&R guys had to put their stamp of approval on it. Since these deals require an inside A&R champion, that person often ends up being the point person in the early stages.

Moses: The song was getting some airplay?

John Brodey: Yes, but off of the *original* record that we made, not the subsequent masters that Pacific recorded. Then it was like they put the freeze on that. Pacific Records goes out and says, we just picked up the band, why don't you guys ease up on promoting [the songs you own].

Moses: This makes no sense. These are people who have 20 years' experience in the music business? They had the makings of a hit, they also owned the band and the next masters. Why pull the plug?

6 Joint venture: A business model whereby both parties share equally in the risk and rewards of a venture.

John Brodey: It makes no sense in retrospect.

Once the album was pulled from radio it *had* to be pulled from the distribution channels of **ADA**[7] as well so that it could then be re-released by Pacific Records. Milestone already had a distribution deal on ADA when Pacific bought the contract.

[7] Alternative Distribution Alliance: One of the larger independent distributors of CDs and music. Headquartered in Manhattan with 16 branch offices nationwide. Actually owned at the time by Warner Music, a "Pacific Records" competitor. (www.ada-music.com)

John Brodey: And they had to be appeased and compensated for what they had put out, and the cost they had incurred. It seemed easier to make the small amount of units already in the pipeline disappear, and do a re-release on the new distributor, Pacific.

Moses: Isn't that risky? ADA already has people talking about the band, then the units are suddenly not available to the public. The heat could cool. And the public is very fickle.

John Brodey: Well, obviously there were heated discussions and real arguments. Besides, having to go in and ask [ADA] to let us out of our deal felt disingenuous. Ultimately it was Pacific going, "Wait, we have controlling interest in the band, this is what we are going to do." [They thought] if the band is that smoking, what difference is three months going to make? And we didn't have any say at that point. Once you've made a deal with [a major] they have the upper hand and then they start redoing the deal. It happens every time. We said, "You know how hard it is to start a fire? When you finally get it going do you want to put it out and start a new one? No."

Moses: What was their rationalization for it?

John Brodey: They felt that everybody would be more in line with [Pacific Records, over us]. They would have a better [sounding] record, it would be a fresh start, and they'd do the full-court press, reprioritize it. That was their mentality.

Moses: Who was champion of this "bigger is better" philosophy?

John Brodey: It was all the way through the system.

Moses: So this was a united front?

John Brodey: Absolutely. The various departments. Marketing, sales, the programs, everything was out of whack. In a marketing meeting, the only guy with a hammer in his hand is the general manager or the president. Everyone else in there is saying, "Okay, which way is the wind blowing today, who do I have to make friends with? Who is going to make my life miserable? Who do I have to deal with?" You have the marketing guy, the promotional guy, and the A&R guy, each with their turf. Somehow, they have to come out of there with as much of their asses as they can hang on to.

By the time Pacific released the record, the momentum had faded. Truth Seeker was just another band that didn't make its numbers.

John Brodey: I went in there and I got an apology. I couldn't believe that I was getting an apology from the president of the company, saying that they really screwed this up. I obviously feel shitty about it because I am somebody who has had enough experience to know better and we wanted to do right by our band, even though we were in a tricky position. But at that point you have that thing that happens in a record company, where they don't like to be reminded of a bad decision. A hit has a thousand mothers, but a stiff is an orphan. Immediately people are walking away from the wreckage.

Milestone still believed in the act and asked Pacific to allow them to continue to develop Truth Seeker, since they were not going to back the record. The major label was happy to—for twice what they paid to Milestone. This of course would have ensured that Milestone would lose money on the deal. They decided to try anyway. Unfortunately, it was too little too late. Truth Seeker could never recapture the appeal, and ADA, the original independent distributor, wanted nothing to do with Milestone or the band that dissed them for a competitor, Pacific Records. The band eventually broke up. None of the hit songs from either label ever sold more than a few thousand copies.

Kicking Harold

Ben McLane is a Los Angeles–based lawyer who has worked for and with many top gold and platinum and Grammy-winning artists. He brings us this story of label excess and fickle behavior.

Ben McLane: **George Tobin** was a producer who would sign a band and develop the band to a certain point and then try to flip it over to a larger label. He's most famous for breaking **Tiffany**[8] in the '80s. When I was working with him he found this band called **Kicking Harold**, a rock band from L.A. George owned two radio stations; he is extremely wealthy. He produced Kicking Harold and put it on his stations. They sold almost 10,000 copies. Then of course a major label gets interested, and as soon as the band signs, all of the sales stop and all the radio play stops. This was just one case in particular where the label dropped the ball. Why would they spend a lot of money to sign a band and then just kill the record? It just doesn't make any sense to me. Tobin was in a position where, if he wanted to, he

[8] Born Tiffany Darwish. Most of her big hits were remakes: "Delta Dawn" and "I Think We're Alone Now." She emancipated herself from her parents at age 16. Intriguing mistake: while appearing on the *Tonight Show* in 1987, she instructed the band to "stop playing" when she raised her hand. When she raised her hand early in the second verse she had to finish the song a cappella. Debatable mistake: she also appeared nude in *Playboy* (March 2002).

could have inserted things into his agreement to prevent that. But he basically just wanted to get the money. If someone says, "Hey, sign now, here's all this money" versus "Let's spend several months negotiating all of the finer points" — just give me the money and where do I sign? The band dies and breaks up and there were lawsuits galore over lack of promotion and they were supposed to do a second record and they didn't, blah blah blah. The sad part for the band: Tobin can move on to his next project, and so can the label, but the band gets branded as a failure. That kinda kills their career.

⊗ Conclusion

What went wrong, and what can we learn? In the case of most of these stories, was the small label or production company entirely to blame? Was a producer perhaps too eager to upsell the act they had discovered? Were the bands guilty of the same short-sighted greed? Tough call. This is a business and you don't generally turn down a half-million dollars from one of the largest record companies in the world.

But had some of these people not been blinded by the hype of success they might have done things differently. For example, Milestone could have put a clause in the contract that specifically stated that if the major dropped the ball the contract would revert back to the smaller entity. But this would only be something a large corporation would agree to if they were buying the contract completely. In some of these cases, like Milestone, the indie wanted to remain a partner on the project with the major. That's like a marriage. In a marriage, if one side racks up debt the other spouse is still legally responsible for it. Milestone's desire to be "partnered" with a major may have been a serious miscalculation. But it's hard to blame them.

Sometimes the allure of the major label can be so seductive it makes you forget an old Yiddish expression: "A favor that's no favor is no favor." If you need a plumber and your Uncle Louie is a plumber and hears that you're going to call someone, he may jump in and say, "I'm family, I'll fix it for you for free." But then he does a lousy job. You are loath to complain since you don't want to seem ungrateful. But eventually you have to say something. Louie takes offense and says, "But I did it for free!" Louie's free service will now end up costing you more because you have to hire someone to fix his bad work.

Likewise in these cases, a major-label deal that's no major-label deal is no major label deal. Pacific buying a small label's contract case makes little difference if the large label is not going to service the band. Thus these acts were killed by a combination of apathy and ambition.

Next, we'll look at the most fundamental thing to any career: getting hired and its subsequent action, getting fired. Most specifically when it's friends who do both. They say marriage is the prime cause of divorce. Is hiring the prime cause of firing? You might be surprised. Turn the page.

CHAPTER 5

Friendly Firings

"He'll set up a meeting with someone that you absolutely trust, guaranteeing your safety. And at that meeting you'll be assassinated."
—**Mario Puzo,** *The Godfather*

Ben McLane: I worked well with the band and helped them at a time when I didn't have a whole lot of huge credits to my name. As soon as the band got the offer, their heads got big and managers started approaching them, and so they basically blew me out without even telling me. I had to find out from the label.

Has this or something like it happened to you? Then you're reading the right chapter.

There is a complex social dynamic that exists in the entertainment business. It goes like this: you hint that you would like your "good friend" of several years to throw you some much-needed work or produce your record or manage your act. He responds with some version of "I don't like to do business with friends. It can get ugly."

Now, wait a minute, isn't that the entire reason that you were hanging out with this pinhead in the first place? Drinking with him, compromising many of your values, and, let's face it, lowering your standards to new depths of what you would call "a friend"? Only to have him tell you that you don't stand a chance of getting anything commercial out of him.

This would be bad enough. Then you hear he is working with so-and-so and he says in a *Billboard* interview, "Yeah, we're great friends and that really helps the creative process," and you're standing there, listening to this, thinking, "Where can I get my hands on a voodoo doll?"

Then there is the flip side of this bizarre phenomenon—your friend of many years who tosses you a job and then says, "I have to let you go. I really value our friendship and the work is getting in the way." So, to keep a friendship, this person is cutting you off financially? Sign up a few more friends like that and you can quickly go bankrupt.

If you think this only happens to the "little people" in the biz, you're about to learn otherwise. Friendly firings is an industry-wide phenomenon.

➤ Style over Substance: The Shelf Life of an "Old Friend"

Professionals in the music space spend years building up contacts. When someone we barely know casually approaches and asks for an introduction to someone, it's a dead giveaway that they don't have a clue about how the business works. Why make a hard-earned connection for a total stranger? What if they are a crook? That could damage the contact for the future. Even if the neophyte is not a crook, where is the consideration for all the time and effort (and money, let's be honest) invested in establishing the contact? There is nothing more valuable than a great connection. It's just too important to give away for free.

Before we go into how one can avoid closing a door and what to do right to open it wide and sweet, let's hear from a music journalist who tells us why good connections we make on the way up have a shelf life. And why, once that shelf life expires, they can be a serious detriment.

Journalist: I have been very good friends for years with the general manager of **Cleopatra**. He recently took over as general manager for [a major label]. When I was managing a major act, we got them signed to **Metal Blade/Warner**. In those years he was the head of retail for Warners Metal Blade, I helped him many times when *I* had the power and the leverage. I have helped his acts out and written stories about him. He was a good "friend." Then, when he was in position, he in turn helped a million new people. But he has never one time given me help. He has never given the artists I manage a moment. Not even like, "Let me get this over to those people." He felt like it would look like nepotism of some sort, or maybe that I am too strong of a personality at times, maybe that I was hustling him now that he got big.

Lesson Learned?

It doesn't really matter how much you do for someone. To expect a quid pro quo if they don't appreciate your "style" is unrealistic, especially if they have a preconceived notion of you from years back, when your style was not as refined as it might be today.

> *Journalist*: As a matter of fact, I am a big believer that old connections are not that valuable, because they have history and the history makes them see you as you *were,* not as you are today.

In the Family Way

The value of an old friend? How about the value of an old relative? **Jay Jay French**, who was on **Atlantic Records** with **Twisted Sister** for about a decade and helped sell over 10,000,000 records for that company, offers some positive spin on the subject of nepotism.

> *Jay Jay French:* I have seen [hiring friends] hurt. I know a chairman of a music label who, because of his nationality, brought people in, and unfortunately through the ineptness of the people he brought in, probably spent millions of dollars pushing garbage. Have I ever seen it help? I can't say that I have, but there are some people in the business that have brought in relatives and it did work. Look at **Steve Winwood**, from **Traffic**.[1] His brother **Muff** was in Traffic and quit to be on the business side and turned out to be an extremely talented executive.[2] **Warner Brothers/Columbia** in England: **Jane Asher**[3] was **Paul McCartney**'s[4] girlfriend; her brother went on to become an extremely successful producer and music company executive.

To my eyes there has been a shift in emphasis in the music-business job market. It used to be a place where eccentricities were not only tolerated, but often admired. Stories of **Irving Azoff** wrecking hotel rooms and **Walter Yetnikoff**'s[5] party habits

---

[1] Traffic: Had a string of major hits from the late 1960s to early 1970s, including *Mr. Fantasy, John Barleycorn Must Die, Feelin' Alright,* and *The Low Spark of High Heeled Boys.* However, there were about ten revolving members in the group. Even rock journalists had trouble keeping the names in the lineup straight. Chris Wood (flute/saxophone) died of liver failure in 1983. Jim Gordon (drummer number two) suffered from schizophrenia and was convicted in 1984 of killing his mother. The only superstar solo career to emerge from the group was Steve Winwood (with Dave Mason a close second). He tried to re-form Traffic in 1994 with a comeback record. The album's sales were considered poor.

[2] Muff Winwood: After a touch-and-go career as a musician, he went to work as an A&R man for Island Records. The first signing was Traffic—his brother's band. His follow-up signings were not

lined the halls of record companies like folklore. These days a wave of conservatism has washed over the business. And why not? As large corporations add "stability" to the business, they also bring their first cousins—the insurance companies. One day you wake up and there's an "efficiency expert" hired by corporate headquarters saying things to you like, "It's not what you say, but how you say it. Say it calmly, show restraint." Yesterday's swashbuckling screamer, who motivated people to meet the challenges, is today's potential liability in need of "sensitivity training."

In the journalist's case above, the fact that he's managed big acts and written reviews for *Billboard* holds less currency to some in power than the fear that if you invite him to a dinner party, he might eat with his elbows on the table.

What about when the job you get is because somebody who's been close to you for years recommends you? Such is the case often with attorneys, who in many cases are legally allowed to *pay* each other for referrals. Often a particular manager, lawyer, agent, or publicist winds up with an artist as a client because they were referred by a friend. This system works in favor of the professionals and not necessarily for the artist. In fact, it can be a disservice for the artist because if that relationship is too cozy, the professional representing the artist doesn't necessarily have your best interests at heart. His priority is protecting the source of the referral, often the major label or friend. The artists tend to come and go, but the referrals could be forever if you keep that relationship. **Paul Menes**, Los Angeles music lawyer, gives us some insight on this hustle.

Paul Menes: We used to represent a jazz artist. Originally, their manager referred them to us. So, when they fired the manager they fired us also because we were his referral. I think it disadvantaged them because their career went directly into the toilet after that. When they left they had a deal with a major label; now I don't know what deal they have. I certainly don't see their name or see them perform or hear about them half as much as I used to. That mistake cost them hundreds of thousands of dollars. If not more.

> Firing Your Best Friend When He's Your Mother

Who's your daddy? We know the answer to that—the record company, if you're signed to a major. Your investor, if you're doing the indie thing. So if the money is your daddy, who is your mamma? The manager.

Manager is a mamma's job. As the manager you are the one taking calls at three in the morning about bail for statutory rape charges, finding new drum skins at 5 A.M., fixing a broken tour bus in the middle of Sandusky, Ohio. You'd think that after all that you have some job security. I mean, after all, they say you can't choose your family. Well, whoever said that has not worked in the music biz.

A Change of Heart, or "I don't know, I just think you're not nice to me anymore, now that I don't need you as much."

Witness this anonymous story by a man who broke one of the biggest pop divas ever and created the business model for all others. To protect the innocent (and my publishing company) we'll call our diva Bethany and our source, who was fired after personally investing in her and taking her to the top, Johnny D.

Johnny D: If your manager proves to be a thief, has absconded with millions of dollars, you don't have the frickin' choice—you fire them and prosecute. But if you just don't like them anymore… think twice.

Moses: You were never accused of stealing from Bethany. What happened there? She just decided that she didn't like you?

Johnny D: Considering my age and lack of experience at the time, I think I was a brilliant manager of her career. But I was probably less than likeable. I would not have wanted to deal with me back then. But [I thought] the bottom line was that the trains ran on time and I generated the success. And I believed that as long as I did my job that I didn't have to deal with the intangibles of the interpersonal shit between a manager and an artist. I was completely focused on the mechanical and technical aspects of the execution of managing her career. I didn't pay attention to the human dynamic.

Moses: Isn't that just a fancy way of saying, "Look, if you don't stroke the artist's ego, no matter how good of a job you're doing, you're fired"?

Johnny D: Absolutely. I should have been doing that if I was doing my job properly. She was working her ass off. There was no sleep, I was driving her hard.

Moses: If she was right, why was it a mistake for her to fire you?

Johnny D: Because I built a winning *team*. There were publishing relationships, label relationships. We had several hits. She was number one worldwide. We had a national-brand cosmetics company endorsement. If she knew all of that would go away within a year by firing me, would she have done it? The artist never, ever thinks in those terms when they're thinking of firing their manager. They decide they've had it with somebody for whatever reason, and they go, "You're fired."

[5] Walter Yetnikoff: Presided over CBS Records (now Sony Music) in the Wild West days from 1975 to 1990. He was given a $25 million go-away fee to leave CBS. He took it and had a breakdown shortly thereafter. A quote from his autobiography, *Howling at the Moon*: "I created a mutual balance of terror between me and my artists." Michael Jackson calls him "Good Daddy."

Moses: Is there an ultimate truth here or is this just one of those things where you have competing truths?

Johnny D: Competing truths, and here is the nexus of those competing truths: You are confronted with the artist not wanting to do something which is critical to her professional health, and [her not doing it] has huge financial ramifications. [In other words, you'll be in breach of contract.] This comes up every day in a manager's life with an artist that has *any* success. Like taking off and going to Vegas and getting married without telling anybody; bailing out in the middle of a promotional tour across Europe. [*mimicking*] "I don't want to do four radio station stops in a foreign country, I want to go with **Michael Jackson**[6] to his new aquatic petting zoo. I just want to have a good time." An artist isn't exactly smart and savvy about whether it is a good or bad thing to cancel out on a commitment or whatever. They just know that they are burning the midnight oil, they've done six countries in four days. They have not had enough sleep, and they are *cranky.* They haven't slept in their own bed, and it's like, are *you* taking care of them? I thought I was taking care of Bethany pretty good. Obviously not good enough or she would have been happy and we would have still been working together today.

Moses: What did that mistake cost you?

Johnny D: Good question. I wasn't screwed out of money in that situation because what I had invested I got back and then some. But potentially millions of dollars because there were intangible losses. I had goals and visions for her career—transitions into movie and TV.

Although I was not involved with this situation personally, I knew Johnny D and was able to watch it fall apart from the outside. I had always wondered how a guy as smart and connected as him could let a cancer like this develop. He had mastered the biggest hurdles in the business, sold millions of records, and taken her from a small-town child to a nationwide sensation. What was the Achilles' heel? I asked him several times, but he would never talk about it. In public interviews he avoided it. But I told him, this book is a chance to teach tomorrow's version of him a lesson. He opened up.

Johnny D: The inducement in this situation was not another manager. I was very careful to make sure that the team was not going to be disrupted from outside of the group. But I never anticipated the attack from within: the [close relative]. Someone on my team was opportunistic and, coming from the dark side, persuaded [the close relative] to believe that she could do my job better than me. The one thing

[6] Jackson has named all his children Michael. (Sons one and two: Prince Michael and Prince Michael II. His daughter is Paris Michael.) Prince Michael Jackson II was held over a balcony in Berlin in full view of the media.

that can absolutely defeat you is if the *artist starts to manage herself*.

Moses: Does the person that induces the breach[7] have to have a vested interest in order to be guilty of a tort?

Johnny D: I am not sure if they have to have a vested interest to be liable for it. We liquidated what I was entitled to based on what business was currently on the table and I walked away, clean.

Johnny D did his job, but forgot about the human elements of being in the service business: if they don't like you, no matter how good at your job you are, you're out. So make an effort to listen to your client (who is usually much younger than you) when she wants to talk to you about "boys 'n' stuff."

❯ Firing Your God: Why Artists Replace a Hit Producer

"The reality is that if the manager and the A&R person think the producer needs to go and the artist wants to keep the producer… if push comes to shove the label has more juice than the artist."

—Geza X, Producer

In an industry where a formula for success is so nebulous to begin with, one would think that when an artist or label did finally arrive at one, you would stick with it. Would Hostess change the recipe for Twinkies[8] once they became popular? Would Coca-Cola change the recipe for the world's most popular soft drink? You'd have to be nuts.[9] Yet, when we examine the credits on the back of albums, we rarely see the same producer twice with the same artist. Even after they created hits for them. There are some important exceptions: **James Taylor**[10] comes to mind, or the **Beatles**,[11] who used the same producer for all of their albums. But, in general, this is unheard of.

Don't artists know and appreciate a producer's value? They see firsthand how the producer takes a raw demo and turns it into a hit master. Why change the recipe when they have a match that works?

To learn why, we have to examine a little-understood dynamic about the music business: who actually *hires* the producer. Most people outside the business think

[7] Inducement to breach: A fancy legalese way of saying if A and B have a contact and C convinces B that he doesn't need A, A can sue C for getting him fired.

[8] Twinkie: A popular Hostess pastry that according to rumor would take almost 10,000 years to deteriorate completely if left on a window sill. Eating them (along with other junk snacks) has also been used as a defense to murder in one high-profile case, creating the so-called "Twinkie defense."

[9] Of course they did just that in 1985 with New Coke. It was a flop. They then softened the switchback with Classic Coke, and now we're back to just plain Coke.

[10] James Taylor: In 1966, he formed a bubblegum pop group called the Flying Machine, which lasted only one year. Soon afterwards, he be-

[11] George Martin produced all the Beatles' albums.

[12] The list of the top ten female pop producers with platinum records and Grammys is only four names long.

[13] Suzanne Vega was turned down twice by A&M, and finally got a deal with them in 1983. A graduate of Barnard College in 1982, she claims that other than CNN, she only watches *The Sopranos*.

[14] Shawn Colvin: In 1998, "Sunny Came Home" won Grammy Awards for Record of the Year and Song of the Year.

that producers are in charge. This is due to the role of the producer in the movie industry, where the producer really is the *auteur*, deal maker, and, in a real sense, the "manufacturer" of the product. In music, the artist hires the producer at the request (or insistence) of the label. Yet, even though the artist is the producer's employer, it is the artist who is expected to take orders from *him*. It's more akin to a movie star turned producer who then hires a director from whom he must then take direction. Who is the actual boss? The potential tension is obvious and manifests in interesting ways. Especially when the artist is a woman and the producer is (and almost always is) a man.[12] Let's look at two stories.

Folk Rock and Rocky Folk: Sleeping with the Talent

I sought wisdom on this issue from a longtime friend and multi-platinum producer, **Steve Addabbo**, who launched two of the biggest post-1960s female folk artists: **Suzanne Vega**[13] and **Shawn Colvin**.[14] Some say, and I agree, that his productions of these artists are what revitalized the folk-rock genre in the 1980s and made it possible for people like **Tracy Chapman**, the **Indigo Girls**,[15] and, more recently, **Norah Jones**[16] to have a place in the world of pop when the music around them was generated by electronicized beatboxes. Yet, neither of his two famous artists retained him for their follow-up albums.

> *Moses:* So, Steve, produce a hit and you're out? What up?
>
> *Steve Addabbo:* Who knows? There could be pressure from the record company to try something different. When you have success, you think that it will carry on regardless of what you do. When I was going through my hit period and we had a success, [the record company] always seemed to be looking for the next person to bring it to the next level, even though it could be totally inappropriate for the music.

Steve has class. I've been a producer of female artists and I know the sexual tension that exists. One side or the other usually wants more than just a professional relationship. And in a business where promiscuity is often a norm I was sure there was something he could teach us. So I punted.

> *Moses:* You've produced some of the most talented and reputedly temperamental female artists of your day. Do you think there is some kind of dynamic that a female recording artist brings into the room with a male producer that a male recording artist wouldn't bring?

Long pause.

Steve Addabbo: There have been mistakes where unnamed producers have done something that they should not have been doing with their female artist and their wives walked in on them. That shatters marriages. You are in close quarters with people for long hours, you are seeing them all of the time, nights go late, and you're dealing with emotional material. I am sure plenty of stuff happens. That's a minefield I do not want to enter. I've never gone there. I am a married man.

It would be easy to simply blame producers for taking advantage of their young "impressionable" female artists. But this would be an oversimplification of the problem. One should bear in mind a few other variables. Most successful producers are in their early 40s to mid-50s. The older ones came from an era where casual sex in the music business, even among employees, was tolerated to a far greater extent than it is today. Old dogs rarely learn new tricks. This does not excuse anybody's actions, but it could mitigate how harshly we estimate what is "normal" behavior. Conversely, artists are not immune to using their "buying power" to control a situation either. When the normal tension of disagreements surfaces in the recording process, the dynamics of male/female relationships are tested to their limits. Producers are fired, or, more accurately, not rehired even though their contributions were salient.[17]

To grasp the importance of this point, it's important to remember why a producer is hired in the first place. One does not need a producer to help an artist be creative. (Hopefully.) He is hired to keep the product consistent and commercial. His commercial sensibilities are his commodity. But many artists look to producers to give them approval about their talent. This is similar to wanting your doctor to approve of your diet. If you fire your doctor because he reminds you of an old boyfriend or your father who used to tell you not to eat so much fat and sugar, who are you hurting?

The male/female dynamic in the recording studio is a complex and intense one. Bottom-line advice: don't repeat the mistakes of other artists. If you're firing your producer, make sure it's for the right reasons. If you're an artist, don't bring your baggage into that room and ask your producer to solve your personal issues. Save that for your shrink, your friends, or your spiritual advisor. For producers, mixing business with pleasure may be unavoidable 100 percent of the time, but you can limit your liability; be more selective than the opportunities that your power presents.

[15] Indigo Girls (1989): Their national debut album featured R.E.M.'s Michael Stipe. Tracy Chapman (1988): Her first album went multi-platinum.

[16] Norah Jones (2002): *Come Away with Me*, recorded by legendary producer Arif Mardin (Aretha Franklin, Dusty Springfield, the Bee Gees), eventually sold 18 million copies worldwide and won eight Grammy awards.

[17] Suzanne Vega: After firing Addabbo she used a band member she was involved with to produce her next recordings. The direction was far off her established style and the records did not sell as well as her previous ones. She then married producer Mitchell Froom (Joan Osborne). They divorced years later, allegedly over his infidelity with a new artist he produced.

Fired Before You're Hired

Record companies don't like to appear to be ramming their choice of a producer down the artist's throat. So they will give them a list of "approved" producers. The artist meets with several and chooses one. But often the deck is stacked.

> *Steve Addabbo:* [The label] brought me in to [meet with a new] artist so that she would see she had another choice of producer. All along they had their good ol' boy that was going to produce the record for them. I also had another project that got pulled out from under me because of a relationship that existed between the A&R department and some other producers. I didn't stand a chance. The artist wanted me to do it and the record company said no. And I was the hot guy at the time. But I lost it to the guy who produced **Tracy Chapman**.
>
> *Moses:* Do you think that passing on Tracy earlier had something to do with that?[18] Are they connected in some way?
>
> *Steve Addabbo:* No. Different record labels. I don't think it had anything to do with it. I think it was just one of those things that are part of a good ol' boy network. They really had no intention of letting me do the record. They just wanted the artist to think, "Oh, look at the choice they are giving me." When in fact they weren't.

[18] Steve passed on an opportunity to produce the first Tracy Chapman record. See Chapter 2.

Record companies enjoy manipulating (consciously or not) this illusion of choice. It keeps producers' fees competitive. But they will never tell the artist this. To the new artist, it seems like a full palette of choices is being presented. This illusion of choice is fairly transparent and a well-practiced con.

In one situation I can recall, I was asked to participate in a scheme whereby the A&R person would influence the artist's decision to go with my company if I was willing to kickback the A&R person (acting outside of the record company's knowledge) a percentage of the budget. Such relationships used to be more common in the pre-corporatizing of the business. Now they are not as prevalent, but it would be naive to presume that they have vanished completely.

Today, the label's motivation for stacking the producer deck is based mostly on creating hits. Artists typically want to break the mold; corporations want to establish it and then maintain a status quo. It's far easier to make next quarter's numbers if you can maintain order. So far, this new method has not worked out so well for the big labels. We'll learn why in Chapter 10, called *The Future of Music and Its Enemies*. Don't skip ahead.

Leaving alone the dynamics of the sexes, Steve brings to light in his interview another important trend in the music business that is eroding the creative process.

The idea of corporatizing the marketing of records and influencing an artist's creative choices to match that agenda.

Steve Addabbo: Now it is even worse because all of the companies seem to be controlled by the bean counters, and they really want quarterly success. People buy a record because there is something unusual about it. But corporations think: everyone loves hamburgers. Then they say, "Well, McDonalds is doing something right; if we want to sell hamburgers we should look at what they're doing." Unfortunately, music can't be marketed that way because you never know where success is going to come from. It is not predictable. It's not a Big Mac. Who would have predicted **Norah Jones**? Who would have predicted **Suzanne Vega**? You would never, and those are the ones that are usually the big success. The ones that are kind of off the wall. It's not like, well, if we just put a new dressing on this hamburger we are going to sell 12 billion of them. However, you look at the world of the mixers [or re-mixers].[19] There you have an elite group. They basically mix about 90 percent of the stuff you hear on the radio. That's where the "consistency" is happening.

It is weirdly contradictory. You have bean counters who went to the same business school as the ones working for McDonalds now running the business, yet they don't follow the classic business acumen that says you don't change your winning formula. Instead, they constantly look for new combinations. Steve feels that this is because a creative product *demands* change. It demands—to continue on the hamburger analogy—new dressing, a different bun. He's probably right, but this will mean that a producer's job security will always be tenuous. He will always be victim to the "flavor of the minute" syndrome, just like an artist.[20]

Meredith Brooks and Her Single Bitch

Okay, so in some cases it's not clear who was the real star, the producer or the artist. But how about when the producer puts a clear hit on the desk of an A&R person, with someone who is still an emerging artist. Any guarantees then? Let's see what **Geza X** has to say about **Meredith Brooks**[21] after he produced her million-seller hit single "Bitch" and was fired for it. There might be some irony here.

Geza X: I was probably the first person to hear "Bitch." I heard some of her songs and I thought, this chick can write, she can sing, she can play the guitar, but her songs sound a little dated. She had been in a band called the **Graces**,[22] which was a follow-up to the **Go-Go's**.[23] The Graces had a couple of albums that went

[19] Re-mixers: Audio engineering "wizards" who can make and manipulate the elements of the recording to sound good on only one format—radio. These "radio mixes" cost a major anywhere from $10,000 to $50,000 per song.

[20] In November of 2004, I was informed that Jimmy Jam and Terry Lewis, who produced many of the biggest hits in the 1990s, could not find a distribution deal for their own label.

[21] Meredith Brooks: She was one of the first headlining acts on the Lilith Fair (an all-women traveling rock show), but earlier in her career she was booked to open for the Rolling Stones. Whoever made that match made a serious boo-boo. Brooks's strong feminist philosophy wasn't a great mix with the "let's party" tradition of the Stones' audience. She was booed off the stage.

22 The Graces was a project put together by Go-Go's guitarist Charlotte Caffey and Gia Ciambotti, following that band's mid-'80s breakup. Their 1989 debut album, *A Perfect View*, eked out a modest single, "Lay Down Your Arms." In early 1991, the Graces were dropped from their label and Brooks left to pursue a solo career.

23 See Chapters 2 and 6 for more Go-Go's facts.

24 Shelly Piken: Author of Christina Aguilera's hit "What a Girl Wants" as well as several other hits.

25 Christina Aguilera: Unlike Mariah Carey, who is famous for insisting on Evian water for her dog, backstage Aguilera insists on bottled water but it must *not* be Evian. She also named her dog Jackson in honor of Michael Jackson.

nowhere. After that, Meredith had been kind of kicking around for years. She was a little older than most when they fall into their first major-label success and just really couldn't get signed. Everyone thought that she was over. The industry is not sexist, but it is definitely ageist. But even though she was older and having trouble getting a deal, I saw potential. I saw talent; I saw a pretty girl who could really rock out on the guitar. Almost too good, because it goes into that metal girl kind of thing. She had written some songs, most of which I had liked, but I didn't hear the slam dunk [hit]. And I told her, "Your stuff is good but it just needs to be updated or modernized a bit." A week later she had gotten together with this girl named **Shelly Piken**,[24] a great writer, she has written songs for **Christina Aguilera**[25] and others. Meredith came back a week or two later with "Bitch." She was kind of embarrassed because she was a feminist and it seems like she wrote an anti-women song.[26] She played it on the acoustic guitar, and after she finished I scraped my jaw off of the floor. I told her she was so wrong. The whole point of taking a word like "bitch" and putting it right upfront there is that it defuses it and takes all of its power away and puts it back in the hands of the person that is brave enough to own it. I had cut the song on spec and when we finished recording, I cried. I knew that it was really going to hit a nerve.

Moses: Sounds like you should have gotten to do the rest of the album from that. What happened?

Geza X: The single I produced on spec is what [finally] got her signed. The label was going gaga over it. Meanwhile, I had started the [rest of] the album. I had rough tracks on four or five songs at that point. "Bitch" sounded like **Alanis Morissette**, not deliberately, but that was the sound of the moment. I wanted to open her horizons a little bit [with the other cuts]. We were experimenting with interesting guitar sounds and a lot of different ways of phasing out vocals and things that were interesting sounding. It would have been more of a hybrid of different-sounding things. Examples would be just dashes of **Enya**[27] and **Sarah McLachlan** combined with Meredith's really strong voice and guitar playing.

Unfortunately, none of that work ever saw the light of day.

Geza X: This is what happens with labels. Once they know they have their hit, they don't really care that much about the identity of the album as long as they think it supports the image of the artist. [The A&R man] said, "This is bombastic, this is over the top, I am sorry, but I have to fire you." He then hired this guy who had *never produced a major album in his life,*[28] someone he used to manage. He finished a sort of adequate but very ordinary-sounding album. They didn't care. They already had their hit.

Moses: Didn't she have any say in it?

Geza X: That is the perfect question. Technically, the artist hires the producer, but the artist is signed to a record company that can drop them or fuck with them, hold them back for the duration of their contract. The artist can get suffocated legally. The reality is that if the manager and the A&R person think the producer needs to go and the artist wants to keep the producer but is fearing losing their recording contract, if push comes to shove the label has more juice than the artist. They are paying the bills and holding the one card, which is that most artists know they have maybe a couple albums' shot at it for their entire career.

Moses: Who told you that they weren't going to use you for the rest of the record?

Geza X: [Meredith and the A&R exec] had a luncheon and afterwards she was kind enough to call me and tell me. "Just put up the best rough mixes that you have. Just make sure that everything is on," she said. She was tipping me off [that I needed to prove myself again]. I put up the best rough mixes. But it didn't matter. The decision had already been made.

Moses: The album did really well. At that point there is going to be a second album. Doesn't the artist have some pull at that point?

Geza X: In this case I think there might have been bad blood. We didn't talk for a long time afterwards. I would have been willing to discuss it, but I think that either she or the label thought that was untenable—I am not sure.

Moses: What did this cost you?

Geza X: She wrote all of the songs on that album, she was the artist. Based on what I made, which was fairly substantial, she probably made several million dollars.

Moses: What would you do differently if you had to do it all again?

Geza X: I didn't have a deal memo that stated that if she got a deal I would end up doing the whole album. I did start doing more tracks, but somehow or another I was getting phased out. It's kind of a shame, because there were some amazing songs in the works.

In Geza's case a deal memo with Meredith would not have guaranteed him the slot to produce the entire album, but it would have forced the label and the artist to deal with him more fairly and offer him some "go away" money.

One also has to consider that had Geza tried to get Meredith Brooks to sign a deal memo *before* he invested his time, she might have balked, as many artists do when confronted with commitment papers.

26 Funny. Because when retailers asked her to change the art on her album cover she said, "I don't care if it says 'Bitch' on the cover or not."

27 Enya: Born Eithne Ní Bhraonáin. Celtic singer. She changed her name because it's easier to spell. (Thank you.) Her songs have appeared in many movie soundtracks, yet she turned down the composing gig for the 2000 blockbuster *Titanic*, a mistake that probably cost her tens of millions. The director hired James Horner to compose Celtic music very much in her style.

28 Her album was produced by David Ricketts, formerly of David & David and also the Tuesday Music Club of which Sheryl Crow was a member. Reviewers claimed that Ricketts gave her album a "commercial polish," but the only cut to chart was the one song he didn't produce, "Bitch."

***Actors Find God, Musicians Find Jazz, or "I thought I mattered!"* —The Captain & Tennille Comeback**

After their super-hits "Love Will Keep Us Together" and the indelible "Muskrat Love," which concluded a two-year hot streak from 1974 and 1976, **The Captain & Tennille** contributed very little to the tapestry of pop music. However, life does go on even after your hit sinks off the charts. You're still a musician and you have to do something. It's been said that actors find God as they mature, but musicians find jazz.

Enter veteran jazz producer and extraordinary music-business professor at UCLA, **Jeff Weber**. His body of work includes artists like **Nancy Wilson, Jackson Browne, Michael McDonald, Chick Corea, Stanley Clarke, Luther Vandross**, and **David Crosby**. He echoes a familiar lamentation of producers' war stories: thinking that because you are of use to the artist or can provide a service, that somehow you matter to them.

Jeff Weber: I went to **Toni Tennille** with an idea that she loved. Her husband (**Daryl Dragon**, aka **The Captain**) declined to be involved because, according to him, he didn't know much about jazz. So I produced a jazz record for them, but I had to raise the money for the record first. The record was very successful. It was one of the few jazz records that was played on pop radio. We did a live, two-track recording with no mixing, no editing, and no overdubbing. Twenty-two songs were recorded in 11 hours with the finest musicians available anywhere. At the conclusion of the sessions, Toni started to cry tears of joy. We did it on spec, but it came out so well that the first record company that heard it, **Mirage**, an imprint of **Atlantic**, bought it. All of the investors received their money back, plus interest within 30 days. Eventually, Mirage was folded into Atlantic; The Captain & Tennille bought the masters from them and released it themselves under their own label as part of a double album entitled *Do It Again*.

Moses: A rare DIY success story. What happened next?

Jeff Weber: So when it came time to do the next record, while Toni initially wanted me to produce it, I got a nice note from someone in their company saying, "Dear Jeff, I am very sorry, but you cannot produce the next record because you're not the husband."

Moses: Can I print that?

Jeff Weber: Yeah, you can print that. The thing about it is, Daryl Dragon happens to be a very nice guy. You can print that too. I was really bitter back then because for the next record, they simply hired all of *my people*, and they took all of my ideas, and did it again.

Moses: What was the mistake that you think you made there?

Jeff Weber: I really thought I mattered! I thought I mattered to them because I believed I helped give her a new career. She is still doing stuff based on that record. Still, they did try to find me to let me know that they purchased the first record and recorded another record (the one I didn't produce). They wanted to send me a contract so that I could get royalties if the double album did well.

Moses: Royalties off of album number two, that you *didn't* produce, to make up for the fact that they fired you off album number one, which you *did* produce, and for which they paid you no royalties?

Jeff Weber: What they did was put the two records together in one package. But I got nothing from either release.

Moses: You thought you mattered. What do you think this mistake cost you in dollars and cents?

Jeff Weber: Probably twenty to fifty thousand dollars. Because I could have done all these other records, you know.

Moses: You are basing that on fees you would have made as a producer?

Jeff Weber: Fees and potential royalties. Well, let's put it this way, I never got a royalty statement from the first record label, Mirage. I never got credit for thinking of the concept on the second record. I never got any of the royalties off any of the released product. I created a concept that allowed her to have a revitalized career. Not just an album, a career.

Moses: It sounds more like a mistake that she made, not that you made.

Jeff Weber: The day we finished the recording she cried, and her comment to me was, "If I die tomorrow at least I have something that I am proud of." Well, the mistake that I made was that I thought that I mattered to her, but I didn't.

Yes, it's true, artists can be a bit pathological when it comes to expressing gratitude. They thank you, but memory fades fast. Or perhaps it's just a "what-have-you-done-for-me-lately" world. If you don't continue to stay necessary, your replaceability grows like a herpes sore right before your big date.

Moses: Okay, so knowing that they don't matter, what can up-and-coming producers do to protect themselves?

Jeff Weber: I would just say look at each deal with an artist as an individual album and not as a string of pearls (multiple albums). Think of the album you're being hired to work on as the first, last, and only. Don't think long term. Don't even think that if you have a contract for X amount of albums with a particular artist you will do them. If the artist doesn't want it to happen it's not going to happen.

⊳ Extraction Jackson

When dealing with producers we tend to think of them as irreplaceable, invincible. But the above stories show us how vulnerable they can be. How about the producer's point person—the engineer? If the producer can be usurped, how difficult is it for the engineer to maintain some status? **Matt Forger** worked as one of **Michael Jackson**'s key engineers for almost 20 years. Matt is one of the warmest people I've met in my many years in this snake pit of a business. In this very revealing interview he takes us inside the camp of the enigmatic performer and shows us exactly how politics can affect your employment in the world of a superstar.

Matt Forger: At the conclusion of the [name of project withheld], when the album was released, I of course was eager to get the first copy off of the presses. Lo and behold, when I read through the credits, my name was absent. And it wasn't just my own credits. Everyone I had involvement with, their names were also omitted. The first [place] I called was the Jackson production office. They said, "We just submit the credits for the work and the head engineer [name withheld] would be in charge of editing and submitting them." I was getting the runaround and being told my name was dropped "inadvertently." I spent three years of my life [on the project] and it was a high-profile job.

Moses: What did you do next?

Matt Forger: I talked to the head engineer and he said, "Oh, y'know, somebody has it in for you." He was referring to a person who was a mere cog in the wheel, and I can't say the name, but I got along with him very well. I confronted him and he said, "That is ridiculous, who told you that?" I said, "The head engineer, [name withheld]."

Moses: Usually the producer is in charge of submitting the credits. Who was the producer of this record?

Matt Forger: Michael was. And there were several producers that worked on individual songs on the album.

This is quite typical in a large camp. Although Jackson was the producer in credit and name, in fact each song on an R&B record generally has an individual producer and then a chief engineer who acts as an overseer to coordinate all the elements. Matt's multiple role is one that exists in every large organization—part engineer, part project coordinator, part line producer. So the chain of command is a confusing zigzag, and who takes responsibility is far more nebulous than in a smaller, more traditional production. In this case it was clear that Matt had stepped on someone's toes. But how? If Matt's opponent here was such a giant in the industry, why would he care about one other credit?

> *Matt Forger:* One of my tracks made it on the album. That's one less track that he got on the album.
>
> *Moses:* I can see the argument if you're a producer. Producers get points based on album placement. But engineers just get an hourly or weekly fee whether the song gets on the record or not.
>
> *Matt Forger:* That's true. But there is a matter of prestige. Obviously I bruised his ego. It isn't something that I would do intentionally, because my job was to support the work of the other engineers and producers.
>
> *Moses:* Was there any justice here? I must think that this damaged your ability to work for Jackson in the future.
>
> *Matt Forger:* No. The situation was rectified. My name was present in subsequent releases. This is the nature of working for someone like Michael Jackson. These are the landmines that you constantly have to navigate.

◉ Warning Signs

It seems almost incomprehensible. Managers who put their personal money into projects and get screwed, producers who spend hundreds of development hours and yet the artists fire them on a whim, major artists who have no idea what's going on in their own professional backyard.

Whenever I hear artists accepting their Grammys they seem to spend a few seconds thanking Jesus. Don't Christian ethics include the concept of loyalty? And isn't that what this chapter is really about? Where is the loyalty?

> *Jay Jay French:* Loyalty is, for the most part, a myth. Most people will just stab you in the back if given a shot, so you have to be extremely vigilant.

From punk to folk to pop, the personality of the music doesn't seem to matter. Don't be lulled into a false sense of security because you're dealing with a Christian rock band or with a folk artist who spreads crystals in a circle at each meeting. At the end of the day it's about dollars, politics, and personalities.

> *Matt Forger:* One of the things I've come to understand is that friendship, loyalty, and integrity are all matters of convenience in the music business, regardless

of what relationships that you think have a lot of depth and integrity. There is a real difference between a person as an individual and as a person as a part of "the business." Because the business is cutthroat, it's mean; if you take the people out of the business as individuals they might not be bad, evil people.

So what protection can be offered? What lessons can be learned? How do you prepare for the coming freight train before it hits you in the face. **Johnny D** (see earlier in this chapter for his credentials) offers a psychological profiling approach.

Johnny D: The "writing on the wall" is in changes in behavior in any part of the team, where all of a sudden somebody is adopting an attitude that is adversarial [to you] or just out of character. You are looking at them and going, "I gave you this job." But all of a sudden they are disagreeing with you. Where is the license coming from that is enabling that person to believe that they are *not* going to get fired? It's coming from the artist and there is mischief afoot. Example: There is a steady dialog between a manager and artist. You are talking several times a day. Then, all of a sudden, a phone call isn't getting returned for some time. Then something crosses your desk and you know nothing about it. And all of a sudden you are being invited to a *second meeting* between the artist and *somebody*. You are in trouble.

⊗ Conclusion

Jay Jay French: If you get hired because you are a good friend and you are not equipped to do the job, it's the biggest disaster. You hurt your talent base because these people aren't talented and it demoralizes the people around you. They feel like they can kill themselves, and it's not going to matter because they are not related.

One thing that I noticed when I was editing the stories in this chapter: each of the people who was fired continued to have long successful careers. In many of the cases, the ones who did the firing did not. When I look back at all the jobs I was fired from, most of those people who fired me are not in the music business anymore. I'm still here.

Stick to your guns. Everyone gets fired. If you're not getting fired, you're probably not trying too hard to move up the ladder. It means you're probably complacent with where you are. If that's the case, then you have no problems. But if you dream of being a maverick or even someone who sees a better way to do things and wants to get involved, you're going to be a threat to someone who likes things the way they are. Here's a personal example.

Some years back I contacted a small learning institution that catered to recording artists and musicians. I had some innovative ideas for teaching the business to musicians and wanted to see if there was a way I could beta-test my method with their still-fledgling music business program. I'll never forget what the school's music business dean said: "We're trying to sell the dream to these kids. You're going to scare them." This was a person who had claimed to once manage big rock acts and national tours. If anyone should be sensitive to teaching the cautions of the business to young students, it should have been him.

Some time after that, the same school's marketing director brought me in to do my workshop. Students were given free passes or huge discounts on the tickets for a full two-day event I put together with the help of **Jay Frank**, the VP of Label Relations for Yahoo! Music.[29] The workshop attracted some major industry producers, lawyers, and managers. People hooked up for jobs through the workshop and obtained internships. But only several students from the institute itself registered. The dean, still pissed at me, had never advertised the workshop or given away the free tickets.

I guessed, given my reputation for telling it like it is, he was afraid that some of the things I was teaching would conflict with his Pollyannaish picture. He tried everything to shut me up, including telling teachers they shouldn't have me as guest speaker and bullying the campus bookstore to not carry my books, even though two professors used one of them as required text in their courses at that school. Regardless, we survived over a year and a half in that venue until several of the dean's allies conspired to get my advocate fired, and with him out of the picture, I was "fired" too. But not before my workshop achieved the highest amount of State Bar MCLE credits[30] of any music business workshop in the US. Since leaving that institution, the Confessions Workshop has been booked at Harvard and New York University. This dean, once the manager of national acts, is still administering at the school. It's his fiefdom. I wish him well.

So, if you were fired for being ambitious and wanting to make things better, take it as a compliment. It means you actually have a chance to end up more successful than the person who torpedoed you. Keep trying.

[29] Yahoo! Music is quickly becoming the new way for artists to promote themselves on the Web. In 2005 they began to compete directly with iTunes and other digital distribution outlets.

[30] MCLE: Minimum Continuing Legal Education credits. Lawyers are required to take a certain amount of courses each year to maintain their license in most states. Most courses offer about 3 credits. The Confessions of a Record Producer Workshop offered 13.5 participatory credits and 8 ethics credits, a record in California.

CHAPTER 6

Massaging the Talent

"You don't actually have to be able to understand the lyrics, you've just got to feel like you could if you wanted to."
—**Chuck Plotkin (producer for Bruce Springsteen)**

"There is a dynamic to the whole major-label experience; everybody goes down the road of best intentions...in flames."
—**John Brodey**

"All you need in this life is ignorance and confidence; then success is sure."
—**Mark Twain**

Take a man with no money and put him on a street corner wearing mostly a trench coat. He takes to wiping windows for a living. He's a bum, or, to use a more PC term, "homeless." Nothing interesting. Nothing new. But take that same person and put 100 million dollars in his bank account, now he's "eccentric." A news story. Exotic.

The story goes that in her *hospitality rider*[1] **Mariah Carey**, probably the best-selling female artist of the 1990s,[2] insisted that backstage at every show there be Evian water for her dog. Another famous request was by **Van Halen**,[3] who wanted all the green M&Ms segregated from the rest and put in each dressing room. In

[1] Hospitality rider: A part of the performance contract that states what goodies are to go in the star's dressing room or entourage lounge.

2 Mariah Carey:
A couple of her
whaler mistakes are
in the PR area. Feel-
ing put off by the
fact that some
other divas'
recorded perfor-
mances were en-
hanced by
computers (Britney
Spears in particu-
lar), she vocifer-
ously condemned
the use of comput-
ers in the produc-
tion process, saying
that if an artist's
sound depended on
computers, the
album cover art
should feature the
computers instead
of the artist. She
was probably un-
aware (as many
artists are) that her
voice is enhanced
by those same ma-
chines. Also, her
movie vehicle, *Glit-
ter*, designed to
launch her acting
career, was deemed
too low-grade to be
put in the discount
bin at one super-
store, so it was
given away with any
purchase. People
still returned it.

3 Van Halen: Only
major act to
change lead vocal-
ists four times:
David Lee Roth
(1974–1985, 1996),
Sammy Hagar
(1985–1996), Gary
Cherone
(1996–1999). (Five,
if you count Hagar
coming back for
the 2004 tour.)

New York, a concert presenter was asked to send a production assistant to Montreal to pick up a certain type of cheese to satisfy a certain singer.

From concert promoters to labels to managers, the industry seems to bend over backward to put up with absurd requests by artists. When the artist is riding high these requests are appeased, even encouraged by their managers: "You deserve it, you worked hard." When the hit drops into position 150 on the top 200 the requests start to sound asinine. Sometimes those crazy requests come back to haunt the artist in ironic ways. The exotic "interesting" artist becomes the window-washing bum. And it's their attitudes that can be a bigger barrier to their success than talent or creative blocks.

André Fischer: When I joined **MCA** I was in charge of 105 artists, including certain Uptown business with **Mary J. Blige, Heavy D**, and with all kinds of satellite and production deals. What outsiders to the industry don't get is when the president of the company has internal financial needs, he says, "Drop 15 to 25 percent of your roster." Not only does it mean "drop," it means you have to deal with the legal department to see if it's contractually possible and how much it will cost to do it. The artists that they keep are the ones that are selling or the ones that were politically placed in the company and have a champion watching out for them. There are a lot of artists signed for political payback. Like a production house: because one or two of their artists were successful, they took on a third artist for the record company, the major label signed additional artists [from the production company], which wasn't really always prudent. That is how **Bobby Brown**'s label was started in Atlanta.[4] Bobby was successful for the label, so [the major label] fronted him [money for his label]. But when he didn't deliver his solo record on time they were pissed. Yet they kept sending his label large amounts of money to produce acts that they knew they would just let sit on the shelf. Nothing was ever going to happen with the artists until Bobby gave them what they wanted—which, sorry to say, never happened while I was there.

Yesss! And when a cut needs to be made, all things being equal (meaning sales) the artist's quirks can be the final nail in the coffin. How does this happen? How do you go from being so grateful to have a deal that you'd lick a star off the sidewalk on the Hollywood Walk of Fame, to being the kind of artist who will walk out unless they have Evian for their dog? Let's see.

⊜ The Pygmalion Effect

Producers tend to fall in love many times early in their career. They see a great act with great songs and pursue, hoping that they can smooth out the rough edges and get the artist signed so he can get paid.

Then reality sets in. Well…

- The songs are only half-written by the artist. Some of the songs are left over from the act the artist used to be with. He doesn't speak to them anymore.
- The artist has an eating problem and gains and then loses many pounds in a month.
- The artist is scared of live performances.
- The artist is still signed to an old contract.
- The artist has a bad drug habit.
- The artist wants you sexually, but you don't want him/her.
- You want the artist sexually, but he/she is underage.
- The artists can't get along with others in a band situation.
- The artists has no understanding of how business works.
- The artist is lazy, combined with a strong sense of entitlement.

And the all-time favorite… The artist has a great look but their singing is more like a mating call for a smoke alarm.

Individually, each of these is a surmountable problem. Any two combined spell trouble. Three is a recipe for failure. Regardless, if you like the overall potential of the project your human psyche will rationalize that the problem can be worked around. Never underestimate the power of denial. The Pygmalion effect[5] is one where the producer convinces himself that an artist who is lacking one of the fundamental components necessary for success can be worked around with a bit of coaching.

Most of the examples below could be printed here only if I promised to allow the subjects to talk off the record. It seems when it comes to artists and their shortcomings, producers are on the down low.

Sex and the City

The fact that this is a business with its roots firmly entrenched in debauched behavior is a subject that cannot be avoided if we are to write a candid book. Just how

[4] Bobby Brown: His record company, Bosstown, went bankrupt. Soon after he checked into the Betty Ford Clinic. A few days after "completing a program" he was seen drinking beer.

[5] Pygmalion: From Greek mythology, a king who commissioned a statue of a woman and then fell in love with it. He had Aphrodite bring the sculpture to life as Galatea.

do producers find (and keep) their talent? Sometimes it's just the way the press release reads: at a club. Other times it's something that is often left out of the MTV interview. This story from a platinum R&B producer, who we'll call "Ladies' Man," brings a different slant to the title of this chapter, *Massaging the Talent.*

Ladies' Man: I'll tell you something that will really help your female readers, but it's got to be off the record.

Moses: (Sigh) It's off the record. Go on.

Ladies' Man: I get a call from my mom one day in January. She's vacationing in the Cayman Islands in a time-share. She made some friends who had a daughter that they said was a great singer. My mom wanted me to take a look at her and be honest. I can't say no to my mom, y'know. So I said, "Send her to my office." She walks in and she's a real looker. Hot body. Now I'm going to tell you what goes through the mind of every producer out there, but they won't talk about it. The first thing they are thinking is, she better be a *great* singer. Not good, great. If not, we all know how this girl is going to get signed.

Moses: You mean she'll have to buy a lot of dinners for A&R men so they will overlook her shortcomings?

Ladies' Man: Uh, yeah. That's exactly what I mean. So, I sit at the keyboard and have her sing a blues song. That's how I audition all my talent. Blues has everything in it. If you can sing great blues, you can sing almost anything pop.

Moses: And can she sing?

Ladies' Man: Not bad. I give her an eight. Good pipes, fair range, decent style.

Moses: So this is good news for her. No buying dinners, right?

Ladies' Man: Wrong. Y'see, and this is the truth, eight ain't good enough to skate. Nine is fine. Ten is done [pronounced *"den"*]. But eight or below means you're "buying dinner." A lot of dinner.

Moses: So are you saying that if you're not a nine or a ten vocally then give it up?

Ladies' Man: No, I'm saying you have to reevaluate how badly you want a career in pop. Remember there are always jingles, wedding bands, and other ways to make a living as a singer besides a major-label deal.

Moses: So what did you tell her?

Ladies' Man: This girl is the daughter of a friend of my mom's, so I know anything I do has to be straight up. I told her, "Look, this is a funny business. And a lot of the time it doesn't really matter how talented you are. A lot of the time it can boil down to you and a record executive in a limo, alone. He puts his hand on your knee. You know what he wants. What do you do?" I said, "You can't decide at that moment what you think is the right thing to do. You have to be prepared *now*, to know what your policy is going to be. It doesn't pay for your parents to spend fifty grand to develop you as an artist if, at the end of the day, it boils down to you offending some dude because he thinks you're a prude or a tease, or are just not willing to play the game."

Moses: Was she crying at this point?

Ladies' Man: No, I told her, this is the same advice I would give my daughter if she wanted to go into pop. I didn't tell her she was an eight, and all that. She doesn't need to hear that shit anyway. She sat there for a full minute in absolute silence. Then she said, "I can do it. It's no big deal." She was a tough girl. Spent time in the street even though her parents had some dough. I was very impressed.

Moses: What happened?

Ladies' Man: I got her four gigs singing demos for four different producers. All top guys. It was my way of getting her introduced around town. She did well. They liked her. One of them liked her a bit too much. He made a move on her. She showed up on my doorstep that night freaked out. She freaked out on him. That was pretty much it.

Moses: It was over?

Ladies' Man: There's always *Star Search*. [*laughs*] Word gets out. It was fucked. I never spoke to that producer again. I couldn't believe he couldn't keep it in his pants. But this shit happens, and I think if you're trying to break into pop, you need to be ready for it. You can't say, "I'll deal with that scenario when it happens." You need to train yourself mentally for it *before* you get in too deep, before you get on the bus to New York or L.A.

Moses: Do you think this is true of all women trying to break in?

Ladies' Man: You know I don't mean that. You've been there, Moses, you know what I'm talking about. It's not a business that tolerates prudes.

Moses: Yes, but I want the readers to know it too.

Ladies' Man: If you're **Whitney Houston** [6] or **Mariah Carey**, you can get away with it. (And even Mariah didn't. [7]) If you've got family in the business, you can dodge this bullet. But for most—coming from the outside, from some town in the Midwest, getting off the bus, with great homecoming-queen looks and marginal voice—you may avoid the casting couch, especially if you have integrity, but to *not* be prepared for it is just naive. It's more likely that it's going to happen than not. And when it does, you can't just simply reject the dude. You have to finesse it. Work it somehow. I don't know how. You'll have to talk to **Madonna**, [8] she's the queen of that shit. Back in New York at **Danceteria** [9] she was doing anyone it took

[6] **Whitney Houston:** Her reputation in the press is that of a very difficult personality. She's canceled performances on a whim.

[7] **Mariah Carey:** Married her A&R man, Tommy Mottola, who later became the president of Sony Music. When she filed for divorce the label stopped supporting her releases. She changed labels, getting a $21 million advance from EMI. Apparently they felt this was a big mistake. They then dropped her a year later without releasing a record. See Chapters 3 and 5 for more on this.

[8] **Madonna:** Back in the day, she seemed to find it easy to mix business with pleasure.

[9] **Danceteria:** Club in downtown New York City. Its heyday was the late-seventies to mid-eighties.

10 **You never know.
Among Madonna's
career boners: she
appeared in the
low-budget "ma-
ture rated" movie,
A Certain Sacrifice.**

to get to the next level. You think she cares a bit about it now?[10] And I'm sure she learned how to say no to some of the freaks, without really saying no. That's what you need to learn. Mothers, you need to talk to your daughters and explain the facts of life about men. Train them to finesse a rejection so they don't burn a bridge.

Okay. I need a smoke after that one.

Look at the list at the beginning of this chapter. If you're thinking of getting into producing make sure the act you're signing doesn't have more than one of these flaws. A very big mistake many producers make is thinking that they have the power to fundamentally change the person they are producing. Only in movies do people change that quickly and severely. In life it takes many years to accomplish real growth and have the right stuff.

Force-Feeding Opportunity

How about when the producer wants to get the act signed more so than the act it-self? Impossible, you think? This person we'll call "The Pusher" has worked with mega-producers **Jimmy Jam** and **Terry Lewis**, writers for **Usher** and **Janet Jackson** and others.

The Pusher: This project was very important for me. It was my first develop-ment deal, and the first record I *hadn't* done for a major label. I was really trying to groom my sound, as a producer, as I had been taking money gigs from labels, which wasn't exactly for me stylistically. So this project would hopefully push me in a slightly different direction, and I really loved the songs. I signed an artist to a small label which I co-owned with one other person. The artist was/is extremely talented… but the drive to make a record did not come from the artist, it came from us. Once we got into the record, I found that the artist wasn't very present through the process past a certain point. This became a problem. As I was doing the work, the artist watched satellite TV in the lounge. I constantly encouraged more involvement, but the motivation from them was simply not there. Prior to starting we'd agreed to shop to majors, so I kept that in mind, which was one mis-take. The artist was all over the map directionally. In the end, we ended up with a record in between a more mainstream sound and an indie sound (no-man's land), and an artist who didn't know if they liked it, didn't feel like they'd had enough of a part of it, and had become more aware through the process of the sound they now wanted to pursue, which wasn't what we had. Tragedy was, I agreed with them. All that work and pushing, and in the end… too "produced." I learned a lot.

Producer Punditry

Producers are also artists in their own right. In many cases their contribution to the work is every bit as "artistic" as the writers and musicians. And as will be the nature of artists, they want to be heard. In truth many a producer is a frustrated artist. They may lack the looks or the time needed to be a star, but that in no way diminishes their ability to write and perform a hit record. Sometimes the producer forgets, though, that he is not the star. That he is working toward another's vision. If he's persuasive and the artist is inexperienced he can convince the artist to side with his view and abandon his creative vision in favor of the producer's. With a new artist this is almost always a mistake.

Ben McLane: I worked with a band called **Clear Static**. The members were in their late teens and had just signed to **Island Records**. Their initial demos were very power pop, you know, just real crisp, with background harmonies and hand claps, really cool-sounding stuff. That was pretty much what the label signed the band for. Then as soon as they hooked up with the producer, who is a very good producer, he had a vision to make everything very '80s and new wave. Maybe he was right, but maybe his timing was off. By the time they turned in the record it was a complete 180 of the sound that the label signed the band to do. The band gets dropped, the record never comes out. I think maybe the label felt like they switched it up on them. I am not sure what the moral of the story is, other than, as a band, try to have a little more input and control over your sound. You know, if a label is going to mention spending over a million dollars on you, I really think you should act like their partner and not their adversary.

A&R Optimism: When Ego Battles with a Label Do Not Pay Off

In the stories above it's the talent being pushed by the pro. But here's one where you had a major-label A&R person who fought to keep the band *as is*. Was it worth it?

Jim Barber: A huge mistake I made was in 1996 at **Geffen Records**. I saw the **Blink 182** moment and I really felt that the pop/punk revival '80s nostalgia was about to happen. I was approached by a pop/punk L.A. punk band called **Frosted**.[11] They sounded absolutely commercial. They had great hooks; the songs to me were as great as anything that Geffen has ever had.

Moses: What was your mistake?

Jim Barber: Over the objections of the label, I signed the band.

[11] Frosted is a pop-punk outfit from Los Angeles fronted by ex-Go-Go's guitarist Jane Wiedlin. Their debut album, *Cold*, was released in 1996 by DGC.

Really!?! A&R people are paid mid-six-figure salaries for their forecasting. Shouldn't the posture then be, if a starchy senior exec who hasn't bought a record in a record store in years, or been in a club past 11 P.M. since his second child was born, wants to assert that he knows better, to tell him to take a hike? Isn't that what the "hip" executive is for?

> *Jim Barber:* I knew I could make a great record that would definitely get radio play. The mistake was not realizing that a record company can bury a record because they feel like it. I made the record, I got a video made for next to nothing that was MTV playable, and the record company buried the project. My mistake was not understanding that unless you have a stroke of incredible luck, a great record can't transcend the indifference or outright hostility of its own record company. It was my sense of "I'm right, you're wrong, and I am going to prove you wrong." I sacrificed an artist's career.

Narrow Minds and Narrow Demos

This final note about the complex and competitive world of the producer comes from **Mervyn Warren**,[12] vocal arranger, writer, and member of the famous a cappella group **Take 6**. Warren has written many songs for a variety of artists. At a panel in Los Angeles he talked about the politics involved in that process and the massaging that your song demo has to undergo because of the industry's limited imagination and preconceptions about music.

[12] No relation to songwriter Diane Warren, who wrote more than 90 *Billboard* Top Ten hits.

> *Mervyn Warren:* I have finished great arrangements for songs sometimes, but if you put a female vocal on a demo and the A&R person is looking for a song for *a man*, they don't get it. That is really frustrating. If you are not careful you could spin your wheels doing 12 different demos, because if you're pitching **Whitney [Houston]** you want one type of demo and **Luther [Vandross]** is another type of demo. I am always trying to do the most versatile demo that I can, but you can never please everyone and a lot of times the demo, in their mind, *is* the record. The business really has changed. Many years ago when an artist started to record a song he or she sat down with the producer and they made decisions about the arrangement of the song. Depending on the style of the music they might bring in an arranger who said, "Let's try this or that." But the song itself is about *the lyrics and the melody.* Today the emphasis is much more on the rhythm tracks, and this changes what I have to do in demos.

⊙ Stockho' Syndrome

The term "Stockholm Syndrome" was coined by criminologist **Nils Bejerot** in the early 1970s to describe the "bonding" reactions of four bank employees after they were taken hostage by robbers. They were held for six days in August of 1973. To the shock of many, the hostages resisted the government's efforts to rescue them, claiming they were more afraid of authorities than of the robbers. Soon after, researchers discovered that captor/hostage bonding is a common phenomenon. The most famous incident in the US involved the kidnapped newspaper heiress **Patty Hearst** (granddaughter of **William Randolph Hearst**[13]). Held against her will by a small group of radicals that called themselves the **Symbionese Liberation Army**, Ms. Hearst eventually joined the group and assisted them by wielding a loaded machine gun in a 1974 bank robbery. The syndrome has also been linked to bonding between concentration camp prisoners and Nazis, incest victims/battered spouses and their abusers, prisoners of war and their guards, victims of hijackings and the hijackers, and now, thanks to me, musicians and their professional team.

[13] The subject of the classic film *Citizen Kane*, by Orson Welles. Hearst used his publishing empire to try to kill Welles's career. Welles is considered one of America's greatest cinema talents.

According to one website, this is what causes Stockholm Syndrome: "Captives begin to identify with their captors initially as a defensive mechanism, out of fear. Small acts of kindness by the captor are magnified, since finding perspective in a hostage situation is by definition impossible. Rescue attempts are also seen as a threat, since it's likely the captive would be injured during such attempts."

Interesting. Sounds a lot like what goes on when an artist gets ground into the star-making machinery. Shrinks love to come up with acronyms. Like ADD. The "D" almost always stands for "disorder." So here's one I came up with: SDD, or Sell-out Dependency Disorder, when the artist wants to get rich and famous and therefore becomes dependent on those they think can get them there. Call it the "Stock*ho'* Syndrome." Let's see how it works.

Promotion Paranoia Disorder

It's a fact of commerce that you can't sell something if no one knows it exists, no matter how good a product it is. That's where the marketing department comes in. If charity begins in the home, then Stock*ho'* Syndrome begins in the label's boardroom. **John Brodey**, former national director of promotion for **Geffen Records** who oversaw the campaigns of such artists as **Vanessa Williams, Tears for Fears, Tony! Toni! Toné!, Color Me Badd, Jade,** the **Eagles, Peter Gabriel**'s *So* album, **Whitesnake, Guns N' Roses, Cher, Def Leppard**, and **John Mellencamp**, brings us ringside

STOCKING UP ON
STOCKHO' SYNDROME

re you suffering in some small way from music industry Stock*ho'* Syndrome? Check this list. Virtually any music business profesional or musician can get it once they sell out.

Stockholm Syndrome Symptom	Stock*ho'* Manifestation
Perceived threat to survival and the belief that one's captor is willing to act on that threat.	Record company hints to the artist that they are delaying the release of the first record until the time is right. Meanwhile, they ask the artist to do some kind of humiliating publicity.
The captive's perception of small acts of kindness from the captor within a context of terror.	Throwing the artist high-profile parties and spending money on limos and videos, only to then charge them back to the artist's account.
Isolation from perspectives other than those of the captor.	Long hours in the studio and tours, which separates the artist from family and friends for extended periods of time. Then the label referring to themselves as their "new family," and talking shit to the artist about the others to inspire insecurity.
Perceived inability to escape. Stockholm Syndrome is a survival mechanism.	The clear implication given by managers and lawyers that if the artist wants to think outside the box they will be abandoned.

at the conference table and how labels "think" about what to promote and what to drop and how this starts to affect the artist's loyalties.

> *John Brodey*: One of biggest mistake by artists, writers, or producers who have already been in the business for over five years? They start thinking like the major labels. They buy into the system, and they start saying, "Well, you have to have radio, so everything is going to be about that, we saw how that worked last time." The problem is that you are thrilled to have the interest from the label that signed you, but it's not a given that the whole company is going to get excited all the way through the building. You get to the point where, no matter what idea they come up with, you are down with it regardless.

Many new managers and artists are often intimidated by the apparent size and prestige of the label. The building is large, there are many employees. It's not readily apparent that most of the building is rented out to other companies and many of the people working at the label are interns or working for very little. The illusion is a strong one. As a result they enter into a premature assumption that the label must know how to market the act since they've been in business for so many years and have a lot of success.

> *John Brodey:* If you are lucky enough to have gotten a deal for your client, now you have to deal with "the building."[14] If you are a new, inexperienced manager they are going to look at you and chew you up if you don't have a plan of your own. Walking in there hoping to *make friends* and then seeing what they can do for you isn't going to cut it.
>
> *Moses:* Can you elaborate as to why this is a mistake?
>
> *John Brodey:* Big labels don't spend money very wisely and they tend to overspend. One of the problem areas is the marketing meeting. You go into a marketing meeting and no department head wants to be the guy who doesn't have a plan. You're being paid to do something and the obligatory shopping list can add up. People are spending money because it's part of how they do their job, not necessarily because they're convinced it's good for the band or because they have an incredible idea. Yet, they are spending the *band's money*.[15] There is very little control on the part of the artist as to how much is spent and for what. A lot of people are just protecting their asses at the band's expense. This has eased a bit as labels have streamlined budgets and they have finally started to ask basic marketing questions such as, who is going to buy this CD? But they still make some baffling decisions.

[14] The building: Slang for the entire company.

[15] Because the band must pay back most of this money out of their royalties. This is usually renegotiated out of the deal once the band get a hit. See Chapter 7 for more.

It does seem ironic that a company generally hires a person with expertise so that they don't overspend in an area. But what Brodey is suggesting is that in the major label area that same person *needs* to spend money to justify their existence. Seems kind of ass-backwards.

Moses: Can you give us a personal example?

John Brodey: There was a band on **Warner Brothers** that I was managing. Warner Brothers was the artist-oriented label back then. It was a brand-new punk rock band. They had a great marketing concept for a video, but it was going to cost $175,000. This was 1996. People were doing videos but not on that level. And given the fact that contractually the label did not have to do a video, you immediately find yourself with business-affairs guys hedging their bet, saying, "Okay, here's the deal, we will put up the first seventy-five grand; everything over that is 50 percent recoupable against the band." Immediately, the band is going, "Geez, we want a great video," and they are excited, and it's a great idea. Now all of a sudden, you're on tilt.[16] The budget is out of control and we are on the hook for half of the overage.[17] These are traps that you fall into. When they step up in a situation like that, you are sort of swept along thinking that you have a great level of support. You lose sight of the fact that [$175,000] isn't a lot of money to them. They are used to pissing that kind of money away. What you are mistaking for a heightened sense of commitment is really business as usual. In the case of this band, the record and video came out and nothing clicked in 15 minutes, and they didn't even put out a second track.

It's not uncommon for an artist to go over budget for reasons that are completely out of their control and completely within the control of the label. Then the axe gets lowered.

André Fischer: **Jacki Magee**[18] was signed to **MCA**. She was a wonderful singer and had been barely able to finish her album because of some *reforecasts*. A reforecast is when someone gives you a budget, and there is a misappropriation of funds, or it is spent incorrectly, or because of some unknown X factor causing the need for more money. They come back to the company with a reforecast of the budget, which has to be approved by the department that issued it, which usually means there has to be money in their account. If you go to an urban department and say, "I need more money for the album, I know I said that I only need $300,000, but I need another $50,000," that department has to find out if that hurts the budget for

[16] **Tilt:** Poker terminology meaning out of control or caught up in the momentum of the moment and betting when you shouldn't.

[17] **Overage:** The amount over the allotted budget. Usually the artist has to pay for this 100 percent, either out of his pocket or through a withholding of royalties.

[18] **Jacki Magee:** Signed to MCA and dropped, has earned numerous credits as a background singer on high-end projects like Toto.

the [total year]. A major company has many acts signed and there is only so much money allocated to a promotion and marketing department. Which acts get the money? Because of someone's mistake at a company there are careers and artists you've never heard from again. Great artists you've never heard of get dropped.

Norwegian Would

It's been said that small people make small mistakes and big people make big mistakes. Meaning that everyone has a bad day at the races, but when the moguls' bad day comes the fallout can be extreme. **Clive Davis** has probably the best reputation in the business as a real "record man." In the old-school vernacular this meant he had "ears." He wasn't just an executive like Geffen is reputed to be—he was involved with the music and personally hand-picked most of the artists on his label,[19] relegating his team of A&R "executives" to mere talent scouts. This is what has justified his record-breaking $4,000,000 a year salary (without bonus).

But in the late 1990s he signed an act that would bust the development bank at **Arista Records**. When people talk about Clive Davis and his impeccable track record, I've got two words for them: **the Tuesdays.**[20] **Paul Menes** was counsel for the Norwegian rock act and tells their tale.

> *Paul Menes:* They were signed to a two-record guarantee deal with Arista. The label loved them, they played their own instruments,[21] they wrote most of their own songs. Arista paid them a great advance and broke their butts trying to break this band. I was so excited having this artist, I thought that they were going to be huge and have a long career.

Four hot girls from Norway who played songs reminiscent of the **Beatles.** Perhaps too reminiscent. And perhaps it was Clive's personal nostalgia that got the better of his business sense. In a time when the radio was flooded with hard-edged metal and gangster hip-hop, the airwaves may not have been right for a bubblegum wet-dream team.

Clive hired co-writers to polish the girls' material and the top re-mixer in the business, whose normal fees were about $15,000 per song, to give the record a "radio ready" sound. Clive wanted the best for the Tuesdays. And the girls never objected. Nor did their management. All believed in the same Stock*ho'* mantra repeated in this temple of commerce:

money = love

[19] Clive Davis: Some of Clive's big picks: Barry Manilow, Janis Joplin, Bruce Springsteen, the Grateful Dead, Whitney Houston.

[20] Two other words could be Anita Baker, who was released from her Arista contract after executives there told her she had no talent. Two years later she signed with Elektra and had a smash hit, *Rapture*.

[21] Unusual for an all-girl band at the time.

The more the label spent, the larger their commitment. The video debuted on MTV, didn't catch on, and two weeks later it was over.

Paul Menes: The girls never did a second record [on Arista]. To this day, I believe the reason was the label just decided to cut their losses. That is an example of, after spending so much money on the band, that's what happens. With this artist they, we, and their management all thought it was the way to go. The label offered the deal. They took it. We never even thought twice, or that they would not have at least a second record to establish themselves.[22]

[22] The Tuesdays' catchy single "It's Up to You" (not written by the band) peaked at No. 55 on *Billboard*'s Hot 100 chart. They played MTV live and went on a two-month festival tour with the Backstreet Boys, 'N Sync, and Matchbox 20. Arista then dropped them and the group decided to split up.

Your Own Marketing Plan

It's easy to forget that the marketing people you're dealing with may not have been working for many years. Some may be new to their jobs, and even if they are not the best, most experienced ones are usually straining to remain hip. Many may not be up on the newest ways to reaching a new market. You, on the other hand, have been in the clubs with your act for a while. You know the crowd. You know the fans.

Moses: What do you think a new manager out there needs to be thinking about first and foremost?

Steve Addabbo: Long term—how this is all feeding into the long-term career development of their artist and of their own management career. Both of those things go hand in hand.

John Brodey: [Labels] come up with a plan because everyone wants to keep their jobs and in a very basic way they realize the need for direction. Once the album is finished you have a release schedule. Eventually, the label is going to be spending a bunch of money, so you better be ready to challenge them and offer ideas or you're at their mercy. Once the label's plan is in place, the manager has no leverage, he has no bargaining power. If you didn't offer much, then the marketing guys, regardless of their experience or creativity, are going to forge ahead even if it's a vision that doesn't sync with the act.

Moses: What's the best way to get a plan?

John Brodey: A plan is knowing what is going to work for your artist. You get that from being savvy, looking at your audience and knowing what connects with them. You obviously need to understand your artist thoroughly and be prepared to fight to make sure nothing happens that compromises what they're about.

Jim Barber: What was it [about your act] that connected with people, what does your audience tell you when you are playing live? Why are you getting a response?

John Brodey: When it comes down to artistic aspects, a band is often told what is expected for the next record based on the label's perception. If you look at guys like **Tommy Mottola**, they've made a career out of doing the same thing over and over again with immediate results, but nothing lasting.[23] The same cookie-cutter stuff, that's what you often get from a major label. You are going to get their version of reality; unless you have a vision of your own, you are going in there with the same kind of mentality that the labels have, which is let's throw all of this stuff together and see which things work. Maybe we can get a little spark over here or a little spark over there.

Moses: The artist has to pretty much cooperate with the label, and you're saying the artist shouldn't cooperate with the label. Isn't that what you are saying?

John Brodey: The artist has to have a sense of when they are getting bad advice or when they are being led down the wrong path. They have to be true to themselves to a certain point. It's one thing to be good about doing your business, and it's another thing to be thinking with a corporate mentality. There are people out there that hear the music and connect with it. It's real, there is a thing about it that speaks the truth. You look at these bands, you look at **Velvet Revolver**[24] and all this crap. They all used to be in great bands and it's this ridiculously fabricated thing that really doesn't speak to anybody. I think at a certain point those guys are victims of that system. They can't do anything apart from that. It's all geared to the machine.

Seems like everyone is basically saying, look far down the road and know how you're getting from A to B before the label takes control of your career. Once they think they know what is best, you stand little chance of convincing them otherwise. They'll want to spend gobs of money on things that you are going to have to pay them back for, and Stockho' Syndrome will be in effect.

❯ Payola Patronizing Dementia: The Story of Debbie Gibson's Secret of Success

Now here is an interesting phenomenon. A thing every artist feels on a gut level is wrong, but yet every artist eventually gives into the reality of. Don't think that be-

[23] Tommy Mottola: Earned $10,000,000 a year. He is considered responsible for development of several top acts, including Mariah Carey. He was asked to resign from Sony in 2003 after huge loses for the company's record division. The company subsequently fired another 1,000 people and consolidated its two main labels, Columbia and Epic. His ex-wife Mariah Carey claims he is trying to destroy her career. Michael Jackson called him "the Devil."

[24] Velvet Revolver: Fabricated supergroup that includes Scott Weiland, Slash, Duff McKagen.

cause you have a killer record that's going to be enough to get you on the charts. Don't get your feelings hurt when you find out that in order to make you a star, people were *shmeared*[25] along the way. Does *shmearing* do damage to the ethics of the artist and in some way contribute to Stockho' Syndrome?

Payola has several meanings.[26] It should also be noted that one person's "payola" is another person's legitimate "promotion expense." Recent criminal investigations by the New York District Attorney's office are going to more clearly define what is allowable under the law in the next few years. But in the context of the artist it means that thing they don't want to know about how they get famous. It's too upsetting to think that after all their hard work, who flies and who dies boils down to a payoff. In the 1980s independent promotion broke down to five regions, syndicated to about five "radio consultants," and they charged about a quarter of a million dollars to "break" a single. **Doug Breitbart**, former manager of **Debbie Gibson**,[27] is a get-it-done type who is not afraid to bend rules a bit to satisfy his objectives. He was new to the music business when he worked with Gibson and tells us here why "indie promotion" (what some would call "payola") is necessary and how he helped reinvent the model of it that permeated the 1980s.

> *Doug Breitbart:* If I had counted on **Atlantic Records** to do their job, to come up with the funds and do the promotion work, Debbie Gibson never would have happened. I capitalized Debbie Gibson's first album production and independent promotion. Both things that Atlantic Records was supposed to do. Now, back then, if you were doing old school, your numbers [$250,000] are right. You'd hire those guys, they then start at small stations in each market, build up, scratching and clawing, station by station, ad by ad. It was a huge effort. It was truly working, building a base, building a foundation process. The amount of the check didn't guarantee success. Sure, you have things like a national contest for a trip to Bermuda for program directors that play this record X amount of times, sponsored by record companies, and lo and behold every PD "won" a trip to Bermuda. But ultimately the record had to generate audience response.

This was the state of things as Doug found them when his artist Debbie Gibson was first signed to Atlantic Records in 1985. At the time Atlantic was one of the largest and most respected record companies in the business. However, they had a reputation for signing many acts and releasing relatively few. This left many acts on their roster dangling in limbo, as **André Fischer** pointed out earlier in this chapter. During this limbo many acts get dropped unless the manager steps in and does something radical.

[25] Shmeared: Yiddish for bribed. Originates from the act of spreading (or shmearing) cream cheese on a bagel. Likewise the image is that of greasing a palm with cash.

[26] Payola: Technically it only means illegal pay-for-play, but has evolved colloquially to mean any form of pay-for-play, illegal or not. Also an interesting side note: it is a misconception that paying a radio station to play music is illegal. It's only illegal if it's not disclosed to the public. For a good history on the subject, see Fredric Dannen's book *Hit Men*.

[27] Debbie Gibson: Teen idol with several Top Ten hits in the mid-eighties.

Doug Breitbart: A week before her first single was positioned for the pop crossover from the dance charts, a couple of significant independent promoters came under investigation. Every independent promoter across the country, within seven to ten days, was out of work. Every major label dropped all independent promotion to make sure that whatever the investigation produced as a result did not trace back to them. So they, by policy, wouldn't hire independents anymore. I was a bright, young, newly minted lawyer and manager and I went to the Atlantic exec who signed [Gibson], and I said I needed to hire an indie for New York who I had met with the week before. He said I can't give it to you, we aren't doing that anymore. I can give you money for anything else, but I can't give you money for that.

Without promotion money, Doug and Debbie would have stood about a zero percent chance of success.

Doug Breitbart: Around that time, the independent promoters had been put out of business and the P1's[28] didn't know what to play. Also a new format had arrived on the scene. Stations began to play 12-inch dance mixes.[29] Suddenly you had *dance* records being played on these "hot" or "power" stations. And they were just blowing up. They were crossing over to pop and going to the top of the charts. Once it hit the top of the charts in major markets the rest of the country would follow without any benefit or need for independent promotion. So I said, "Can you give me money for marketing?" He goes, "Maybe a mix-and-match actually. Some cash and maybe some free goods." The stock-in-trade and currency and commerce of the music industry was *free records* and their convertibility to cash. Record companies are really mints. They manufacture things for the cost of pennies that have the value of dollars. They print money. It used to be vinyl and now it's CDs... same difference.

To clarify, for those new to the business, Doug is referring to the fact that an album could be returned to the record company for a credit of about $9 each. So if you were given a free box of albums that contained about 35 units, in effect this was like paying you $315. The cost to the label was less than $40. Of course, the artist would never see royalties on these, and often a restocking fee for records that were returned was charged against their account at the label.

Doug Breitbart: I go home and I write a letter, a proposal for marketing services on the Debbie Gibson project. It called for X amount of cash and Y amount of

[28] P1: Industry jargon for the radio stations that have the most amount of listeners. Indie promoters make their bread and butter marketing to these types of stations, more so than smaller local and college stations.

[29] 12-inch singles, they were sometimes called. Soon to be coming to a museum near you. Now a relic of the analog age, replaced by CDs. Some diehard vinyl stores still sell them. Bless their hearts.

30 One-stop: A sub-
distributor that
would give you
cash for the box of
records. They were
supposed to try to
sell the record to
smaller record
stores but often
would simply re-
turn the box for a
credit themselves.

product. I sent it to him and he said, [*sarcastically*] "Boy, Doug, you do good law."
It went through. I turned around and gave the independent promoter cash and
"free goods" which he converted into cash at his local one-stop.[30] Within a week
of me doing that every independent promoter in the country had a "marketing
company." By using a marketing concept, I enabled the independent promoters to
get back to work. I paid the independent promoter and we went about our business. The indie promoters were out of work, they were lost and looking for other
things to do. I came up with a device, by using the word "marketing," which traditionally in the music industry was associated with free goods, retail space, end
caps, in-store displays, and co-op advertising, as a device to get the means to
promote my records. We broke the record; that particular single went top five.

Payola Then Versus Now

Doug Breitbart: Today, a pop single [nationally] is a million-dollar promotion bill.
It's a handful of checks. Major radio syndicates play the record.

Moses: Are independent promoters still in use?

Doug Breitbart: Yes. **Clear Channel**[31] doesn't have corporate headquarters
with a monolithic control panel where they push a button and every station they
own is playing the record. You still have the [individual indie promoter]. I think the
line is blurred as to whether that is "independent promotions" or just "promotion
costs." If you sort of think of it from a network-like model it makes sense because
a record company's [promotion] staff isn't large. The independent promoter tends
to be more radio-station-relationship centered. The independent promoter was
working with the program director, saying, here are all the releases you are con-
tending with from all the major labels. Which one does it make sense to give the
shots to now, and how do we coordinate them to maximize exposure and gener-
ate a hit, which is radio's job. The independent promoters were truly intermedi-
aries that facilitated and helped programming directors. You can [be cynical and]
focus exclusively on the economics around independent promoters, but as a
practical matter they were serving a critical industry function. I clearly used independent promotion to help break Debbie Gibson's records at radio. I assure you I
did not have the resources, nor did the indie promoter I hired, to pay anyone anything for that airplay. Effective indie promotion, absolutely. Payola, not a drop.

31 Clear Channel:
Concert promotion
company turned
radio conglomer-
ate that rolled up
over 1,200 stations
nationwide. Many
in the industry feel
that this homoge-
nized radio and
connected the
radio industry to
the concert promo-
tion industry in
ways that are too
incestuous.

> Changing the Voice of the Artist

In many cases artists don't see themselves the same way the label or even the fans do. **Joan Osborne**[32] was a fabulous blues/soul singer before she signed her deal to be a pop artist. The labels went through two versions of her album before they came out with a single that hit. When they did, she was singing anything but blues. **Alanis Morissette** was also very different prior to her big release in the US. She was a bubblegum singer from Canada before **Glen Ballard**[33] worked his magic on her.

The transition an artist goes through when they cross that bridge from up-and-coming to signed (or branded) by a label to the final stage—stardom—is a radical one. Most artists start out wanting to do something different from everyone else or do the opposite, something classic. When they see that "different" often means hard, and "classic" means something nobody cares about, they compromise and try to fit into one the several prepackaged and narrow mediums of music genres. In the parlance of the industry this is called a "format." It relates to radio formats and what songs they will play. Some formats are listed in the sidebar, but the names of these formats change over time.

After some success, however, many artists try to use their leverage to get "back to their roots." They persuade the record company to let them try their hand at what they think they do best. It usually meets with disaster.

Wrestling with Your Career

Steve Addabbo: I think one of the biggest mistakes **Cyndi Lauper**[34] ever made was getting involved with that wrestling stuff. People forgot what a great singer she was. Look at **Joan Osborne**, huge success with **Rick Chertoff**[35] as producer, had that song "What If God Was One of Us." The next record, totally bails on it. Now she is there, but she is very much under the covers. I think on that particular one it is almost like she wanted to prove that she was a jazz singer. Some people aren't comfortable with the pop stardom. When they see what it is like they go, forget it, I don't want to do that again.

[32] Osborne has been nominated for a Grammy seven times but has never won.

[33] Glen Ballard: His first "hit" was 1990's release of *Wilson Phillips*, although it's questionable that this was a success. It's believed that the record company spent far more promoting it than was eventually made on sales. His unmitigated success is the co-writing and producing of *Jagged Little Pill* with Alanis Morissette, for which he received several Grammy awards.

[34] Cyndi Lauper: Recorded "Girls Just Want to Have Fun," "True Colors," and "Time After Time." Won the 1984 Grammy for Best New Artist. Even though Lauper claimed in an interview that she was color-blind, her song "True Colors" was used in a Kodak commercial to emphasize the film's vividness.

35 Rick Chertoff: Produced the Hooters' *And We Danced* (1985) and Cyndi Lauper's debut album *She's So Unusual,* both multi-platinum successes. Despite a phenomenal career, he has never won a Grammy. He was Grammy nominated for Osborne's album but lost to Alanis Morissette's "You Oughta Know."

RADIO FORMATS

Name of Format	What It Means
Top 40	Crossover hits from one of the other formats below.
Classic Rock	Rock that was recorded over ten years ago or sounds like it was.
Hot 100	Code for mostly black music or artists who are white but sound black. Includes hip-hop, R&B.
Easy Listening	The name says it all. Snooze music.
AC (formally AAA)	Adult Contemporary: Code for white music. Sting 'n' stuff like that.
Jazz	Not really straightahead jazz except for a few shifts at night. Really, it's more "fuzak" and a blend of "smooth" instrumental music.
Classical	Orchestral music written by people usually long dead.
Power or Hot	High-energy music, mostly dance oriented. Power pop.

It's also worth noting that songs move from format to format over the course of their lifespan. For example, **Led Zeppelin**'s "Stairway to Heaven" has been on AC, Classic Rock, and Top 40 over the course of its life. Someday we might find it on Easy Listening or "smooth" stations as baby boomers reach their twilight years. Astounding.

Young v. Geffen: The War of the Roses

Labels have little choice but to indulge artists when they want to "experiment," but they have a big stick to regulate how far. No contract requires a label to release and promote a record. So, if the artist decides to totally change directions, the label can bite back hard. In the famous case of folk rocker **Neil Young**[36] and **David Geffen** the sparks became a bonfire.

> *Jim Barber:* It always amazed me to see people shocked and upset by the Neil Young, **Joni Mitchell**,[37] David Geffen wars in the 1980s. Neil delivered records that David Geffen and his staff deemed to be not representative of being Neil Young records. He changed his style every single record. After three or four of these Geffen lost his temper. Not sitting down and saying, "Neil, this isn't working for us because people aren't able to follow you, people aren't going with you 'cause they've lost your plot and you need to do something to re-explain yourself so that they understand what is going on." That's not how Geffen handled it. Geffen sued him. You could say that one of the most fascinating things about David Geffen is that, for all of his charisma and how dynamic he is, he really doesn't give a fuck about music, and he really doesn't care much for musicians. To me the classic guy in the business these days is [name withheld],[38] who, if you deliver a record to his [major] label and he isn't happy, he will say something like, "I don't hear a single, go write me some more songs." Not "What are these lyrics about?" or "This song would be great if I understood what was going on." You get nothing. You get zero and it's incredibly cold. I think it's evil.

Because I Got Dropped

Defying a label to get out of a deal has been tried by artists of every genre. Taking a tip from some of his contemporaries, such as Prince, in 2001 an obscure performer named **Afroman** spit in the eye of **Universal Music**. His lawyer, **Ben McLane**, gives us this little-known inside scoop about the one-hit wonder.

> *Ben McLane:* The label kind of expects a certain sound from you, and if you don't cooperate... Afroman[39] had the song "Because I Got High." It was the number one song in the country and all over the world basically. He got a huge deal with **Universal** because the song was already an independent hit. He went out and got it played on local stations and it was just one of those things that blew up. But Universal only saw him as a novelty rapper, which is pretty much what his specialty is. As soon as he became a big star there were a lot of demands on him

[36] Neil Young: Formerly of the groups Buffalo Springfield, Crosby, Stills, Nash, & Young, and Crazy Horse. Recorded the songs "After the Gold Rush," "Alabama," "Cinnamon Girl," "Old Man," "Down by the River," "Southern Man," "Keep on Rockin' in the Free World," "Like a Hurricane," "Heart of Gold," and "Ohio."

[37] Joni Mitchell: Biggest hit, "Big Yellow Taxi" in 1970. It was redone as a hip-hop/rock song in 2003 by Counting Crows, charting for far longer than Mitchell's original version. Tori Amos, Sarah McLachlan, Shawn Colvin, and Madonna claim her as a musical influence. In a recent interview Mitchell, known for her wordsmithing, called the music industry a "corrupt cesspool," adding in a reference to singers like Madonna and Britney Spears that "record companies are not looking for talent. They're looking for a look and a willingness to cooperate."

[38] Co-chairman of several major labels and included on the list "100 Most Successful Entertainment Executives." While at Warner Brothers, the label lost its reputation as being "artist friendly."

[39] Afroman: L.A. rapper, born Joseph Foreman. Most of his songs are about getting high or selling dope. Because his music was inadvertently and illegally distributed on Napster, some say that Afroman may be the first artist broken on the Internet. He was signed shortly after that to Universal.

as far as touring and having to come up with a follow-up and keeping schedules and all that kind of stuff, which he wasn't accustomed to and didn't want to be like that, so he intentionally made a gospel record as his follow-up and turned that in. Of course the label didn't accept it and dropped him. They could tell he was being difficult, and they had spent a full budget on a record that had nothing to do with his genre.

⊳ Conclusion

It's a shame that professionals can't just speak their minds to their clients, the artist. Things would probably be a bit easier for all concerned. Artists are very sensitive. Many simply refuse to learn about the realities of selling their music. They will hate the system for being what it is, but without it they would be performing in cafés.

Producers hype their talent to get them in the studio and to get great performances out of them. A&R people do the same to both the talent and to themselves to muster the strength to sell it to their bosses. When the record is done, the promotions department tells them how great they are. And if all this doesn't screw with their head enough, the artist usually has a different perception of who they are than the label does. When the artist gets the power (and is now drunk on hype) they often want to change their image and sound, alienating fans.

In the end, massaging the talent is necessary, but it can have its dark side. It can turn the artist into a prima donna and destroy what we hold dear about their work. The line is blurry and wiggles from side to side, but learning which side you are on can be the difference between success and failure. What keeps it all together? The contract. Yes, at the end of the day, the lawyers and their product—the binding agreement—are basically all that keeps chaos from erupting. But things can and do go horribly wrong there as well, as you'll see in the next chapter where the lawyer is our focus.

CHAPTER 7

Lawyer Lamentations

"We know there are known knowns: there are things we know we know. We also know there are known unknowns: that is to say, we know there are things we know we don't know. But there are also unknown unknowns — the ones we don't know we don't know."
—**Secretary of State Donald Rumsfeld during a briefing on Iraq**

"Liars when they speak the truth are not believed."
—**Aristotle (384–322 BC)**

"Bad lawyering is standard in the music business."
—**Some guy**

A s a kid I learned that in a restaurant the customer is always right. In just about every service scenario this philosophy is practiced in some form, except the law. The law is contrary to this fundamental law of commerce: *treat your customer with respect.* (However, in defense of lawyers, given the circumstances of their need, sometimes that can be hard to do.)

In the law, an attempt is made to make the client feel that he is wrong and has been wrong for most of his life. But now… now that you've met the lawyer, now your life will start to turn around. Heck, the mere fact that you need a lawyer implies that something important is *finally* happening to you. Right?

Given this fact, it should seem fairly transparent that you can only be a truly effective client to a lawyer if you know as much about your rights as the lawyer you are hiring. How can you do that? There are two ways. One of them is the wrong way, but it is the one that many employ: you find a lawyer who is slightly less ignorant than you about the law. That way you are almost on an equal footing, but you still feel like you've hired someone competent.

The smart way, and the way least chosen in the music business, is to choose a lawyer who not only knows more than you'll ever forget about this business, but one who also has the skills to manage your expectations. He should also educate you as best he can about what your rights are, not just ram some version of the industry standard down your throat that is designed to "handle you."

This is hard because the "best" lawyers are well entrenched in traditional ways of doing things, meaning that they make their money by being aligned with the interests of the major labels, the same ones who lost millions in the past few years and downsized the entire industry by a third. (More on this later.) When one considers that following old patterns could lead to failure just as easily as to success, we get a paradox: the "best" lawyers don't always give the best advice. Assuming reasonable odds, they will probably only give good advice about half the time. And they charge the most all of the time. (Still, someone who is right about half the time is probably better than your drinking buddy, spouse, bandmate, or parent, whose batting average is nowhere near as good, despite what they recall.)

Also consider that artists and attorneys solve problems in opposite ways. Attorneys, when faced with a challenge, are trained to look to the past and ask, "How was this problem solved last time? What precedents are there?" Artists are the opposite. They say, "Forget the past, let's look ahead. Let's try something that's never been tried."

Two polar opposites, and yet they have to work together to make the wheels of the commercial music business work. But does it work? An "attorney's mentality" is what caused record companies to make shortsighted decisions in the late 1990s that have resulted in the worst opportunity loss in the business's history, and a confusing future about how they will continue to make money (see Chapter 10).

So, should we have artists running labels? Well, that also has a huge downside. Even many artists agree that this would probably lead to as much, if not more, disaster than we've seen in recent years, as they can be a bit trigger-happy about litigation, often even more so than attorneys.

A disturbing example of how artists can use the law as therapy comes from **Andrea Brauer**, who has been in the music business for 25 years and has practiced entertainment law for 12 of these. She is a legal consultant to several music organizations in Los Angeles such as the **Songwriters Guild** and **Los Angeles Women in Music**.

Andrea Brauer: The litigation that some of my clients have gotten themselves into seems not to be based on any sort of economic rationality or even greed. The emotional agendas that governed the litigant's behavior were utterly confounding. For example, when a daughter sued her mother for failing to obtain a talent agent license even though the daughter received all the money she asked for.

Nice. If it's a litigious world we're going to live in, then the "attorney's mentality" seems to become the lesser of two evils. Maybe, one day, when the element of human nature that makes us volatile is somehow weeded out, we can also adjust our priorities.

How to interact with your attorney—and bludgeoning examples of what can happen if you ignore this advice—is what you're about to experience.

Note: You'll notice that in many interviews I "argue" with the lawyers. This is because one can't get a straight answer out of people trained to be ambiguous.

Jay Jay French: Ambiguity in the contract is *deliberate*. It invites lawsuits, which makes lawyers a lot of money.

❯ Conflicts of Interest and Interests of Conflict

Artists, labels, and producers screw each other every day. Lawyers pick up the pieces. When an artist needs a contract looked over he rarely considers whether or not the lawyer he's using to represent his side is suspected of selling him out to the opposing side. But this is a real possibility because of conflicts of interest.[1] It's been said that in the world of the blind, the one-eyed man is king. So music lawyers who show the minimal amount of compassion have no difficulty appearing ethical given their environment.

[1] See *Confessions of a Record Producer*'s chapter on *Lawyers* for more on the dynamics of this.

Over time I've had lawyers who read my other books come up to me and defend this point that I've raised many times in the past. They say, "Moses, the reason the artist hires us in the first place is *because* of that conflict of interest." They mean that it's the lawyers' connections that make them valuable to the artists. But the tradeoff for the artist creates for them a lower standard of professional care, and this is the number one reason why artists claim to be "ripped off."

Paul Menes: A lot of law firms make their livelihood off of conflicts of interest. They used to represent the label on one side and a couple of artists on that label on the other side, or both the artist and their manager(s). There is no way you can divide your allegiance properly. I could give you a bunch of examples, but I would get the crap sued out of me for defamation.

Joey Akles: Bad lawyering is standard. Conflict of interest is standard. You have to understand these lawyers negotiate constantly with the [record companies].

Can this be true? Do lawyers help create the conflicts of interest even with the best of intentions? **Barbara Graham**, a St. Louis entertainment attorney whose clients and alliances include **Potzee, Starr 47, Louie V,** and **Erika Johnson**, elaborates:

Barbara Graham: In the past, if an artist came to me with a contract given to them by a manager, and the artist had no ability to pay attorney fees, I would actually call the manager and say, "Why don't you pay my retainer for them so that we can get this thing done?" (I no longer do this—I end up the bad guy in those situations.)
Moses: How successful is that technique?
Barbara Graham: It actually worked out all right, sometimes. But it's not necessarily a great idea. What happens of course is that the lawyer is now *not* acting in the artist's best interest because he usually was with the manager first, or the label, or the production company [who's referring him/her]. The manager of course is getting 20 percent or 15 percent off the top of everything and the lawyer is going to be looking to protect that. And if there comes a point that the artist wants to get rid of the manager, then what is the lawyer going to do? Basically they have to get out of the whole deal entirely because they cannot represent one of their clients in an adversarial relationship against the other.

The standard in the industry has developed to the point where most lawyers make clients sign a "conflict of interest waiver." This is a piece of paper that basically says, even though you know that I sometimes work for the other side we're negotiating with, you're okay with that. People routinely sign them, thinking they have no choice. They do.

But the crafty attorney trying to insulate himself will bring pressure on the artists, especially if there's a deal offer on the table.

Barbara Graham: I see it almost as a duress[2] type of situation. The label will put it in front of you and say, "Look, you have five days to get this thing signed and back to us, otherwise we are going on to the next person. And here is an attorney that can explain it to you." "Explain" is always dangerous because it means the lawyer will only tell you how badly you are being screwed but not do anything about it.

Moses: But does it really meet the legal standards of duress? It's just a record deal, not life or death.

Barbara Graham: I would say that anytime that somebody gives you [only] a couple of days, or five days, to me not only is it BS, it means that they just want the artist to sign the thing without getting legal counsel.

Or without educating themselves about the realities of conflicts of interest. The pressure of time puts everyone on notice and fosters an environment where hasty and poor decisions are made.

Barbara Graham: Artists tend to be very desperate and just want to get this deal closed. Rather than going out and forking over five hundred bucks to have somebody [impartial] review the contract for them, they will just go to whoever and do it on the cheap.

In most cases the attorney is getting a 5 percent commission if the artist signs the deal. But to the artist it feels free. He is not usually inclined to spend a few hundred dollars on a second opinion when he's got his star lawyer (whose interests are conflicted) sitting right there "representing" him.

Barbara Graham: My artist wrote a song that she recorded with another artist. The other artist's label wants to use this song and wants her to deliver the Pro Tools sessions.[3] I said the only way you are going to get this is if we get a song-writer agreement drawn up first so that we know she is going to retain ownership of this song. Then there is this whole thing that time is of the essence, "we have to get these sessions to the people in New York," and all that. Meanwhile it's not going to happen for at least another six months. That's just the way the industry moves. People love to say time is of the essence. But it usually isn't.

[2] **Duress: In some situations if a person can prove that they signed a contract under pressure the contract can be voided.**

[3] **Pro Tools sessions: The computer file that contains the actual musical performances. The "tracks," as the saying goes in the biz.**

⯈ A Conspiracy of Apathy

Two people who have been on both sides of an artist negotiation, former Geffen exec **Jim Barber** and **Twisted Sister** founder **Jay Jay French**, tell us this:

> *Jim Barber:* I have been in at least half a dozen situations where a band had a complete freakout after a successful record when they realized that their producer was getting royalty checks and they weren't. No one bothered to explain to them what a "record one" royalty[4] was or what they were signing meant.

> *Jay Jay French:* You don't see any [real money] until you get into the multi-platinum area. I would have to say a five-man band on every dollar grossed will probably see about a penny and a half per person. If you understand that economy ultimately you can start to be realistic with your projections. That is the single greatest misunderstanding.

> *Jim Barber:* I think the biggest mistake is to not ask enough questions about how the business is structured and what the contracts mean. People don't know what they are signing and the [lawyers] sometimes don't know what they are asking people to sign. That is the standard practice in the business. I think the lawyers that do try to explain things to artists don't have very much luck.

Largely true. I can attest that many artists' eyes glaze over when their attorney tries to educate them about the deal. We shouldn't judge attorneys too harshly for their failure here. They are not trained to be educators. However, in the defense of all those who don't want to educate the artist too much there's this to consider: many artists seem to think that the rules of the music business do not apply to them. They feel their talent will somehow transcend the nature of the business. Lawyers who do many deals a year know that sometimes being too good a negotiator will kill a deal.

For example, in my workshop[5] I often stress that when an artist signs to a small label, they should request to see *the distribution agreement* that the small label claims to have with their major distributor. This sends everyone in the class into a trundle. Artists rock in their seats—it never occurred to them. Lawyers cringe, because they know that the label will react as if this request is bad faith—like asking for proof of virginity on the eve of marriage.

Unfortunately the word "label" has no legal standard. Anyone can call themselves a label even when they are nothing more than a business card and cell phone.

[4] **Record one royalty:** A structure of a record deal whereby the producer gets paid his royalty starting from the first record sold. But usually the artists do not start to see royalties until after the complete recoupment of the advance they are given from the label. Paying the producer from the first record sold increases the "moving goalpost" until the artist's debt is paid off. See my website *www.mosesavalon.com* and click on the Royalty Calculator for more on this.

[5] For info on workshops go to *www.mosesavalon.com.*

Real labels have distribution agreements with legitimate record distributors. When it comes to large deals on larger labels it's not necessary to make the request to see the distribution contract. Everyone knows who distributes them. But a smaller, newer label called, say, "Bob's Records," needs to prove its credibility if they're claiming to have Sony as their distributor. If they are operating without a distribution contract (or one that is about to expire), then they have a moral (and perhaps legal) obligation to disclose this fact, lest the artists lock themselves into a binding agreement where they have zero hope of getting their product on the street. Yet when asked to show their distribution agreement, many small labels will take offense and give a lame excuse like "it's confidential."[6] This is crap and every lawyer knows it, yet attorneys will often not rock the boat or even inform their clients about this withholding in most cases. A former VP at **Universal Music Group** would not allow me to use his name in connection with this quote on this subject:

[6] "It's confidential": Nonsense. They do not have to show the entire agreement to prove an agreement exists. Just the last page (signature page) will do.

> *UMG Mug:* If you go to work at a big entertainment law firm, you are encouraged to *not* get into details with the artist. You push that off on the manager, and the manager pushes that off on the lawyer, and no one ever explains anything to the artist.
>
> *Moses:* Do you think it's an actual conspiracy?
>
> *UMG Mug:* No, I don't think people are that smart.
>
> *Moses:* So it is more like a conspiracy of apathy?
>
> *UMG Mug:* Yes. And a few years ago there was a lot of rhetoric from the artists' side about the "conspiracy" of the record companies. I think there were a lot of record execs that considered themselves to be really decent guys that were really offended and hurt by the fact that artists were talking about them this way. When, in fact, everything that the artists were saying was essentially true.

> Manager Misalignments

Just about every unsigned artist I deal with asks me, "How do I get a manager?" As if this is the thing that is separating them from their big dream. The quotes below should be enough to add some depth to that viewpoint.

> *Doug Breitbart:* The greatest mistake made by most new artists is to assume that procurement or collection of people to assist them through the signing of contracts—the manager, production company, or publisher—actually means that you have in fact made progress toward earning your living from the record business.

Jay Jay French: My mistake when entering the business was signing a horrible management deal. In the very earliest stages of my career, I had no clue what was going on.

There is a perception that this all-important person is necessary in order to get to the coveted prize—a major label deal. Although I have always heard (and admittedly have repeated) that one does *not* need a manager to succeed, I have yet to see an act signed to a major where a manager or producer backing the artist was absent. Contradicting? Oh, y'betcha.

An important fact to assimilate is that a manager's contract never says, "I'll get you a deal." It states simply that the manager's job is to "advise and give career advice." Kinda vague. It's so vague that these deals are hard to enforce without a good legal budget.

This exchange between myself and an attorney to many artists and labels, **Ben McLane**, manages to cover a lot of ground on this subject. As you can see, even two well-informed people will not always agree.

To Sign or Not to Sign

Los Angeles attorney Ben McLane, who's worked with the **Dixie Chicks** and **Guns N' Roses**, has a rather interesting viewpoint on whether a emerging band *ever* really needs a manager.

[7] Strip band: Slang for a local Los Angeles band that tours the Sunset Strip in West Hollywood.

Ben McLane: Go to the **Whiskey**, in L.A., [and] every strip band [7] says they've got a manager! Think about it: why would anybody be interested in managing a strip band that has no deal?

Moses: What if you are playing the clubs, but your strategy is to get on a major label?

Ben McLane: I think by and large the major labels are kind of forcing you to go with somebody that they know. Some labels now won't even sign you if you don't have a manager that they approve of, because they just don't want to take the risk. Look at the rosters of the major labels, you just see the same names over and over again, with few exceptions: **The Firm**, **Sanctuary**, **Azoff Management**, or …

Moses: I am sure that those strip bands would sign with The Firm or Sodenberg or Azoff [8] if they could get to them. The strip band probably feels as though they have to work their way up to those guys by starting out with someone smaller.

[8] All top management firms.

Ben McLane: If a manager comes to you and they don't have any current hits on the chart and is a one-man show without a staff and doesn't have big relationships, if I were a band why would I think they could really do anything for me?

Moses: So… hits on the charts, a big staff, solid relationships with majors. That's a manager worth signing with? You just narrowed the field down to about ten individuals. Up-and-coming managers don't deserve a chance? And what about indie deals? The Irving Azoffs of tomorrow have to start somewhere. But you would have the strip band tell them to take a hike until they get big credits.

Ben McLane: Because nine times out of ten that entry-level guy isn't going to do anything but make some phone calls or book some shows or whatever, things a band can do on their own.

Moses: Sometimes those phone calls add up to real progress for the act. Besides, I've seen that same scenario happen when an act signs with a big manager, too. They don't get much attention. Then they get dropped after a few months. Try to get another big manager or label to take you seriously after that.

Ben McLane: Absolutely, of course. That happens a lot too, but what is a safer bet? Here's the bigger point: If you're going to sign with an up-and-coming manager, you need to have your contract structured to where if a label deal becomes a reality, that the up-and-coming manager will agree to partner up with somebody bigger or bow out of the picture.

Moses: Isn't it implied in the standard language of the manager's contract? The manager is supposed to "advise you" and that is the service that he provides. If that up-and-coming manager has an Azoff that wants to partner with him, then he's going to see that as his ticket upstairs. If he refuses to partner up, the artist could sue him for breach of contract, because how could he advise against it? The artist can sue the manager because the advice he is giving you is self-serving and not serving you.

Ben McLane: Okay, but who has the money for lawyers to argue that point?

Moses: If there are big people interested, everybody has money for lawyers. I have seen this exact scenario countless times. In fact, it is usually the Azoff that is saying to the up-and-coming manager, "Look, take fifteen thousand dollars and collect a point for your finder's fee. If you don't I will bury you."

Ben McLane: But why would an outfit with the prestige of an Azoff want to get involved with a band where there's going to be litigation right from the get-go?

Moses: Because there's always litigation when it comes to anything good. Guys like Azoff bathe in litigations every morning.

Ben McLane: Probably so. Probably so. Good point. Anybody who's successful is probably going to get sued eventually.

How unfortunate and what a roundabout, right?

Let's recap: labels won't sign an artist without a manager they approve of. They only approve of a few managers. And artists can't get to those managers, and even if they can in many cases they will not get the attention they need because they are too small-time and the big manager has other acts to deal with who earn him big commissions. So the artist finds an up-and-coming manager who will work his butt off only to be disapproved of by the label and have to be pried away from the band come payday by a lawyer the band hires to find grounds to terminate the manager's contract.

A reality check. Lawyers of note, like Ben, deal mostly with acts that are already on the label radar. In my opinion this makes it hard for them to understand the needs of most young bands when starting out. It also doesn't take into consideration that on smaller indie deals the scope of "approved managers" expands greatly to include anyone who can show up on time (well, most of the time) and has a valid driver's license to drive the tour van.

As a side note, I hope **Irving Azoff** appreciates us turning his name into industry jargon: Azoff = big successful manager.

Freeloading on the Gravy Train

Sunset clauses are part of almost every manager's contract. Called "sunset" because it allows the manager to enjoy commissions after he's been fired, or the sun has "set" on the relationship, usually for a year or two. Sometimes certain provisions of the sunset clause can survive the contract forever. With new artists, many low-budget, corner-cutting, and DIY improvisations are experimented with. Who wants to spend thousands on a lawyer for an artist that may not break wind, let alone the Top 40? In situations like this, sneaky subtle clauses that are not scrutinized by a pro can really come back to hurt the artist.

Doug Breitbart managed and developed one of the biggest singer-songwriters of the 1980s, **Debbie Gibson**.[9] He offers this about overreaching sunset clauses:

[9] The precursor to the Britney Spears model. Gibson had a string of hits before she was 17. By 19 she was producing her own hits. Before her popularity faded she sold over 10,000,000 albums.

Doug Breitbart: Okay, Artist X is getting acknowledgment, recognition, and label interest. A manager/publisher comes in that's established in the business and has them sign a bunch of papers and ends up with his hooks firmly planted into a major chunk of the artist's [songwriting] catalog, often songs and demo recordings. Then he never generates a deal, never generates anything. When Artist X fires him, Artist X does not walk away with those copyrights—often they've been left behind. The standout single, the most amazing smash ballad for his or her career [Artist X] is administered, owned, controlled by a former [manager] and left behind [with the manager]. Artist X has a serious problem. Number one, that song isn't available to [provide an incentive for] the new manager the artist needs now. The guy who has the publishing and administrative control over it is a dead weight that sits back and makes money in his sleep. In the case of Artist X, it wasn't even a big publisher. It was a guy that was occupying a management position in a publishing company, and the operating principle of the deal was grabbing as much as you can and holding on forever. That is a crime. That is a frickin' crime. If you are not going to deliver the results, then don't hold the children [songs and recordings] hostage.

Major Label Rejects AM Radio

Many times, successful and famous musicians try their hand at management. In most cases they come away from that experience with two things:

- A major headache from lack of sleep
- A newfound appreciation for their own manager

A celebrity as a manager or liaison can be a sharp, double-edged sword in these cases. It makes everybody pay attention to the situation, but it can also mean that other obligations for that celebrity can get in the way and make it hard for him or her to do their job. This story, from the archives of an anonymous L.A. manager who works with bands from national level to emerging garage acts, illustrates perfectly how a having a celebrity manager can be a bittersweet experience. We'll call him "Player Hater."

Player Hater: The singer from **Weezer**,[10] **Rivers Cuomo**, was touting this emerging band called **AM Radio**. Weezer was a big cult band, and Cuomo, the singer, was well respected. He was instrumental in AM Radio's deal with **Elektra** because the label sort of *assumed* that Cuomo was going to be involved in managing AM Radio and use his clout to help them piggyback on the Weezer brand. Y'know, have the band second stage[11] for them, things like that. That was a picture-perfect situation that was just prime success if everything would have worked as planned. But nothing did. Cuomo is really famous for being undercover. He didn't do interviews. Stayed to himself and kept a low profile. He had this whole persona about being ultra cool and mysterious.

Moses: It's tough to be a manager of an act on a major label and stay in the background. Especially when you have a major act you're involved in as a primary responsibility.

[10] Weezer: Big hit *Buddy Holly* produced by Ric Ocasek of the Cars. Despite a huge cult following that crossed over to mainstream, their follow-up effort *Pinkerton* did not resonate as well with their fan base, according to *Rolling Stone*, who called it "the Worst Album of 1996."

[11] Second stage: It used to be called an "opening slot" or a warm-up act that went on before the headliner. Now big acts sell a spot to emerging acts on a "second stage" located near the main stage.

Player Hater: Unfortunately he didn't get to spend the time that the label felt was necessary with the act, and because of that they basically pulled the plug on the project.

Moses: I am confused, because when a band gets signed to a major, there are a million managers that would step in and take over.

Player Hater: By the time it had got to that point the record had already come out and was starting to lose its juice. Sure, a new manager could come in, but it's kind of like resurrecting a project that is already dead, and most people don't want to do that. I know the attorneys spoke to every major manager in town that they knew. Pretty much all of them said, "No way, this is a sinking ship, we are not getting involved." The problem also was, when this all happened Elektra was being absorbed into Atlantic and pretty much every act was getting cut, unless you were **AC/DC** or somebody very, very big. Cuomo is a great guy. He probably just bit off more then he could chew.

Even with the best of intentions and with contact galore, management is a job that, as people learn the hard way, requires 100 percent focus. Always assess to yourself:

- Why do I think I need a manager?
- What are they going to do for me that I cannot do myself if I put a little elbow grease into it?
- If I have to sign a deal with someone, does the contract have sufficient safety provisions in case things fall apart?

⊜ URL Hell

The digital age brought with it a whole new set of things for lawyers to fight over: Web rights. Every artist has a Web site. You can no longer even be taken seriously without one. Like stenciling your band's name on the kick drum was the cheap branding of the sixties, so too is a Web site the poor man's trademarking of a pop artist or group.

When a group is signed by a major these days, they already have a Web site in most cases. Many are already selling their music and merchandise on their site. They are in a sense a mini–record company. It's this professionalism that often attracts labels to the act. And it's the first thing they try to take away when they make an offer.

Paul Menes: A couple years ago some record companies were putting into their contracts that the artist had to give up their domain name (and some of them signed it). A [URL] is your trademark. It's like publishing. It's intellectual property and unique to you, something that you can utilize to make money. You need to be very careful about giving up your rights to something that earns you money down the road for a fast buck now.

Moses: In my recollection, when labels ask for domain names—and it's still pretty standard—they claim they want to create that brand footprint for the artist. That it's part of developing the artist, and I know lawyers at some pretty big firms who yield on that point. We all know it's a mistake—ultimately you want to keep as much as you can—but at the end of the day are you saying that an artist should walk rather than give up their domain right?

Paul Menes: There's a difference between ownership and profit participation. The label saying they *need* to *own* the rights, because they want to make the Web site and the Internet experience of that artist as fabulous as possible, is crap. They don't need to own the name to do that. They can *lease* the name. The last couple of deals that I negotiated, the label will have the exclusive right during the term of the record contract to the artist's domain name to put stuff on the site, promote the artist on the site, and direct people to the site, but it doesn't give them the right after the term to that name. It only gives them the nonexclusive right to use the name as long as they are selling records and things related to the record or the artist.

Moses: Why do you think that the label wants this right, then, if it's nothing they need?

Paul Menes: Intellectual property is very valuable. The biggest component of gross national product in the United States is intellectual property, copyrights, trademarks, and patents.

Moses: There are a lot of other things they could spend their time going after. Why do they need a domain name? They must spend a good $5,000 just negotiating that one point per negotiation, when many of these artists are not even going to be released.

Paul Menes: For the one artist that does well. If they own the domain name and that artist is famous, it sort of forces the artist to deal with them for as long as the artist is around. The digital age is a little more entrenched and a little more realistic.

Moses: Sure, but the artist still owns their name as an artist, and if the record company wants to maintain a Web site on the artist's behalf why would they care?

Paul Menes: They can't use it on the Web.

Moses: So if they are called the Beatles and they signed away TheBeatles.com, they can't start a Web site called TheNewBeatles.com?

Paul Menes: Well, usually the wording in the contracts is not that specific. What the wording traditionally says is that the artist is granting the label the exclusive right to utilize their name on Web sites on the Internet. Also, how would fans of the Beatles know that the band's controlled Web site was TheNewBeatles.com, when those fans had known it was at TheBeatles.com for many years? It's logical to look for them at TheBeatles.com.

Good points.

Contract Do-Overs: The Realities of Renegotiating After the Fact

Back in the day (whenever that was), managers and lawyers would routinely tell their clients that they should not worry about the first deal they sign. That the contract was merely a suggestion. The reality was that if they proved themselves, a renegotiation would be triggered. One where they would start to get a better share of profits and more amenities, like a bigger advance for the second record.

Jay Jay French: The minute you have a hit record, you should just sit down with the label and renegotiate the deal.

André Fischer: As long as you don't take them to the brink they will renegotiate with you. It has to do with popularity and sales.

Then in the mid-nineties, after some consolidation of the music business in the US, the policy began to curtail. Several companies (mostly from the **Universal** family) put their foot down and said no. Stuck with the old contracts, several of the more successful artists began a quiet revolt.

Moses: Explain to the readers what leverage a band has against the label to renegotiate.
Jay Jay French: You stop recording.
Moses: If a label is playing the odds, chances are you are not going to have a second hit anyway.

Jay Jay French: They don't know that and their shareholders don't know that. Their marquee value is that you are a hit, because they sign another act based on you being a hit. They need *you* to be successful so that they can go get other bands.

Moses: Let me play devil's advocate. If I was the label and you are Twisted Sister and you came to me and said, "We had a hit record; we want to negotiate these points," I would say, "No, live with the deal you made." Twisted says if you don't renegotiate we are *not* going to make another record for you. Well, then, I say they are in breach of contract.

Jay Jay French: No, they're not. There is no such thing as indentured servitude. You don't have to do anything.

Moses: You can't go anywhere else and make a record. Because of the exclusivity clause. So you're basically giving up your recording career.

Jay Jay French: True, so you pay the price on that.

Moses: Then where is your leverage?

Jay Jay French: Look, every record company sits down and says, "What do we have for the next quarter?" If you are already guaranteed X amount of sales because you had a hit last quarter, they can then guarantee to their rack jobbers [12] X amount of units. They become beholden to a percentage of it, not that they believe you are going to sell the same amount in the next album, but they will believe that you are going to do 30 or 40 or 50 percent of it, which is 20 or 30 percent more than a new act that they are bringing on.

Basically, a tried-and-true act is a better risk than a new one. Sounds like a simple enough game. However, in the new record industry the role of the rack jobber[13] and other secondary sales outlets (especially ones where the label can get out of paying royalties) will be greatly diminished now that a significant percentage of records will be sold through downloads and not returnable to the distributor. Digital sales will one day soon increase the profit margins. Higher profits could reduce the leverage that a new hit artist has in intimidating the label. In fact, remove the nebulous cloud for royalty-free sales, make royalty reporting accurate, and the record company could find itself adopting a new business philosophy: a successful artist can be a liability. They may want you to quit so that they don't have to give in to your demands. Much like a company firing middle management as they come up for promotion. Instead they give the now vacant executive job to an underling in the form of a "trial promotion," with no increase in pay.

André Fischer: The real leverage the label has is suspension.[14]

[12] Rack jobbers: Companies who buy consignment returns for about $1 a unit and resell them to discount outlets and scrap recycling plants. These records often end up in music clubs and Amoeba record stores. Artists get no royalties for these sales, and it is for this reason that the use of rack jobbers as a substantial portion of the business model for profits at a record company is considered highly controversial.

[13] There is still a lot of controversy about the transition from brick-and-mortar sales to Internet-based sales. Although there was a setback initially due to piracy, this will not be a big issue in the future.

[14] Suspension: Considered the purgatory of record deals. The term does not progress, so you can't run out the clock and yet there is no money forthcoming, including in many cases royalties that are due.

Moses: Doesn't a suspension hurt the artist more than the label?

André Fischer: Only if the artist lives off of record sales and does not perform live. It only hurts those that do not do direct marketing. The people that live off of videos and really can't perform live.

Moses: Do you think that the renegotiation dynamic will survive tomorrow?

Jay Jay French: Let's put it this way: every manager has to assess individually where their artist stands in terms of the ability to renegotiate. If you just sold a lot of records and you have no relation to the label and you just go in and go, "Fuck you, let's renegotiate or I'm gonna stop recording"—just like an athlete that sits out a season—if you do that to the wrong person at the wrong label, then you've cut your nose off to spite your face. It's still a human business even if we start selling records with machines. If you feel that the people you are dealing with can be per-suaded, then you have to make your move. But you have to be careful as a man-ager because if you advise your lawyers to do something and they get screwed in the end, then you are screwed in the end. Don't forget that the lawyers are all from the same law firm. So who is kidding who anyway? They are going to have lunch together, they are going to make a phone call. "Frank, what are you selling Bill for?" "What are you fucking doing?" It's behind-the-scenes bullshit, you figure it out.

So the old-boy network gets the last word on this subject. Not only can you not get a deal without a lawyer, but you can't renegotiate your deal without one. In other words, the lawyer charges you to get you a crappy deal, then charges you again to get you a proper one, once you've proved worthy. The customer is always wrong, until proven otherwise.

I'm reminded of an argument I once had with a general contractor who was fixing my house, who, halfway through the job, began to make excuses as to why he could not complete the work as promised. He said I wasn't paying him enough, even though I gave him his full bid. I asked him, "You mean to tell me there is a price for doing it and then another price for doing it right?" With a bold straight face he said, "Of course."

⊙ The Rapture Vulture

Ben McLane: I was involved with a client named **Garry Glenn**,[15] a great song-writer. He wrote "Rapture" for **Anita Baker**.[16] It was probably his biggest song. A few

[15] Garry Glenn: Toured with his sister, gospel singer Beverly Glenn, as a teenager, but turned to writing in 1983, penning songs for Earth, Wind & Fire and Freddie Jackson, among others.

[16] Anita Baker: Arista executives told her she could not sing and had no talent, and would not renew her contract with her first group, Chapter 8. The ex-perience made her gun-shy and she was hesitant to give up her job as a legal secretary when offered a new contract by Elektra in 1985. This contract yielded *Rapture* in 1986, a platinum, Grammy-winning smash selling more than 1,000,000 copies in less than six months.

years before that, he wrote a song that **Eddie Kendricks** from the **Temptations**[17] recorded, which became his last big hit, "Intimate Friends." The problem happened when "Intimate Friends" was later sampled in a song by **Sweet Sable** called "Old Times' Sake," which was included in the *Above the Rim* soundtrack, starring **Tupac Shakur** (2Pac).[18] It became a very big hit again. But by this time (in the 1990s), Garry had passed away. When Sweet Sable's record came out, we noticed that Garry's name was listed as a writer with another person that had nothing do with writing the song, but who had acted as the original music publisher of "Intimate Friends." This publisher had some songs that were getting sampled, but none of them were getting sampled like "Intimate Friends." It was the sample clearance[19] that triggered the whole thing. We had to sue to take that other guy's name off the credits and to get paid for the other half. We finally won the case because the guy couldn't prove that he co-wrote the song. He was trying to take advantage of a dead guy. I suppose he thought nobody would notice, and put his name down as a co-writer. But by the time we were finished with all the appeals and the bankruptcy, ten years had gone by.

Moses: What advice could you give to a songwriter signing a publishing deal to avoid having that happen to them or their heirs?

Ben McLane: You have to be very careful about paperwork and staying on top of things like copyright registrations. Always be in the loop on getting copies of any documentation that is filed or copies of title clearance forms that are sent to BMI [or ASCAP or whoever your performing rights organization is]. You can only do the best you can. Try to put language in your contract where you are as protected as possible and that you receive copies of *everything*.

> Selling Your Vital Organs to Multiple Hospitals

The word "exclusive" exists in most every contract where rights are being bought for a large sum. In recording contracts, artists give rights to their recordings "exclusively" in almost every case. Knowing this, you'd think artists would be very careful about who gets those rights. In many cases, they are not.

Like signing a donor card, an artist's rights are the vital organs of his career. You can't promise the same organ to two hospitals. So it's important to know what the agenda of a particular company is. For example, what if a label intended to keep the act in the minor leagues and trade them up to a major label when one came a-knockin'? Why, you might ask. There are many reasons.

[17] **The Temptations:** Despite financial success and astounding talent (releasing over 35 Top Ten songs including "Papa Was a Rollin' Stone" and "Just My Imagination" and being inducted into the Rock and Roll Hall of Fame in 1989), the group interpersonally had many challenges. They had a rotating lineup of over 20 members. Founding member David Ruffin was fired when he was MIA for a concert in 1968, and he died from a cocaine overdose in 1991. Paul Williams became an alcoholic and committed suicide in 1973.

[18] **Tupac Shakur:** The top-selling rap artist of all time (more than 36 million copies) and one of the inaugural members of the Hip-Hop Hall of Fame (2002). He was engaged to Quincy Jones's daughter when he was killed. Years after his death his label continued to issue "new releases," which were recorded and archived allegedly because he knew that he would die young.

[19] Sample clearance: The license that is required *before* you can commercially distribute a recording containing the sample. Many people skip this step, thinking forgiveness is often easier to get than permission. This used to be the case but has changed of late.

Leslie Zigel has been a presenter at the *Billboard* **Latin Music Conference**, and sits on the Board of Governors for the **Recording Academy** (the company that owns the Grammy awards). He offers this:

Leslie Zigel: One group called [name withheld] had numerous hits in the Latin world and they were barred from signing a new recording agreement with a major. They had signed with an independent label in South America and did not have a lawyer review the contract. This label did nothing for them but prevent them from signing with the majors. The group almost broke up but worked out a deal in the end or they would never have had a career.

Moses: There is actually a famous story of a famous record executive, I wouldn't say which, who actually put out a record of an artist that was signed to another label in America. He said, "Let this other label try to stop us, I don't care." There was a massive lawsuit; he knew he'd lose, but it would take five or six years to lose that case, at which point he would have made his money on the artist. I would think that even with a contract with the label in Colombia that the American label just wouldn't care.

Leslie Zigel: [In most cases] an American label has someone in their legal and business affairs department, and he is not going to intentionally interfere with another contract that is going to cost the label a couple hundred thousand dollars in legal fees. Unless they think it's going to be a Michael Jackson.[20]

Moses: Was this group signed to a Latin label and then got an offer from an American label?

Leslie Zigel: Yes. Eventually they ended up working on a settlement with the former label and getting out of that deal.

Moses: It sounds like this was one of those "happy accidents." Most artists reading this book would say, "That should be my biggest problem, that label A wants me so bad that they have to buy out label B."

Leslie Zigel: I have a different perspective on that. I think it's a major problem if you are the artist. In this case, these guys could not afford to hire a lawyer and they were basically stalled for over two years.

Moses: What do you estimate this mistake cost them in dollars and cents?

Leslie Zigel: It could easily have been a couple hundred thousand dollars.

[20] During a 2004 *60 Minutes* interview, Jackson claimed his new CD was No. 1 in every country except the US; however, *Court TV* reported it was not No. 1 on any *Billboard* chart in any country.

> When It Comes to Law Firms, Size Doesn't Matter

One artist I worked with years back was very excited about the fact that his parents had given him a generous gift, $5,000. The gift did not come in the form of a check but as a fee to a lawyer.

Y'see, his parents wanted to make a contribution to his career, but they were not really comfortable with the idea of buying him a musical instrument or something as vaporous as studio time. Instead, being professionals themselves, they felt the best way to make a contribution to their son's career was to donate to a commodity.

Having a powerful lawyer is a serious commodity. The only reason that every talented musical group doesn't have the best lawyer in town "shopping" their project is because most people cannot afford them. Lawyers in this category generally want about $5,000 as a retainer to cover expenses and then 5 percent of the back end. This leaves out most up-and-coming acts.[21]

This artist's parents, however, could afford it and were willing to do so under the condition that the lawyers be the best. These are not hard to find. There are only a few top firms that represent the big artists, but there are hidden drawbacks.

Paul Menes: Practicing in a small firm as long as I did, there is perception among a lot of artists that if they're famous they have to have a big, famous firm representing them. What they don't realize a lot of times is it is not the firm. It's who the lawyer is in the firm that is representing them. In a big firm, the artist hires a specific attorney and they end up with an associate or newer lawyer a little further down the food chain, who is far less knowledgeable and who really has no clue about issues that recently have gotten to be very important in entertainment law, which are intellectual property issues, copyright, and trademarks. I am appalled when I talk to some of my contemporaries how little they know about intellectual properties and trademarks. It is a very important facet, especially now as label deals are changing. Label deals are more like partnerships with artists than they are traditional sorts of record deals. Labels want a piece of the merchandise and a piece of the touring income and a piece of the publishing before they give a lot of bread to the artist. **Robbie Williams**,[22] signed to **EMI**, is one example; I think his lawyers didn't let him give up ownership of anything. I think what they wound up doing is giving profit participation, which is the way it should be done. Unless you understand those sorts of concepts and the value of intel-

[21] There are lawyers who charge less. While some are a bargain at twice the price, in most cases, keep in mind a basic rule of commerce: you get what you pay for.

[22] Robbie Williams: Big British pop star. Lost a significant copyright dispute in 2000. The dispute centered on how much Ludlow Music, who owned the rights to a 1961 Woody Guthrie song "I Am the Way," should earn for allowing Williams and his record company to borrow ideas from the late US folk singer. Ludlow has earned a reputation for suing over use of Guthrie's material. In 2004, they sued over a parody of "This Land Is Your Land" when Jib Jab, a Web site, used it for a political parody, Guthrie's exact intent when he wrote the song. The matter is still in litigation as of this writing.

lectual property, you could hurt your artist client. When a lot of artists decide that they want some famous entertainment lawyer representing them it is not necessarily a good thing. A lot of huge artists have fired those lawyers and gone elsewhere to a lawyer just as knowledgeable and experienced, but without a good publicist, because the artist realized that they weren't being serviced to their best advantage.

⊙ DIY "Free" Contracts that Can Cost a Fortune

Do you think it's possible for two little words in a contract to end up costing you millions? It's very possible. Do you think you're saving money if you write the contract yourself? Would you fly in an airplane that you built yourself from a kit?

For several years there have been a host of books that offer do-it-yourself contracts. Books with templates to cover just about every situation you're likely to encounter in music. Songwriter agreements, producer engagements, and many more. It seems like an easy way out: why pay a lawyer for something you can get for free?

One company, NoLo Press, who has the most complete library of such books, was sued by the Texas Unauthorized Practice of Law Committee for "practicing law without a license." Despite the fact that NoLo's books have appeared in law libraries, the Committee felt that the publishing of such books was the same as giving legal advice. Texas lost their case on the grounds of the First Amendment— freedom of speech. Can you imagine if they had won? Only lawyers would be able to write books about the law. This would of course leave out all the works of James Madison, the "Father of the Constitution," who was not a lawyer. This chapter could also fall under such standards as I am not a lawyer either.

Lawyers being threatened by DIY contract books is really a myth, because the secret fact is that these books actually create *more* work for lawyers.

Barbara Graham: You end up with a lot of clients in the music business that do [contract] drafts themselves. They are all doing it supposedly to save money. You hate to say to the client, "Look, you can't use this, this [clause] sucks and you need to give me fifteen hundred dollars to redraft this thing." What I do is say, "If I am going to represent you I have to see every single contract that you have and I am going to review each one, and if I tell you we need to redo these contracts we are going to do it."

This will end up costing far more than $1,500 and far more than the cost of the do-it-yourself contract book that the template came from. However, the lawyer really has little choice. It would probably be legal malpractice *not* to do as Barbara Graham suggests. Even the slightest change in language could mean an interpretation that alters the financial picture completely.

Barbara Graham: I had a manager client who brought in four guys that had a lot of potential. This manager was all excited about them and had signed a [DIY contract] with them as *"a group,"* not individually. So, if this group broke up, the members were free to do whatever they wanted. One of them signed a separate production deal after the group broke up which was well-funded by a professional athlete, which meant he got an advance. He was free from the [DIY] contract.

Moses: How much did that end up costing that manager client of yours?

Barbara Graham: Had she signed them with language that said "individually and collectively" instead of just collectively as a group, she would have been getting 20 [percent] of what each guy made. The advance for that production deal was around $100,000, so it cost her around twenty grand, right off the top.

Moses: Two words for twenty grand!

COMMA CHAMELEON
(WITH APOLOGIES TO BOY GEORGE)

How much difference can a single comma make? Observe:

"Woman, without her, man is a beast."

versus

"Woman, without her man, is a beast."

⊘ Conclusion

It would be nice if lawyers really knew as much as they sometimes pretend to know. I use some of the best lawyers in the business and I catch even them trying to sell me an assumption from time to time. I think it's an occupational hazard that comes with the authority that we often empower them with. So a bit of tolerance is in order. But when they screw up it can cost their clients a fortune. In the next chapter, we're going to see how this can hit an artist where it really can hurt forever—their copyrights.

CHAPTER 8

Copyright Con-fiscations

"I have learned throughout my life as a composer chiefly through my mistakes and pursuits of false assumptions, not by my exposure to founts of wisdom and knowledge."
——**Igor Stravinsky, Russian composer in US (1882–1971)**

Song publishing royalties, rather than sales of CDs, are the key to most of the big money in the US music business. It can take several years for a songwriter to figure that out, and during that time big mistakes are often made. Many songwriters I speak to regret being leveraged out of publishing rights early on in their climb to the top.

To those new to the music business, here's a publishing primer: It's common practice for songwriters to give up the copyright of a song to a publishing company. They have the clout and staff to hunt down all the money the writer's song catalog can earn all over the world: movie placements, radio play, Internet streaming, sheet music, halftime performances,[1] even a high school play. In exchange for complete ownership of the copyright, the publishing company usually gives the writer a royalty equal to between 50 percent and 75 percent of the money it collects. (Called the "writer's share." The part the publisher keeps is called the "publisher's share.") In just about every case I've dealt with, the publishing company, as a sign of good faith (and to lure the best writers), will offer an advance that is equal to about half of the prospective money they think the writer's catalog will earn over

[1] Halftime performances as well as radio and airplay money are hunted down and collected by a collection agent called a PRO (performing rights organization, or society). ASCAP and BMI are the two main societies in the US. For this reason a misconception is created that ASCAP and BMI are publishers. They are not. They are vendors to publishers that collect a portion of the money publishers are entitled to from public performances.

the next five years. If they think the writer's catalog will earn about $500,000, then the writer could expect an initial advance of about $250,000.

Up till 2004 the "appropriate" advance for a writer was a fairly easy number to calculate. Especially if the songwriter is also the artist. Because of events triggered by the advent of the Internet (which is the focus of Chapter 10), how much an artist's catalog is worth is now harder to evaluate. But putting that aside, most albums have between 12 and 14 songs on them. Each song is worth about 8 cents for each copy made.[2] If a label was hot for the artist, then a big pressing (about 250,000 copies) can easily be qualified financially (.08 × 14 × 250,000). (There are some other adjustments that I won't go into here.) This does not include the money that will be earned from radio play and other public performances of the song. These could easily be triple.

In the olden days (1930s to 1960s), writers rarely recorded the songs they wrote. That was the job of recording artists. Publishers would shop their song catalogs to record companies and producers in hopes that the artists signed to them would cover the publisher's songs on their next record. When an artist agreed to record a song, the number of pressings planned by the label would heavily influence the size of the publishing advance. If the writer had a track record of writing hits, the advance might be based on all songs they would write over the next five years.

Starting in the mid-1960s it became more normal for record companies to sign songwriters *as* recording artists. This was done mostly because of new legislation that increased the cost of royalties that labels had to pay writers.[3] Most writers secretly (and many not-so-secretly) want to be artists, and many would gladly give up a portion of their royalties in exchange for a chance at fame. Record companies were happy to oblige them.

Over time (about ten years) this cut off the music publishing industry at its knees. The financial power base of publishers weakened because writers were willing to forgo receiving millions in royalties in order to take a shot at having their own careers as performers. The law of averages (and the basic chances of success that are common to this business) being what they are, many did not succeed as artists and because of the deal they made had little to no publishing income to fall back on.[4]

Naturally over time this reduced the value of a publishing catalog. Power shifted to the record labels, who then went to the next step and bought many of the publishing companies for far below their book value. To be more accurate, the corporate entity that owned the record company would also buy several publishing companies and merge them (known as a "roll up"). Thus, we saw things like ABC Records buying XYZ Publishing, changing the name to ABC Publishing. (Fictitious

[2] It's currently 9.1 cents as of this writing and goes up every couple of years. But for reasons too complex to go into here, writers rarely see the entire amount. For details as to why, see my other book, *Secrets of Negotiating a Record Contract.*

[3] Rates for licensing of a song (called statutory rates) increased radically in the 1960s from 2 cents a copy to 6 cents a copy. Record companies were required by law to pay at least this much for each song that appeared on each LP manufactured. (Eight songs on an LP meant paying 48 cents a record instead of the previous rate of 16 cents a record.)

[4] Obvious exceptions are singer/songwriters like James Taylor, Joni Mitchell, Neil Young, Bob Dylan, et al.

names used only for example.) Both would then be owned by ABC Holding Company. For example, **Warner Brothers Records** is owned by the same company that owned **Warner Chappell Publishing**. Et cetera, et cetera.[5]

Holding companies who owned both types of entities—record and publishing companies—were now in a leveraged position.[6] They were already tempting new artist/writers to give up the half of the publishing money they were entitled to as songwriters in exchange for a big advance and a chance at fame as an artist. Now that they owned the publishing entity that the artist/writer was signing the other half of their rights over to, they would make even more money by trying to combine the advances from both publishing and recording to be recouped from just record sales. They did this knowing full well that recouping from record sales is virtually impossible unless you sell millions of units. Most did not.

> *Jay Jay French:* It always kills me because when people read [about big advances] in the press, they have no clue as to how it really nets out. If a band gets a gold record, they really owe the label roughly half a million to a million dollars. If their second album is gold, they owe the label between one and two million dollars. If their third album is gold, they owe the label between two and three million, and so on and so forth—there is no getting around it. Gold just means you owe a shitload of money.... Four gold records means you owe anywhere from three to four million dollars.

By getting the artist/writer to agree to pay back the recording advance out of their *songwriter royalties*, the major labels were giving the artist an extra $1 with one hand while taking $1.25 out of their pocket with the other. The term in the industry is "cross-collateralization," paying back debt A&B from revenue source A only. In this case, virtually impossible for an artist/writer to ever recoup unless they hit the platinum benchmark, which in the US is 1,000,000 copies sold.[7] Thus the skilled negotiator representing the artist had one goal above all others when dealing with record/publishing companies: to keep the revenue streams of both publishing and record sales discrete and pure.

In the old days, writers signed publishing deals because the publisher would hawk, or solicit, their material to the big artists. Now that the songwriters were recording their own material, what exactly was the publishing company doing in exchange for the 50 percent that writers were giving them?

Soon writer/artists began to see that there was little reason to give up *any* of their publishing. They began to form their own publishing companies (simple

[5] Because of the many mergers of publishing companies it can be difficult to find out who owns a copyright to a song you may be interested in licensing. (And then your request goes into a giant pile of paperwork that's uncannily ignored until right after your deadline.) Prior to the advent of the Internet there were companies that specialized in locating copyright holders. Now ASCAP and BMI both have databases that can help narrow the search considerably.

[6] A complete list of who owns what is in the back of *Confessions of a Record Producer*.

[7] Myth buster: A platinum record award for 1,000,000 copies shipped is only done in the US. In other countries the benchmark is far smaller, sometimes as low as 10,000. If you find yourself looking at a wall of gold and platinum record awards, before you get too impressed look carefully to see what country they were issued in. There has been a rumor that record

sales in the US have been so bad in the past few years that the RIAA has considered changing the threshold for gold to 250,000 units.

[8] All money given to an artist by the label is a special type of loan that is called an *advance*. An advance is defined as "prepayment of royalties." The artist must pay back the total debt/advance out of their share of the sales. Once this debt/advance is paid off they can begin seeing royalties. However, record companies are notorious for making that goal impossible to reach with their hidden deductions and adjustments.

[9] The reasons why are complex, but to boil it down simply: labels had inherited many new acts during the merger-rich environment of the mid-1970s to mid-1980s. More new artists means spreading out the releases to give each act's marketing window "breathing room."

DBAs) to publish their own songs. The industry countered by offering large publishing advances. Since, as said above, most artists typically never see royalties from the sale of the record due to the "debt" that they owe their label,[8] giving up a large percentage of one's rights to songs in exchange for a much-needed payday started to make sense again.

Once radio and TV spread across the country en masse, songwriters saw a new revenue stream from the public performances of their songs over the airwaves. One problem for labels: they saw none of this money. Because of the way the copyright laws are practiced in the US, there is no royalty paid to the owner of the sound recording of a song when it's played over the air, only to the songwriter. Thus, managers and producers started leveraging publishing rights from writer/artists as well. Each entity chiseled away at the copyright until in many cases, after all commissions are paid, the writer sees less than ten cents on the dollar.

Many artist/writers decided (usually with the aid of their lawyer or manager) that a bird in the hand is worth two in the bush—take the large publishing advance because the future is uncertain. Also lawyers can make understanding publishing very hard for the artist to the point where they hide behind their own self-destructive cliché: "I'm just the artist, I can't be bothered with the business. I have lawyers for that."

This, however, generally benefited the managers and lawyers more than the artist, as their business model lends itself more to upfront commissions than back-end, wait-and-see prospects. In other words, by the time artists realized that they had been taken advantage of by the very people they trusted, it was far, far too late.

Jay Jay French: The biggest mistake is to not care about your business. I hear musicians say, "Oh, I'm not worried about that. Whatever happens, happens." My God, [the industry] loves you for that, and because you are a musician and an artist the chances are that you are dysfunctional enough to not care. Basically, you just get screwed.

Other artist/writers rebelled against this philosophy, keeping their publishing rights intact. They thought they could do a better job of brokering the copyrights themselves. This, as we'll see, can have its drawbacks too.

This should give you a basic understanding of the complex dynamics of publishing and why everybody's so damn greedy for a piece. The stories below reveal how a lack of understanding about all of this could be the downfall of even the biggest artist. If the few pages you've just read existed 30 years ago, most of the stories below would not have. Let's start with one of the most famous examples, the **Billy Joel** story as told by **André Fischer**.

⊘ Breaking the Most Successful Songwriter in History: The Billy Joel Story

André Fischer: To the best of my recollection, during the time when Joel wrote his first couple of hits he was involved with **Artie Ripp**, who was helping him with his music and handled his business dealings as well. He signed a large percentage of the publishing over to Ripp, who convinced him that he was there to help.

Rather than sign a typical publishing deal and management contract—20 percent of revenue—with Ripp, Joel signed a deal which included rights to about 20 percent of the copyrights for all songs he created over the length of the recording contract—eight albums. At that time, artists typically did about an album a year. The length of the deal would have been about eight years in Joel's mind. Every artist signs overreaching deals in the beginning of their career. The expectation is that if and when they make it, several years later, they will be in a better negotiating position, but things were changing in the industry and the time between album releases began to spread apart to roughly 15 to 24 months.[9] Thus an eight-album contract easily spread from 1971 to 1987, during which time virtually all Joel's most famous songs were written and released: "Piano Man," "The Entertainer," "Last of the Big Time Spenders," "The Ballad of Billy the Kid," "New York State of Mind," "Captain Jack," "Stranger," "Scenes from an Italian Restaurant," "Only the Good Die Young," "My Life," "Big Shot," "Honesty," "You May Be Right," "It's Still Rock 'n' Roll to Me," "Don't Ask Me Why," "Sometimes a Fantasy," "Under Pressure," "Allentown," "Uptown Girl," "Tell Her About It," "An Innocent Man," "Keeping the Faith" and, last but not least, "I Love You Just the Way You Are"—still one of the most popular songs ever recorded.[10]

André Fischer: What happened is common knowledge in the musician and songwriter community, that instead of making a publishing deal for the songs contained in the upcoming album [which would limit the amount of the catalog that Ripp would control and would have been more standard], he made a deal for

[10] Billy Joel did not have a hit off of his first record, *Cold Spring Harbor* (though "She's Got a Way" became a hit after the fact) in 1971. His second record, *Piano Man*, had "Piano Man" as a semi-hit, hitting No. 25 in 1974. The album went to No. 27. The third record, *Streetlife Serenade,* also had another semi-hit with "The Entertainer," which hit No. 34 in early 1975. The album went to No. 35. The fourth record, *Turnstiles*, produced no hits in 1976 and never charted. The fifth record, *The Stranger*, was the breakthrough which produced "Just the Way You Are," which went to No. 3 in early 1978, was a gold single, and won the Grammy for Record of the Year. This happened seven years after his first record was released. The album went to No. 2 and has been certified 9x platinum.

all of the songs he would write in a certain time frame. When [Joel] did become successful and he became better informed that his contract was taking advantage of him, it was too late.

Interesting conflict to learn from here: personal service contracts work on a time frame—an artist owes money to a manager for, say, five years. At the end of the term there is a *sunset period*, where the manager can earn a diminished percentage for a few years after they are released from service. But publishing contracts are based on specific titles for which you grant rights, sometimes *forever*. A publishing company might get the rights to "Piano Man" for the entire life of the copyright (about 100 years in some cases).[11] Record deals are almost identical, but instead of songs, they acquire rights to *master recordings* that you record during an "option period."[12] All of these methods of who owns what and for how long can start to overlap in unpredictable ways. No new artist (or manager, for that matter) ever realizes this until years later.

> *André Fischer:* After five years you know just enough to be confused and you've had just enough success to want to keep it going, yet you really don't know how. Five years is not a long time because it takes at least two years to really [get paid] from [record/publishing sales] or the total success of your touring and of your airplay. A lot of things can happen in five years; you can be very successful or you can have one album that was very successful and here you are trying to duplicate yourself.

Joel could not have predicted his stellar long-term appeal, especially in his day, when the lifespan of the average *successful* recording artist's career was about five years. He was almost flat broke at the time he signed with Ripp and couldn't count five months down the road, let alone five years. And because he didn't do a typical personal service agreement with Ripp, which should have been based on a fixed period of time but instead granted a percentage of *all* his songs' copyrights he created during the length of the recording contract (15 years), he ended up giving away far more money than he had to on many of his early hits.

Cost?

Well, let's do some basic assumptions.

In Joel's first five years he penned, and made successful, five songs.[13] If each earned him $1,000,000 in publishing dollars a year (conservative) and he came out with one hit a year, he would have earned $15,000,000 accumulated gross over five years, just from publishing. Had he signed a manager's deal that paid about 20 percent for five years he would owe to the manager only 20 percent for the first five years from the publishing revenue, or $3,000,000.

However, using the same assumptions, the deal he *did* sign ended up costing him 20 percent of the gross over 15 years—$120,000,000—or $24,000,000.

Note: These numbers are probably low.

Withholding Material

> *André Fischer:* One of the mistakes was that some of the decisions you make before becoming successful catch up with you.... Billy would write songs [while] in the studio. [So] he would record whatever [he'd written] in that time frame.

It's common for a publishing contract to cover songs written in a given time period. Joel's write-as-you-record method created a scenario whereby he was creating copyrights controlled by the publisher, whose sound recordings were simultaneously controlled by the record company. In other words, he was providing content for both his record company and his publishing company *at the same time*.[14] This compounded the "Ripp effect." Since then, lawyers have learned that it's better *not* to write songs for an album *while* you're recording it. However, as any artist will tell you, it happens all the time. What should one do?

One of my legal specialists, speaking anonymously, said this: "No lawyer will admit it because many [lawyers who rep artists] also work for the labels and publishers, but I know for a fact that many will tell their clients to 'withhold' material."

By this he means that if an artist comes up with a new song while in the studio recording an album of already approved material, it could be a problem. Since most every contract states that the label owns the "first rights" to release anything written in the recording sessions, the artist should lie and say they wrote it sometime outside of the time frame of that option period or not let anyone know that he wrote it at all. Sing it only in a room of people whom he trusts.

Of course, with this attitude and the effect large amounts of new money have on the human psyche, the number of people he trusts will begin to diminish. The practice can become so common that it creates an environment where co-writers within a group will lie to each other about who wrote what and when. It's a horrendous position to put a creative team into. It stifles the process, turns everybody into lawyers, and destroys trust. Yet, because of cases like Billy Joel's, it's done every day.

[14] These days most of the material that appears on a commercial album is written before the artist goes into a professional recording situation.

◉ A Work-Around for a Bad Publishing Deal

Had **Billy Joel** spoken with **André Fischer** anytime during the tenure of his "bad deal" he would have heard a dazzling piece of "work-around" advice that could have saved him millions. In this segment, Fischer tells how he and other members of the '70s–'80s funk group **Rufus**[15] were left with less than 25 cents on the dollar from their publishing, and how they took it back.

[15] One of the most commercially successful funk groups of the 1970s.

[16] Chaka Khan: Real name, Yvette Marie Stevens. Her solo career yielded a significant hit, "I Feel for You." Winner of seven Grammys.

André Fischer: When **Rufus featuring Chaka Khan**[16] first signed to **ABC Dunhill Records** for a recording contract, we also signed a publishing contract to ABC Dunhill *Publishing*. At the time we were told that it was to get them to commit to two financial areas: one, an advance for the album, and two, an advance for the publishing, and the publishing should only be used as barter.

ABC Dunhill Publishing in the 1970s offered them their standard deal of the day, which was to take about 75 percent of the song's copyrights after 10 percent administrative costs. This left the writers with only 22.5 cents on the dollar. However, it's important to understand that *only* the members of Rufus were bound to this arrangement.

André Fischer: So, on purpose we start writing songs with other people [outside the group], or there were folks [outside the group] that maybe didn't have direct input [into the songs] but their names were listed [as writers] anyway.

Since those "co-writers" are not part of the covenant created with the publishing entity, they get to keep their shares completely. Example: André writes a song, ABC Dunhill Publishing gets 100 percent of the entire song. But if André and Joe Blow (who is not part of the deal) write a song, then ABC Dunhill Publishing only gets 100 percent of André's half of the song. The other 50 percent remains Joe Blow's.

André Fischer: We then formed [our own] publishing company with [the name] Rufus spelled backwards [**Sufur**]. We had other "writers" that would "write" within [Sufur] so that ABC [Dunhill Publishing] didn't get their share of the songs. It doesn't get you out of your bad deal [but] it stops them from taking all of your money.

ABC Dunhill Publishing took the entire publishing share, which is fifty cents on the dollar, and split the writer's share (the remaining 50 percent minus administrative fees) with Rufus, leaving them with a quarter of the copyright. But once Rufus created Sufur, the writer's share and the publishing share of the Sufur portion fell outside of the Rufus/ABC Dunhill deal. This meant that Fischer and Co. (aka Rufus) were able to "take back" about 50 percent of their publishing and turn a deal where they were getting only 22.5 cents on the dollar into one where they now were getting about 67 cents on the dollar. It pays to have friends you can trust.

⊘ When "Nonessential Members" Get Cut Out of the Deal

The example above shows how a good understanding of publishing, complete band cooperation, and some clever lawyering can provide a solution to game the system. In many situations people get a bit greedy about publishing and it ends up screwing everyone. This happens for several reasons, but most of them revolve around facts little known to the public: the band, group, or artist that you see on the album cover is *not* really the legal entity that owns the name.

Usually when a label signs an act with several players, they quickly separate the wheat from the chaff. The label/publisher knows that the songwriter is the most valuable member; second is the lead singer. If the bass player only plays bass and doesn't write the songs he's fairly expendable unless his style is unique.

Often, when an amateur group is about to go pro and a deal is on the table, lawyers create corporate entities that are the legal partnership that makes up the "band." It usually consists of just the irreplaceable members. They are the ones who sign the actual recording contract with the label. The other members (usually the rhythm section) are then signed to an exclusive agreement to "perform" for the artist's corporate entity. Hard pill to swallow when you're a player that's been sweating it out for several years with a group playing the same crappy bars that the singer has. Now he's the center of attention, and you're an "employee." (See "Sleuth Operator" later in this chapter for more on this.)

Jay Jay French: If a band doesn't understand how publishing works and you've got one writer in the band, then you've got yourself a problem. I think if there is a sole writer, or if there are two writers in the band, they owe it to themselves to give

[17] **Lennon-McCart-ney:** Although most of the 150 or so Beatles songs are attributed to Lennon-McCartney, they actually only collaborated on 27 songs according to unauthorized biographies. A staunch animal rights activist, McCartney blocked the showing of *Beatles Anthology* on Italian television because they carry ads of animal-derived products. Mistakes: one of his charities, War Child, has been accused of financial irregularities. Years earlier (1973) he was fined £100 for growing marijuana on his Scotland farm and years later he was sent to a Japanese prison for possession of marijuana.

[18] **Ringo Starr:** Real name Richard Starkey, drummer for the Beatles. Although he is revered as one of the greatest rock drummers ever, rumor has it that he did not play drums—only tambourine—on the first three Beatles singles. His unique way of expressing himself contributed to the Beatles.

and **McCartney**[17] gave publishing to **Ringo**.[18] Five percent, I think.

Moses: Do you think that's a good template for bands to follow in general?

Jay Jay French: That's where you make your money, controlling of copyrights. Buying and owning copyrights under your publishing company. That's where you make the bulk of your money in this business. In my band Dee[19] wrote, and I understood that. He was the writer and he kept the publishing. I understood it so I wasn't surprised. I already knew what that was about.

While the writer sees literally millions a year from the publishing of songs, band members who do not write (or have no publishing) get money only from the sale of albums and every now and then when a recording gets used in a film. It's hard to put a dollar figure on this, but a fair ratio might be about 60:1. Meaning that for every $60 of publishing money earned by the song's writers, the nonwriting members of the group, who see money solely from the master recording exploitation, get about a dollar.[20]

Moses: Did you think that was fair?

Jay Jay French: The fact is that these recordings are the gifts that keep on giving. Because he wrote these songs [that became hits], because these songs are in movies and soundtracks, the band consistently gets licensing money.[21] We are very fortunate that way. It never occurred to me that it was unfair.

Moses: If you were counseling a band who had a similar configuration to **Twisted Sister**, and one guy was doing the writing but the other three guys were together for four or five years, would you counsel that writer to share his publishing?

Jay Jay French: I always advise bands in that situation to do that. I always say, you gotta address the issue.

Sleuth Operator

Paul Cooke was the drummer for the '80s pop star **Sade**, whose hit "Smooth Operator" stayed on the charts for a milestone 81 weeks. He didn't sign any copyright forms or any band agreements. He didn't receive any writer's credit. He didn't write the songs in the traditional sense. After leaving the band he learned that he was entitled to royalties and sued Sade and **Sony Records** (England).

Paul Cooke: I was suing on the basis that it was a partnership initially when I was a member of the band. I should have received writing credits.

The irony is he should have won millions in back royalties, and in the US he probably would have, but because of a technicality in British law he ended up getting nothing.

Paul Cooke: When we started out we were all going to get signed as a band. All five of us. We all went to the studio and recorded *Diamond Life,* the first **Sade** album. That album contained "Smooth Operator." I did all the drum tracks. Sade was signed [without us] to **CBS** after recording the album. These were songs that we spent two years developing. Then we had a meeting with the manager and he said, "Look, the singer is going to sign a contract on her own and that's that. You guys are going to be in the band, but she is going to be signed to the record deal."

Moses: So, then you left the band?

Paul Cooke: I was actually sacked because I just wasn't happy with the deal. I didn't want to be just a "side player." What happened from the beginning was that we formed this partnership. There was no written agreement. It was more or less one of these verbal situations where we created the band "Sade" and the manager of the band held all of the money.

Moses: I don't know about England, but in the United States if there is no written agreement between members I believe the common law is that everything is split equally. Is that the law in England?

Paul Cooke: Not necessarily, no.

Moses: What enlightened you to realize you had a claim?

Paul Cooke: I had established my own publishing company in the early '90s, and I got to understand publishing. I made some inquiry to PRS (Performing Rights Society) that triggered this process of going to solicitors and saying, "Do I have a claim on the basis that it was a partnership?" He thought I was entitled to royalties and we went ahead.

Moses: Even though you were just the drummer?

Paul Cooke: Yeah. We based some stuff on the **Morrissey** case.[22] Five years later we got Queen's Counsel [23] on it. We were using public money [legal aid] to fight the case. We got **Elton John**'s drummer (Mr. Morgan) as the expert witness to assess the music and my contribution [as a drummer]. All the witnesses said that I played on the record. So based on those statements they couldn't argue the fact that I had not performed. There was substantial proof.

Alas, the case never went to the high court. All of the evidence pointed to the fact that they did have a claim, but the next stage was going to cost them over

Phrases of his became song titles like "It's a Hard Day's Night" and "Eight Days a Week."

[19] Dee Snider, lead singer of Twisted Sister. He once used a chainsaw to scare and chase away a guy who tried to damage his mailbox. He became enraged when a Toronto DJ asked him if he surfed the Internet to make himself feel young.

[20] In Europe this ratio would be much different, more like 10:4 due to the difference in copyright laws.

[21] Master licenses are the licenses that a movie producer buys from the record company for the right to use a recording in a movie. Typically a hit can go for anywhere from $50,000 to $5,000,000 depending on the use. This money is supposed to be split 50/50 between artist and label, but the label often keeps the artist's share, saying that the artist owes the label money. Bigger artists have more leverage on this issue.

22 **Morrissey case:**
Morrissey mem-
bers had a prior
band called the
Smiths. On the
basis of that writ-
ten collective
agreement the
drummer should
have been paid
songwriting royal-
ties.

23 **Queen's Counsel:**
In England when
using public money
you get a solicitor
who does the ac-
tual legal research
and assembles the
case (a paralegal in
the US). A barrister
is the person who
represents you in
court (attorney in
the US), and if it
goes to the higher
court then you're
assigned a more
high-level attorney,
called a Queen's
Counsel, who's
sort of a super-
barrister.

100,000 pounds in public money and they had already spent 30,000. Part of the QC's job is to assess whether or not the case is worth the expenditure, since the expectation is that the public money will be paid back out of the proceeds of a successful suit. In this case the QC didn't see the upside.

Paul Cooke: He suggested that we wouldn't be successful because of the delay in bringing the case.

Moses: In other words, you waited too long?

Paul Cooke: Because of the delay there was no worth in it because all of the money from the album had generated income in the first five years and it had all been spent. Because the album is not selling a great deal anymore there wasn't any worth in the case.

Moses: If you won the case would you have gotten back-royalties?

Paul Cooke: No, I wouldn't. Under English law I could only go back six years. The six years that I could go back, the album wasn't selling anything anymore.

Drummers don't usually get songwriting royalties; however, in a case like this in the US, Paul probably would have "won" his case. I put the word "won" in quotes, because the case would probably never have been decided by a judge or jury, but he would have been paid a nice sum to relinquish his claim.

Andy Wickett vs. Duran Duran: The Story of "Girls on Film"

Andy Wickett played keys in the early days of the British pop sensation **Duran Duran.** No one disputes this.

Andy Wickett: Before, I was in the band called **TV Eye.** We were named after an **Iggy Pop** song. **Nick Rhodes** used to come and tape our band. He was fond of the way we looked and our music and everything. Eventually I left TV Eye and joined **Duran Duran** as a vocalist, singer, and keyboardist. One night I wrote this song called "Girls on Film." We did a demo of the song, me, Nigel, Nick Rhodes, and John. **Simon [Le Bon]** wasn't in the band then. **Bob Lamb,** who produced **UB40,** produced the demo. A few weeks later I was told that guys from **EMI** really loved it. They said they would sign the band if they had any more songs like "Girls on Film." I did another song called "Stevie's Radio Station"; they changed some of the words and called it "Rio." My girlfriend (who was managing the band) and I fell out and she started seeing Nick. I left the band and they still had this demo from me. They offered me 200 quid at first, and eventually offered me 600 quid [about $1,000 in 1983]. [In 1981] I signed this paper and I had no further rights to Duran Duran *or any of their material.* The solicitor advised me to sign it. He said, "If you sign it, it proves that you have an interest in the material and once you sign it you'll be able to take them to court."

Moses: Could you have sued him for malpractice?

Andy Wickett: Well, I think you'll find the lawyers in this country [in Birmingham] don't like to go against other lawyers.

Moses: What did he charge you for this advice?

Andy Wickett: I was on legal aid.

Moses: When did you realize you made a bad decision?

Andy Wickett: When I heard the final version they had changed the words in the verses, but I wrote the whole melody, music, and hook to "Girls on Film." My name wasn't on it. I knew I had been fucked. I went back to the solicitor and he wouldn't go to court. He wasn't a music business solicitor; I had used him before for a real estate matter.

I'm sure that lawyers reading this are now falling off their chairs. The lawyer's logic (according to Andy) was that if he signed the release (giving up *all* rights) then it would create a paper trail to Duran Duran, and therefore they would not be able to claim later that he had nothing to do with the recordings. Daft, at best. In retrospect Andy should have brought the contract to a proper attorney who would have at least negotiated a proper publishing deal. Had this happened, and Andy retained even half the profits from "Girls on Film" and "Rio," a conservative estimate of his earnings would been about $3,000,000 American instead of 600 quid.

All is not lost. Andy Wickett does retain rights to the original demo and sells it on his Web site for $10: *www.andywickett.pwp.blueyonder.co.uk*, where you can also see the release he signed in 1981.

Black Lab Rat

In my experience, **Jay Jay French**'s enlightened understating of sharing publishing (told earlier) is not the norm. **Jim Barber**, former **Geffen** exec and manager of several big acts, including **Courtney Love** and **Ryan Adams**, tells us the story of **Black Lab**, a mid-'90s rock group that had it all and lost it because, in the end, the lead writer decided that compensating a band member whose unique sound gave the band its appeal wasn't important.

24 Make its numbers:
Means that the
record company
needed to sell a
minimum amount
in order to meet
corporate expecta-
tions.

25 Chasing the
record: Pushing it
to radio stations.

26 Seagram's
Liquors, the com-
pany that was
looking to buy
PolyGram's parent
company, Universal
Music, and eventu-
ally did in 1999 for
$10.4 billion.

27 Some of these
executives went
on to manage
other labels, one
of which was
Madonna's label,
Maverick. Under
their leadership
Maverick imploded
in 2004.

28 The merger of
PolyGram Records
into Universal,
which resulted in
the creation of the
Interscope/Def
Jam Records
Group in 1998.

29 The owner of
Interscope at the
time was Ted Field:
real name, Freder-
ick Woodruff Field,
heir to the Marshall
Field department
store fortune
(gratuitous bit of
gossip).

Jim Barber: Black Lab was originally a band that was started by singer/song-writer **Paul Durham**, who brought in outside musicians. The album sold about 200,000 copies, but that wasn't enough. It was a classic case where a couple of other groups [on the label] weren't as successful as hoped and the label was try-ing to make its numbers.[24] They chased the record,[25] but because there wasn't enough of a foundation laid the album stalled. **Geffen Records** blew it because they were trying to meet the spreadsheet for Seagram[26] instead of sticking to the record business they had been in for the last 20 years.[27]

Moses: What could the band do about it?

Jim Barber: Nothing. They were complete victims. The **Polygram/Universal** merger happened,[28] and they were a band that I tried to help, but **Interscope**[29] didn't like them and they got dropped.

Black Lab then got picked up again by competing label **Epic**. Here's where the Publishing Dragon began to rear its head. Remember, the band, from a legal point of view, is *only the singer.* The rest are technically "employees." Ones who, by now, are starting to figure out that the writer many times more than the rest of the band, due to money he earns from radio play.

Jim Barber: After they signed to Epic there was a dispute about what the song split should be on the new material. Paul, the lead singer [who is also the writer], had a really rich publishing deal with **EMI Music**. I think that the EMI contract Paul had signed specified that he had to have a certain percentage of the copyrights of the album, but the sound of the band really depended on the weird effects and soulful playing of the [hired] guitarist [**Michael Belfer**], who technically didn't write any songs. The new manager sided with Paul, and Michael felt like he was being mistreated.

This is very common, both for publishers and managers. Most publishing deals of that day and still today depend on the songwriter getting "placements" on records: for example, ten placements over five years. In this typical case, the group's writer was under a lot of pressure to satisfy the terms of his publishing deal, which put him in direct conflict with the ethics of being in a band.

Jim Barber: What the guitar player was looking for was his cut of the songs [writer's share], which *wouldn't* have allowed Paul to fulfill his requirements under his publishing deal.

Paul giving away some of the song's publishing would dilute his writer's share significantly and affect the economics of repaying his publishing advance. A co-written song doesn't count as a full "placement," only "half-placement." If you don't get enough placements, it takes far longer to pay back your advance and you sometimes have to give back a portion. After all, the publishing company only makes money if they can collect royalties from the sale of songs *on records*. If you don't get songs on records, they're screwed.

Moses: How do you boil this down into a mistake?

Jim Barber: The mistake was that neither the [label execs] nor the manager had the sense to come in and broker a deal. You are in a situation where you are having a conflict over publishing and the solution is to figure out a way to either convince the guitar player that this is the way things have to be and make him feel like he's important, or cut a deal with him so that he sticks around. What they decided is that the guitar player is not that important. He quit the band. The band managed to record a song that got on the *Spiderman* soundtrack, but the album that they completed for Epic was sort of session players and random people that got brought in, and the label never released it.

Moses: Who do you think is responsible?

Jim Barber: I think it is always the A&R person's job to know what is going on within the band, but it is absolutely the manager's job more than anyone else. If I was still involved as the producer I would have solved the problem. Maybe you could sign the guitar player to his own publishing deal. There are ways to fix it and it never got fixed. You dump the guitar player, you lose the chemistry and the sound of the band, and they are never able to make a record that captures what got them signed in the first place. It's a heartbreaking story.

If they had followed Jay Jay and Jim's advice, all band members would share everything equally no matter who wrote what in the interest of band harmony. It's what many big acts, like **U2** and **R.E.M.**, do to avoid the inevitable hassles of who wrote what and who is entitled to what, but it doesn't always work out for the best either. Behold the story of **Susan Gibson** and how she lost 75 percent of the money from the song she wrote, a little ditty called "Wide Open Spaces." (One of my personal favorites, I might add.)

Dixie Schtick (A Cautionary Tale on How to Structure a Band Partnership Agreement and Not Give Away the Farm)

In 2004, the **Dixie Chicks** were one of the hottest acts in the world. But before they erupted with several crossover country hits, they were desperately looking for good material. They didn't write their own songs. When the Dixie Chicks first got signed to **Sony** they were a low-priority act on **Monument**, which was a little-recognized imprint of Sony. And then along came Susan.

Ben McLane: **Susan Gibson** was in an Americana band from Texas, just playing local beer joints and stuff. She originally wrote "Wide Open Spaces" for her band the **Groobees**. It turned out that the local guy doing their demos was the father of the new singer from the Dixie Chicks [**Natalie Maines**]. She had just joined the band when they got signed to Sony and were looking for songs. The Groobees played some of their songs for him and he was like, "Wow." It ended up being [the Dixie Chicks'] biggest hit.

It seems like party time. Except…

Ben McLane: The partnership agreement for the Groobees stated everybody in the band shared everything equally because the band members were all equals when the band began. However, Susan wrote that song 100 percent by herself and the band never did anything with it. But once the big money started coming in she had to split it equally. Of course the Groobees eventually broke up, and that was the opposite to the whole point and intent of the partnership agreement—that they were all working as a unit. Millions of dollars were generated on that song, and she could have, theoretically, kept all of it. Of course, there was a lot of fighting about that and I kind of got in the middle of it, because I was representing the band and everybody was at odds. The partnership agreement was in existence before I started to work for the band, but it underscores that you have to be really careful about how you structure those band/partnership agreements.

❯ The Risks of Keeping the Publishing for Yourself

In each case above we saw people being forced into publishing deals that didn't serve them well. It begs the question, why give the publishing rights away at all?

Can it be worth the advance? Many writers started heeding the advice that had become popular in the early '80s, "Never give up your publishing." This can have bad results as well. **Joey Akles**, author of a number of hit records, laments not giving his publishing away on some songs.

Joey Akles: I owned a couple of reasonable-sized records as my own publisher. I was offered publishing deals on them and turned them down to hold my own publishing. Not being an artist, I have never made a dime on the things I've controlled. On the songs that I sold to publishing companies, I am making a living.

Moses: The moral of the story is, 50 percent of something is better than 100 percent of nothing?

Joey Akles: Absolutely. I disagree with the DIY idea. There is a really bad bit of advice that generally goes around unchallenged at industry educational seminars and lectures. Hold your publishing? Bullshit. Now if you are Bob Dylan, of course, because you'll find a lawyer to administer. They know the songs and they'll cover them and put them in movies. I've got seven copyrights that are owned by major publishing companies. Most of it is through Peer Music and I make a living from it. I kept two or three copyrights that were nice records in their day, and no one has ever paid attention to them again. But I have never seen a dime from the songs I kept on my own publishing company, even through BMI.

The DIY Thing

Recently the DIY (do it yourself) movement has become rather avant-garde, with DIY conferences and magazines. However, Joey's point is well taken. You still need companies to help administrate and you still need lawyers to facilitate. So, if you *can't* really "do it yourself," what does DIY really mean? Do it without a label? (DIWL?) One Los Angeles music journalist, who would not allow his name to be connected with this quote, has this to say:

L.A. Journalist: It seems that the concept of DIY is targeted at a group of artists/writers who feel their product is not mainstream. DIY makes them feel like they are part of something "independent." It touts as its hero **Ani DiFranco**.[30] I'd be willing to bet not one person who attends these "conferences"—if you can really call them that—has been to [DiFranco's] Web site and read her own words about how little money she's made. Her determination is admirable, and what she's given back to her community is inescapable, but it's nothing for urban musos to use as a business model. She herself claims she's enjoying "modest

[30] Ani DiFranco released her records through her own indie label, Righteous Babe Records, and steadily built a devout grassroots following on the strength of touring. An ardent feminist and an open bisexual, her songs tackled issues like rape, abortion, and sexism. She is responsible for the restoration of an architectural building in Buffalo and galvanizing its arts scene.

profits." I know how she pays her people. Most live as modestly as students. Her model only works because in Buffalo you can buy and renovate an office building with earnings from an independent release. You can have a small staff because you're only paying them meagerly—and they're probably going to be happy about it. Try doing this in L.A. or New York and you'll quickly see that the model has lo mein[31] for legs. Packaging a conference that sells and profits off the idea that this model is easily possible in a large urban area the way the DIY fad does, is a ruse, plain and simple.

My own opinion is not as extreme, but I sympathize with this journalist. The "DiFranco Model" makes sense if your music is so un-mainstream that you have no choice but to do the DIY thing. To aspire to her model as an ultimate level of success might be setting your sights a bit prematurely low. Many believe that with the Internet affording many new opportunities there will emerge a new business model that will break an artist on a mass scale using the DIY religion. This was being said in 1998 when *Confessions of a Record Producer*[32] came out, and I was criticized for my Doubting Thomas attitude toward how significant the Internet

[31] Lo mein: Chinese noodles. Legend has it that world traveler Marco Polo stole the idea in 1296 and brought it back to Italy where it was renamed spaghetti. Virtually all facts about his life are anecdotal.

[32] *Confessions of a Record Producer*: Currently in its third edition and on the reading list of over 25 schools that have music business programs.

EXCERPT FROM ANI DIFRANCO'S "OPEN LETTER"

Posted in 1997 on her site at http://www.columbia.edu/~marg/ani/. (DiFranco's current site, http://www.righteousbabe.com/ani, does not contain the letter.)

Firstly, this "Hootie and the Blowfish" business was not my doing. The *L.A. Times* financial section wrote an article about my record label, Righteous Babe Records, in which they raved about the business savvy of a singer (me) who thwarted the corporate overhead by choosing to remain independent, thereby pocketing $4.25 per unit, as opposed to the $1.25 made by Hootie or the $2.00 made by Michael Jackson. This story was then picked up and reprinted by the *New York Times*, *Forbes* magazine, the Financial News Network, and (lo and behold) *Ms.*

So here I am, publicly morphing into some kinda Fortune 500-young-entrepreneur-from-hell, and all along I thought I was just a folksinger!

Ok, it's true. I do make a much larger profit (percentage-wise) than the Hootster. What's even more astounding is that there are thousands of musicians out there who make an even higher profit percentage than me! How many local musicians are there in your community who play gigs in bars and coffee shops about town? I bet lots of them have made cassettes or CDs which they'll happily sell to you with a personal smile from the edge of the stage or back at the bar after their set. Would you believe these shrewd, profit-minded wheeler-dealers are pocketing a whopping *100 percent* of the profits on the sales of those puppies?! Wait till the Financial News Network gets a whiff of *them*!

I sell approximately 2.5 percent of the albums that a Joan Jewelanis Morisette sells and get about .05 percent of the airplay royalties, so obviously if it all comes down to dollars and cents, I've led a wholly unremarkable life. Yet I choose relative statistical mediocrity over fame and fortune because I have a bigger purpose in mind. Imagine how strange it must be for a girl who has spent 10 years fighting as hard as she could against the lure of the corporate carrot and the almighty forces of capital, only to be eventually recognized by the power structure as a business pioneer.

I have indeed sold enough records to open a small office on the half-abandoned main street in the dilapidated urban center of my hometown, Buffalo, N.Y. I am able to hire 15 or so folks to run and constantly reinvent the place while I drive around and play music for people. I am able to give stimulating business to local printers and manufacturers and to employ the services of independent distributors, promoters, booking agents and publicists. I was able to quit my day job and devote myself to what I love.

And yes, we are enjoying modest profits these days, affording us the opportunity to reinvest in innumerable political and artistic endeavors. RBR is no Warner Bros. But it is a going concern, and for me, it is a vehicle for redefining the relationship between art and commerce in my own life. It is a record company which is the product not just of my own imagination, but that of my friend and manager Scot Fisher and of all the people who work there. People who incorporate and coordinate politics, art and media every day into a people-friendly, sub-corporate, woman-informed, queer-happy small business that puts music before rock stardom and ideology before profit.

will be in this regard. It's over seven years now, and I'm still in the black on this pre-diction, so maybe I'll be on target with this next one: If the Internet is used as a module to break an artist on a mass scale before this book goes into its second printing, I'll be shocked. But on an indie level the Internet is an invaluable market-ing tool that is maturing every day.

I know it will happen someday, but that day is not so close to the present that one should plan a career around it. The artist who wants to make money off of hot songs will still need the cooperation of larger corporate entities who have the re-sources to track and administrate the income. Thus, the old mantra "don't give up your publishing" can now be amended: "Don't give up your publishing… unless its makes sense."

❯ The New Way to Think About Publishing Rights

Doug Breitbart: Publishing companies today are like Swiss banks. They are not playing a proactive role in helping to break material, and in this country they do al-most nothing. At least in Europe and Japan they make more money than they do here, but they are responsible for promoting and breaking the music. In Japan they buy radio spins. In Germany they kick up the promotion dollars for TV.

This next person we're to hear from has a radical approach. One of the people who I truly feel knows more about the future of music publishing than perhaps anyone in the business. He's on the inside track of most of the new legislation and his company is positioned in such a way that he knows just about everything there is to know about how performance licensing really works. Unfortunately he will not go on the record.

Warning: Much of what follows may be over the head of someone who does not understand how PROs and blanket licensing of music works. I've done my best to reinterpret "X Bot's" comments into layman's language, but rather than try to rewrite his words (which I consider valuable) I suggest that if this is too advanced for you, that you find a lawyer or manager who can explain it in person.

X Bot: These days there is really no reason for a writer signed to a major label as an artist to deal with a publisher. Maintain your own rights.

Moses: The common seduction is usually a large advance. Which at the beginning of a career can seem like a bird in the hand.

X Bot: That used to be, not anymore. Where do you get large advances from publishing? How many people actually get that?

Moses: Do you think publishers are getting burned on large advances?

X Bot: Record companies are guaranteeing less and publishers get advances based on certain records' commitments.[33]

To clarify and expand a bit on what X Bot means, when a record company signs a new artist and is planning on pressing a million units as a first printing, that's a cue for a publisher to get in on the action, offer a big advance against those anticipated sales. However, these days, due to a number of factors (the RIAA blames peer-to-peer file sharing), the amount of units being accepted by record stores on a new artist is far less than before. Stores don't want to stock large amounts of a potential flop. It takes up too much space in their basement. So less consignment means less printing. Less printing means less potential publishing dollars (since the bulk of publishing money was once based off of unit sales), which means lower advances.

X Bot: More and more artists simply want more control over their careers. In that case, why give up half of your income? I couldn't advise anybody to do that anymore.

Moses: What would you advise an artist to do in lieu of signing a traditional publishing deal?

X Bot: Own their own rights.

Moses: Let's say you don't have the facility to track down all of the money and do all of these deals. What would you suggest they do?

X Bot: The first deals you are going to do are going to be with your own label. What is there to track down? You make a deal with ASCAP and BMI and if you have any success you do direct deals in foreign territories and wait to see what happens. If you are having any success there are lawyers you can hire to do publishing deals or become direct members of foreign [performing rights] societies. That's going to sound esoteric, because most lawyers don't know that you can do that. If I were advising somebody I would tell them to deal with ASCAP or BMI for the US *only*; collect your own mechanicals. If you are going to have any foreign distribution, become a member of SACEM[34] for France, maybe MCPF. Maybe a couple of other societies. It is administratively a pain in the ass, but ultimately you are a lot better off.

[33] Korn just inked a deal worth about $14 million, a lot of which was publishing.

[34] The SACEM is the French [version of] ASCAP.

X Bot is not understating this point: Registering with about two dozen performing rights organizations around the world and keeping track with each of them is a full-time job that most songwriters don't want. A publishing company is supposed to take care of that, but in many cases they let money slip by them. (See the sidebar "The Black Box.")

Moses: Why can't I start my own performing rights organization called the Avalon Performing Rights Society, and all we do is collect my royalties, and why can't I make a deal with your company?

X Bot: At some point you probably will. One of the things we are having to figure out here is how to deal with some of the new issues that are coming up. There is a consensus on the revision of Section 115,[35] the mechanical license that's floating around that has been proposed by the copyright office and by the **NMPA**[36] and the **RIAA**.[37] It is probably not going to pass [in 2004], but what it's going to do is dramatically change the way mechanical rights are licensed. In other words, a record company will no longer have to get licenses from individual publishers for three individual songs, but simply send one notice to the Library of Congress and they will be licensed to mechanically reproduce the entire history of American music.

X Bot proposes something very radical. Right now record companies get licenses for every song on a record individually. If three writers wrote the songs on the record and they each have their publishing controlled by different publishers, then the record company spends three times the time (and money) to get a license from each. If the future unfolds the way X thinks it will, then a record company will only have to register once with the Library of Congress and they will have a blanket license for all the songs that are filed there.

In the current system, the **Harry Fox Agency** acts as clearinghouse for record companies for these rights. They charge 5 percent and have a de facto monopoly on the service.

Moses: Won't [this new statute] basically put Harry Fox out of business?

X Bot: No, the **National Music Publishers Association** is proposing that the Fox Agency become the sole and exclusive agents to collect and distribute mechanical royalties from the United States. It would destroy independent music publishing and force all writers to get their money through the Harry Fox Agency. That is what the Harry Fox Agency is trying to do. Get the law on their side.

[35] Sections 114 and 115 are the sections of the Copyright Act of 1976 that deal with musical works.

[36] RIAA: Recording Industry Association of America. The trade organization that protects the interests of record companies and recording artists to the extent that their interests are the same. They also sue people for illegal downloading of music and issue the gold and platinum certificates for sales of records.

[37] NMPA: National Music Publishers Association. The trade organization that protects the interests of publishers and writers to the extent that their interests are the same.

THE BLACK BOX

Each year tens of millions of dollars that are collected for artists never make it into their pockets. Why, when there are so many agencies taking percentages on these monies, does this happen?

PROs collect money for the public performances of the songs and are supposed to pass it on to publishers who control the rights to the songs. The same royalty has a portion that is supposed to go directly to the artists, but artists are usually harder to find than established publishing entities. If the PRO can't find the artist within two years, then the money goes into a "black box"—a bank account, in other words—and it is then distributed proportionally to a consortium of European publishing companies.

On the surface this seems relatively clean, but what one must understand is that the consortium's VPs occupy board seats on many of the European PROs. Many believe that this corrupts the process and radically reduces the incentive for the PRO to "find" the artist.[38] In the recent past artists like Ricky Martin and others of that calibre were "hard to find."

[38] This past year one PRO in Amsterdam broke ranks with this system and engaged the Moses Avalon Company to intervene and facilitate the finding of the artists. As a result tens of thousands that were about to go into the **Black Box** were recovered. This is only a small fraction of the money that disappears annually.

Moses: If they don't succeed at getting that written into the statute, then hasn't the fuse been lit on how long they are going to be necessary?

X Bot: Yeah, as a matter of fact that is one of the things that we are having discussions about right now. We, meaning me, and some of the people I deal with.

Moses: Why is this off the record: What is not public information?

X Bot: We don't want to make our intentions known.

Moses: What are your intentions?

X Bot: At some point there is going to be a need for a performing rights organization, one that handles mechanicals as well. Because the distinction between mechanicals and performances is going to be blurred significantly. We are trying to position ourselves as a *mechanicals* performing rights organization.

To think that the organizations that are supposed to protect the rights of songwriters might actually be in cahoots to confiscate copyrights on a mass scale is rather daunting. That is what X Bot is implying is in play, unless laws are modified.

> Conclusion

The rights of publishing are traded like stocks in corporations among the various entities in the music business. Producers get a slice of the pie to garnish their participation in an artist. Managers get a piece as well. The main reason that everyone goes for the publishing is because industry custom in the US until recently makes it impossible for royalties to be paid on the public performance of the record itself. In Europe the laws are different. Sound recordings as well as songs are paid for plays on the radio and TV. Royalties are paid for performances on radio and TV for sound recordings as well as songs.

Hopefully someday the law in this country will catch up with the laws elsewhere, and then songwriters will not constantly be put in positions of having to give up so much of their property. However, this is not likely, as the broadcast industry (which is far more powerful than the music publishing industry) has spent gobs of cash lobbying to keep a rate from being established. It would be their constituents that would end up paying if sound recording, as well as songs, required licensing for public play.

John Luongo: The people making money today own the copyrights to songs that are used in advertising campaigns, commercials, ringtones, and cable shows. They are making big money on low-investment material and deserve to. A great song is more important than a great production—a good song needs a great production while a great one needs a production that just does not screw it up.

Spousal Abuse

...ore honorable,
...doing nothing."
— Bernard Shaw

...use of divorce."
— ...red E. Neuman

...ding vows may ...ays, "Till death do you part," he probably doesn't anticipate that some might want to accelerate that agenda, or the complex dynamics that come into play when spouses work together in a business that's as litigious as a California divorce court and as ego-driven as a Wall Street sales conference.

❯ Tracking with the Missus

For those who are well invested in a domestic relationship, the idea of ducking for cover when in a row is not a new one. Thank God that in recording studios, the control room is protected by shatterproof glass. Although that has not stopped some singers when taking out their frustration on spouses who produce them.

Many years back, when I was a fledging engineer in my early twenties, I witnessed a situation where **LaToya Jackson**[1] threw a tantrum toward her husband and manager, **Jack Gordon**, who subsequently threw a book at the control room glass.[2] Then, this normally soft-spoken woman began to yell so loud that I had to pull the patch cable leading into very expensive piece of voice processing gear for

[1] LaToya Jackson: Sister of Michael. She's fostered a sexy image with a pictorial in *Playboy* and advertised a Pay Per View of her at a strip club; however, many people wanted their money back when she did not give up the goods. Further weird career choices included a country album and LaToya Jackson's Psychic Friends Network, which she sued for back royalties. She had one Top 20 hit in the US, "Hearts Don't Lie."

[2] Jack Gordon: He once allegedly attacked LaToya with a white leather chair and claimed self-defense against her, saying she attacked him first with a sharp object. They divorced in 1997, although most of the time they were together she claimed they were not married.

fear that she might blow it out. As the patch cable was yanked out of the console LaToya turned into a silent movie without subtitles. Jack supplied the soundtrack of obscenities that could only be described as surreal. That was my first exposure to the lesson that engineer **Matt Forger** will now elaborate upon.

Matt Forger: This is one of the most difficult areas that exist. There was a band that was very famous from Los Angeles called **Missing Persons**.[3] **Dale [Bozzio]** was the singer and **Terry [Bozzio]** was the drummer in the band. They were married. I was involved on a project of theirs in the mid-'80s where they decided that they would self-produce their next album. When it came down to the time to record vocals, Terry produced his wife, Dale. But how do you tell your spouse that "you can do it better" or "it's not good enough"?

Moses: Her vocals became a signature for the '80s style. What did you see?

Matt Forger: I saw husband and wife go to battle about how to get the best vocal. There was this constant deterioration of people being burdened by not only producing their own albums, but also taking on the management of their own band, taking on the writing of all of their material, and then taking on going in the studio and putting this together [themselves]. My gosh, you just put yourselves in a lose-lose situation.

Moses: Did they find a solution?

Matt Forger: I can only tell you that this is the final nail in the coffin. Their marriage split. It's one thing to have friction in your professional career with individuals, but you are able to leave the studio and leave the baggage behind.

Moses: The moral?

Matt Forger: You never want to produce your wife as a vocalist.

Dale and Terry Bozzio divorced and reunited (professionally) for a series of US reunion shows in 2001.

Fleetwood Smack

André Fischer: I used to go see **Lindsey Buckingham**[4] and **Stevie Nicks**[5] perform together before they got in **Fleetwood Mac**.

The stories of this industry couple are well documented, as was their bitter breakup, which was the subject of many of Buckingham's songs during his understated post-Mac solo career.

3
Missing Persons: The quintessential '80s "hair band." Their singles "Words" and "Destination Unknown" both nearly hit the Top 40. Dale appeared nude in both *Hustler* and *Playboy*. Her musical break happened when she met Frank Zappa and he invited her to sing on his epic concept album, *Joe's Garage*.

4 Lindsey Buckingham: Singer/guitarist/writer with Fleetwood Mac. Wrote the number one hits "Go Your Own Way" and "Second Hand News." Biggest career mistake: the album *Tusk,* allegedly the most expensive album ever recorded. A football stadium was rented along with a 100-piece marching band to get the sound Buckingham "needed." The album flopped.

CHAPTER 9: SPOUSAL ABUSE

André Fischer: They were cool before they joined; not only were they a pair, but they played together and they got along. And then when they got in the group and became successful everybody got crazy.[6]

Moses: Any theories?

André Fischer: I think it's the pressure. It seems like when people feel like there is more to lose, if they are in a public situation or a business situation and the person they are intimate with is involved with some big business dealing, then it seems like it puts more pressure on both of them.

Moses: Are you saying that money corrupts them somewhat?

André Fischer: It's like you have something to lose. When you're both doing something together at a certain level you are doing fine, but then you get successful in the public eye and there is a lot of scrutiny, like **Ben Affleck** and **Jennifer Lopez**—it's like the public stopped their relationship. It became so public and so visible that it seemed like a mistake, but it was based upon other people. If the folks aren't cool to begin with and do not have their shit together as far as the relationship…when business gets complicated, personal [matters get] double complicated. There are a lot of folks that when these things happen they don't know who to reach out to. They are not informed about how to help themselves in these situations.

Moses: Can you think of any positive examples?

André Fischer: **Danny Bennett**, who manages his dad, **Tony Bennett**, is real sensitive to his dad's needs and has done really well by him over the past 15 to 20 years. From that aspect I have seen a really positive situation.

Steve Addabbo: You could also look at **Rosanne Cash** and **John Leventhal**; he produced her record and they wound up getting married later on. Look at **Mutt Lange** and **Shania Twain**.[7] They were married, huge success.[8]

Co-writing, Co-dependency, and Heritage Acts

The term most used these days by major-label executives is "heritage acts." This is a polite way of saying "old but respected." My friend calls it "wrinkle rock." I happen to like it, but that's because I'm sentimental about my music. Heritage acts are where much of the money is these days in the music biz. These acts have been around for more than two decades and have a very solid fan base. True, they don't sell as many records as many of the new acts, but that's okay. The record will be marked up to some ridiculous amount because the labels know that baby boomers (who make up a lot of today's record buyers) will shell it out. On the concert side, it

[5] Stevie Nicks: Performed with Fleetwood Mac, and with Tom Petty as a soloist. Her vocals on "Gypsy," "Rhiannon," and "Gold Dust Woman" became a signature sound in the late '70s and early '80s. The secret to her trademark "raspy" voice was the result of smoking three packs of Newports a day for 20 years. She quit smoking in 1997 but not cocaine. Her habit burned a hole through her nose cartilage. Klonopin was prescribed to assist her in getting off the narcotic. It worked at the sacrifice of her becoming addicted to the prescription tranquilizer and gaining much weight. Other "mistakes": she had breast implants, but had them removed, claiming they gave her Epstein-Barr syndrome. She wrote the No. 2 hit "Dreams" and is still very well respected in the industry.

[6] Buckingham agreed to join Fleetwood Mac only if they also took his girlfriend, Stevie Nicks, so the story goes. When he joined the band, he changed the direction from jazzy to folksy and created the sound that made the band famous. However, he wrote fewer hits than either Christine McVie or Stevie Nicks.

[7] Shania Twain: Birth name, Eileen Regina Edwards.

[8] Until they got divorced.

seems like these acts are just about the only thing packing seats. (This will likely change, however, as these acts cannot tour forever.)

There are a few problems with these acts. Mostly, they all have wives that they need to make part of the deal.

Jeff Weber: There is an artist that I worked with that felt that he deserved a lot more than the label was giving him. Here is a guy who has been around, he's done Woodstock and all of this, and yet is extraordinarily bitter. He is a fantastic singer and he really deserves to be heard, but the bitterness takes its toll… I produced one of his records. He felt that when he went to a record company, he needed to let them know of his stature, of his heritage. What happened in my situation was, he tried to be the big man at the label, saying, "I have written my own songs and I am capable of doing everything myself. I just got married and my wife is now going to be the songwriter on the record." Even though she had never written a song in her life.

Moses: You were in the room when he was telling this to record executives?

Jeff Weber: Yes, as a matter of fact, the reason I was there was that the record executives did not want him to produce the record. They did not like the songs that he and his new bride selected. I was in a very poor situation, because the label was adamant about me producing the record, much to the chagrin of the artist. It was kind of a hate/hate relationship. He did not like me from the beginning. I was set up to fail.

Moses: So you were there because the record company was going to convince him to use you instead of producing it himself?

Jeff Weber: Correct. The record company insisted and demanded that he *not* produce the record.

Moses: In front of you? In front of him?

Jeff Weber: Oh yeah! It was a yelling and screaming match. Basically the label won out.

Moses: How did the record come out?

Jeff Weber: While the record came out very well overall, the songs were terrible. I used extraordinary musicians, and the arrangements were terrific. The artist had a great voice, and he did a wonderful job. The material, except for the one or two songs written solely by the artist, was very bad. For example, his wife wrote a song about their pool toys. They had names for pool toys. This is the type of insanity that I was dealing with.

Moses: I can understand that you think you deserve more success so you go in with a stronger head for negotiating, but at the end of the day he did the right thing, didn't he?

Jeff Weber: In his opinion, he lost everything. If he would have soft-sold it then I would not have been the producer. If he would have been more open about the songs, he would have won. He's got a quick temper.

Moses: So the lesson here is: If you're going to be a megalomaniac and your wife doesn't have the talent, soft-sell it.

Jeff Weber: Exactly.

❯ Family Planning

And now for some good news. Spousal problems aside, it is usually necessary to have one in order to progress to a part of life many consider essential—children. As a parent I feel I can summarize parenthood into one line: You spend the first three years teaching them to walk and talk and the next 15 teaching them to sit down and shut up.

The adult world is divided basically into two groups, those who have children and those who do not. The two clubs will never willingly eat dinner in the same restaurant (metaphorically speaking). In addition, those without kids will never understand the sacrifices made to have the little rug rats.

Many women I encounter at seminars and workshops ask me about family planning. I'm never sure exactly what to tell them. Do I tell them what I think is the truth, that if they have a family they can pretty much kiss their chances of a career as a recording artist goodbye? No. They would only become angry and throw examples like **Shania Twain**[9] at me, forgetting that she and others like her are exceptional exceptions. You cannot discuss statistics with someone who has a dream, no matter how unrealistic. Besides, who am I to assume that they won't be the exception? Instead I just say… something vague. On rare occasion I tell them this true story from my archives.

[9] Shania Twain: Mother of two small children. She takes them everywhere she goes. Even on tour.

Privacy and Career in Music

One rarely stops to think how valuable one's privacy can be when they embark on a career in the public eye, like music. Success can have a price—your right to be left alone or treated with courtesy.

In my daily line of work I investigate complaints about companies in the music business. Sort of like the Better Business Bureau. Sometimes the companies I expose bite back. I've brought attention to potential malfeasance in companies like

ASCAP, RIAA, SoundScan, Harry Fox, ASCAP, Sony, Universal Music, and many others. Each time those companies and I have handled it professionally. Because I always check my facts I have good relationships with companies I've vetted.

When I started the **Moses Avalon Company** I had no children. Now, being on the front line of fighting corruption in the business with a family in the background, I have to choose my battles more carefully. Believe it or not, going after big game is less risky. They fight fairly and professionally. They take criticism well because they have a lot riding on their reputations. Despite what the movies tell us, they have too much to lose to do rash things to silence you.

In August of 2002, things went horribly wrong with a small distributor incorporated in Nevada. They were offering to get unsigned artists' music on iTunes. The problem: they did not even have a contract with Apple Computers to do so at the time.[10] In addition, the company's contract took exclusive rights from artists for three years (a lifetime in the world of an up-and-coming band). Desperate and trusting artists signed up in droves paying a $35 sign-up fee and "signing" a click-to-agree contract that made the company their exclusive record/publishing entity. Most had not read the agreement.

I received several complaints about this agreement before I had even become aware of its existence. I read it and was shocked. I knew the CEO of the company. He and I had had several lunches together. I'd done some ad hoc consulting for him about digital distribution. He seemed reasonable enough and I thought that perhaps he was not aware of what his lawyers had drafted. But after several conversations and emails with him it seemed that something odd was afoot.

I solicited the opinions of about 100 other lawyers from my personal rolodex. Most agreed that the company's contract was dangerously worded. I gave this company a chance to change the contract and spent over an hour walking them through its problems. When they refused to make any significant changes, I did what I always do when I find something that disenfranchises artists: I wrote a cautionary article and sent it to my private list of *Moses Supposes* subscribers.[11] Bad news travels fast. My email circled the globe several times in less than 24 hours. No one ever asked my permission to redistribute the article. Ahh, the Internet. A prominent trade magazine picked up the story. The article made the company look kind of foolish and this just made them madder.

The CEO, a former computer programmer, retaliated with a smear campaign, accusing me of extortion and other things on various chatrooms where music business folk congregate. He had posted my IP address on a public bulletin board which gave specific instructions on how to report me to ISPs as a *spammer.* (This is

[10] In fairness to the company, this may have been a misunderstanding between Apple and the company. They may have had a good-faith assumption to think they had a contract. Apple told me that the company had no authority to announce that they had a deal with them. Apple gave them a contract several months later.

[11] At the time we had about 10,000 subscribers.

the Internet equivalent of calling someone a child molester. And even though my list is a subscriber list, this came at a time when the new Spam-in-a-Can law had been passed. ISPs were not taking any chances. I was blocked.) Soon after this, my Web site was hacked and destroyed.

At first I was not completely sure who was responsible. Then, months later, a reporter who worked for a cornerstone Los Angeles–based music magazine told me that the company threatened to rescind advertising support from them if they supported my advocacy efforts, and pressure came down on the reporters: "avoid using Avalon" as a source for their articles. The company also threatened to rescind support from several conferences that booked both of us on panels. For over a year I rarely spoke in public and had to spend a fair amount of time and money rehabilitating the *MosesAvalon.com* URL with AOL, EarthLink, and Yahoo!.

And here's the point of this story. Many of my readers wondered why I didn't fight back as hard as they were fighting to silence me. I naturally thought of suing. God knows I have some of the best lawyers in the business as clients and advisors. But despite having the facts on my side, I was supporting a family. When you sue, especially if it involves slander and libel, your family and private life can and often will come into play, if for no other reason than as a legal strategy.

Lesson learned: *The little mouse will sometimes bite back harder than the big lion.*

I decided that my time was better spent working on the deals I had in process that would help artists in the future. I decided to swallow my pride and let it go.

The CEO's campaign against me continues to this day. When asked in public about what happened between us he paints a one-sided picture that depicts me as a criminal. (He forgets that most of these appearances are taped.) Three months after my article, and heading off rumors that a class action suit was brewing, the company announced that they would be returning the fees they had collected. Thankfully, my reputation when it comes to artist rights and exposing scams remains intact.

Too Busy for Baby

How does the dynamic of having children affect the busy, on-call demands of the music business? I'd rather it come from a different source, one of the most devoted fathers I know in the business, **Matt Forger**.

> *Moses:* What kind of advice would you give someone who is telling you they are 25 years old and they want to be a recording engineer but they are also thinking about getting married and having a kid?

Matt Forger: I would say, reassess your priorities. Evaluate what is important to you in your life. There are those people that are willing to make the sacrifice and work for five to ten years, twelve or thirteen hours a day, six or seven days a week. And there are those people that that's too much of a compromise. They are giving away too much of themselves as a person and too much of their lives. A family is such a large responsibility, you are forced to make decisions. Can I take this gig? It is out of town, I will be away from my family for X amount of time. My daughter is handicapped so on a day-to-day basis I literally have to participate in her life.

Moses: I can print that?

Matt Forger: Yeah. That means that I am not free, for example, to work tremendously long hours or travel out of town without planning and making arrangements ahead of time. I have to turn down some things that are too great a demand on my time. At the end of the day, at the end of your life, you don't want to look back and have regrets. You don't want to be bitter about the fact that "this happened to me" or "that happened to me." You have to understand the nature of the business and what is demanded of you. I know so many marriages that have gone down the tubes and so many families where kids have grown up without their dads because their dad was always working. You know, those are the choices that we all have the ability to make. At the end where the final tally is, at the end of your life, you've got to realize that those are the decisions you've made, that was your choice and you don't want to look back with regret. I have so many friends that got tied down young and didn't have the freedom to pursue something in a career. Maybe they are entirely happy with being middle class and having a family and that kind of job and normal hours. That was never what I decided or wanted so I made sure that at some point in my life that my career, my focus, and all of my direction was very specific. When I got to a certain point I let myself think about having a relationship. Have your eyes open and do the research. Find out if it is going to take you years of work to establish yourself being a recording engineer or producer or some capacity like that, evaluate what the tradeoff is going to be between establishing yourself first and then at least being in a position where your family life should have more stability. As opposed to, "Oh, I've got to get married now and my wife wants to have a baby right away," because some part of it is going to tear you apart. One way or another. If you feel like you've made a bad mistake you are going to regret it for a long time. You are going to be living with it.

 Conclusion

Last words on this subject go to engineer/producer/educator **John Luongo**, whose contribution to this section got me a little misty.

John Luongo: When you get into this business everything is second to your job. You are married to the work and the hours and the principle of being the best at all costs. When you, like I, are lucky enough to find a person in this business that understands the demands and hours (I married **Joy Dorris**, the female half of the group **Lime**), then and only then can you carry on with a clear heart and on a clear path to continued success. No normal person would put up with or understand the job demands and the pressure that they will be under raising a family, primarily on their own, for a period of time. When we had our first son I was overjoyed, and my wife often took him to the studio where I proudly mixed with him on my lap. **Aerosmith, Guns N' Roses**, and many dance songs filled his head even as he was inside my wife's womb. As time progresses you move away from the studio and the business to focus on the family, and sometimes you drift too far away and have to get yourself back in the game (out of sight, out of mind). Eventually you realize (in my case, years after my second son) that you must get back to where you were, as it is what you are and defines you and makes you into who you are and should be. I must say, that to raise a child is the most unselfish act that anyone can undertake. It is also the most rewarding experience you can ever imagine, and when you find the right woman, as I did, it can be the best part of one's life. It is unlike any success or accolade that you might receive in your lifetime and validates you and not just your accomplishments.

CHAPTER 10

The Future of Music and Its Enemies

Things to Consider for a Career in the Early 21st Century Music Business

> *"The future will be better tomorrow."*
> — Dan Quayle, Vice President of the United States, 1989–1993

> *"Irrespective of what any court says, a debate has crystallized: it's legitimate versus illegitimate.... It's whether or not digital music will be enjoyed in a fashion that supports the creative process or one that robs it of its future."*
> — Mitch Bainwol, CEO, Recording Industry Association of America

T he biggest mistake ever made in the music business is how record companies completely misunderstood the power of the Internet and its ability to destroy their business models. This chapter is dedicated to that one mistake and its remedy.

It is also a form of explanation to the general public, who seem to look down on record companies and their agenda. Many feel that the labels owe the public at large an apology, or at the very least an explanation as to why they made such a rash error in judgment in regard to the Internet. But for reasons that are not my area of expertise, they are not issuing one that makes sense to most of us. Instead they sue grandmothers and 12-year-old girls, and the public is even more confused and enraged. So I am going to offer that explanation for them. I'm not expecting a thank-you card. But you never know.

❯ The Shrinking Medium, Nostalgia, and Sales

When I was in college, people were proud of their record collections. You would see everyone using them as shelf liners and wallpaper. Long-playing records, or LPs as they were called, came in large 12" × 12" jackets that were more than just something that held the record. They were works of art in and of themselves. Artists would use it as an auxiliary canvas to express their vision. Record buyers found all kinds of practical uses for the jackets as well. Mostly, to clean weed inside the album fold. (In fact, I am convinced, although I can't prove it, that there is a connection between the decline of pot in US culture during the 1980s and the rise of cocaine with the transition from albums to CDs.)

In the sixties and seventies, if you were a *real* music fan, you memorized the names of producers, musicians, and all of the PR "facts" that went along with the artist. This information was easily accessible because labels printed much of it on the LP's liner notes. The world of the LP was the music industry that I, and many executives operating in the RIAA/ISP war, fell in love with, one that was about making money by affecting culture with something that sounded good and producing it in the form of a tangible product. An album: a 45-minute statement broken down into 10 or 12 three- to four-minute units.

With the advent of the compact disc, artists had to now negotiate with their record companies for extra panels to display credits and art. If the artist wanted something "unusual" they would be charged. It was cruel. Often new artists would buckle, agreeing to fewer liner notes as it cut into their profits. In time the public stopped caring about it as well, and thus the process began, a dwindling spiral of losing touch with the artist's visual identity, MTV notwithstanding. Needless to say, these days on an Internet download or a stream (called a "play event") there is even less attention paid to the artist's visual identity.

Today, we are experiencing a radical transition in the way we relate to music, and music companies are rethinking about how to sell their product. They face a serious obstacle first, though: the fact that no one seems to want to pay for it.

Marshall McLuhan[1] wrote: *"Each medium, independent of the content it mediates, has its own intrinsic effects which are its unique message.... The railway did not introduce movement or transportation or wheel or road into human society, but it accelerated and enlarged the scale of previous human functions, creating totally new kinds of cities and new kinds of work and leisure. The medium is the message because it is the medium that shapes and controls the scale and form of human association and action."*[2]

There is little doubt that the way the medium of music is expressed is changing. Will its message change as well? Given that, it's hard to create a perfectly flawless career path for an industry that is going through such turbulence. But, using some basic laws of commerce and a few McLuhanisms, we can create a roadmap of what to expect and who will be opposing music's progress.

This chapter doesn't have all the answers. But its analysis and predictions will give you a unique look ahead. Rather than taking each conclusion to heart, simply allow them to inspire you. Music is a passion more than a business. It must be pursued in the face of adversity or the product will, to use a technical term, suck.

> Liquid Audio, Liquid World

Before we travel forward in our time machine of imagination, I need to introduce two terms that will become important for describing the twenty-first century music business: "wallpaper" and "liquid." By "wallpaper," we mean that music will become part of your everyday matrix, going unnoticed, something that is simply around you all the time. How many times do you walk into a room and go "Oh, look at the wallpaper"? Rarely, but it is always there, contributing to the aesthetics of your life. "Liquid" means that the music will flow like water and have an amorphous form. It is something that cannot be held in your hand, but you can soak in it. This is in opposition to the way music, until recently, has existed in our lives: as a listening experience, unique to itself and apart from other day-to-day functions. In the liquid/wallpaper world, music will be everywhere almost all the time, but we will not notice it much.

The concept of music becoming ever-present is the sexiest and also the most frightening concept facing the business in the coming years. High-tech companies are pushing the "liquid agenda" because it suits their needs: selling gadgets and Internet-based services. This necessarily means being able to communicate the message to the public that they can provide accessibility and portability to everything you want—legally or not. To them the music is a mere tool to sell technology.

[1] Marshall McLuhan: Famous media analyst and all-around smarty. Wrote the classic book *Understanding Media*, required reading in just about every communications course there is. Also said, "The printing press invented the public."

[2] From *Understanding Media: The Extensions of Man* (New York: McGraw-Hill, 1964).

When you read comments in this chapter by people who work for high-tech companies, remember that this is the viewpoint they are paid to sell and they must make it appear harmless to accomplish that.

Conversely, record companies (and indeed all content companies) have an almost opposite agenda: they need to sell the music itself as an individual unit and a unique experience, which necessarily means controlling copyrights and venues where music is heard and bought. Mired in the traditions of how to do this—specifically, to make money with albums—record companies have been fighting what high-tech companies call "progress" for years. When you read comments in this chapter by label executives, remember that the sanctity of music as an art form and how it should be experienced (as albums and on copy-protected media) is what they are paid to sell.

Between high-tech companies who want to make music a loss leader and content providers who want to preserve their business model, whoever wins this tug-of-war one thing is certain: the future for those making a living with music will probably not be in the selling of discs alone, but in getting your product into as many "liquid" venues as possible in order to get it immersed in the pattern of the "wallpaper." Managers of artists always worked toward this, but where once this was an ancillary consideration for the success of a new artist, it has become a mandatory one. As you will see, this is no small consideration.

Why are record companies so apprehensive, and how will their perspective affect how a person navigates a career in this new job market? To gain some inspiration and insight we need to closely examine the challenge that record/publishing companies (which are the banks of this industry) are facing if they want to continue to exist in a form that resembles their current one. In more conventional terms, how will the industry's "banks" look to lend money and make a return on their investments in a world where the perceived value of their product is ever diminishing?

Warning: If you are a traditionalist, some of this may disturb you. Consider what you are about to read only one possible future, albeit it a likely one.

⊜ Perception and Value

You don't have to scratch your head too much to recall that **Jim Carrey** or **Schwarzenegger** got about $25 million to perform in their movies, or to remember the $280 million it cost to make *Titanic*. I'd like you to ask yourself a question: Why in the hell do you know these facts? They are not important to your day-to-day survival, yet they are part of pop common knowledge.

Now ask yourself this: How much did **Eminem**'s last record cost? What about how much it cost to market and promote **U2**'s integrations into the iPod? What? No answer? The reason you have no idea is because whenever you see a figure of how much an actor is getting paid to appear in a movie, it's not a fact that was uncovered by hard-nosed investigative journalism. Movie companies put it in a press release. They want everyone to know that it's costing them a truckload of cash to entertain the public. Over the last 60 years, while the movie industry has been investing millions a year in educating us about high salaries, the record companies have not invested dime one in communicating the costs of delivering their product. They have not taught us its cash value.

You probably don't even realize it, but one important reason you don't feel easily comfortable sneaking into a blockbuster movie is because subconsciously you figure, "It's only nine bucks, what the heck, they spent $100 million to make it."

When have you heard that **Michael Jackson**'s *History* video cost almost $2,000,000, or that **Mariah Carey**'s second record company paid her close to $29,000,000 to *not* deliver the remaining four albums of her contract[3] and leave the label? Did you hear that a 200-piece orchestra was hired for $20,000 *a day* for an artist who is a known prima donna, instead of using a synthesizer for about $1,500? Do you think that hiring an orchestra helped sell more records than the synth? No, but the record companies did all these things anyway. They just don't advertise it. They don't educate the public about their woes. Instead, they produce music videos about the high lifestyle the artists enjoy, and they give away the music for free in various venues such as radio and TV, hoping we'll get hooked on their new prodigy. The same business model used by drug dealers.

So when a technology comes along that allows anyone with a computer to pilfer a record company's inventory, who would think twice about using it? Music already *feels free* and many feel as though they have a right to it.

It is a law of commerce: You cannot sell something if there is no perceived value in it. You simply can't. Suing people who steal music off the Internet, as the RIAA began doing in 2003, is not really educating the public. It scares them a little, and perhaps this was necessary, but the conceptual effect is probably no different than TV companies suing viewers for making a tape (or DVD) of a movie shown on the air and then lending it to a friend who can't afford their own TiVo.

I concede, the analogy is not a perfectly parallel one in terms of the legal merits, but to the legally unsophisticated public it feels the same. They walk away thinking, "Wait a minute, I'm not stealing. You already give this to me for free. It was free when I heard it at the mall and on the radio and on *my* MTV. I'm just ripping it and sharing my tastes with friends."

[3] Mariah Carey's deal: A five-album deal for $20,000,000 each. She did the first one and then was bought out. The combined monies for both the first CD and the buyout was $49,000,000. The CD sold about 550,000 units, making it the most expensive artist deal in the history of pop music.

Of course, from a copyright perceptive, this is ridiculous. Copyrights were designed to give authors almost absolute authority and monopoly over the use of their work. Regardless, record companies simply cannot get people to voluntarily abide by the law at this late date in the game. The law itself and the concept of intellectual property is too complex.

So how do they reverse this? How do they get people to see the monetary value of music when they've spent 60 years getting you to believe that you are entitled to it for free? They could try to re-educate the public. This would probably take another 15 years, if they start today, assuming there were no obstacles. And there are several.

And Along Came Napster

John Luongo: In about 1999 I had lunch with one of the top business affairs executives at one of the big labels. I asked what his company was doing about the Internet and the fact that people were getting [free] music from it. He said that they were going to just ignore it for now because there was enough on their plate already. He said that he thought that the other labels would take the lead and his would just wait and see how they dealt with the problem.

"Not true," says **Michael Ostroff**, executive vice president of Business and Legal Affairs for the **Universal Music Group**. Mr. Ostroff serves as UMG's chief legal officer, worldwide.

Michael Ostroff: [At Universal] we started looking into the Internet as an opportunity in the late 1990s.[4] One of the opportunities that we thought we would have was like the models they have in the film business. Physical product at one point, then streaming to different sources, and then buying the permanent download. Like video, pay cable, pay per view, and network broadcasts. I think we also thought that we would be able to preserve the album format.[5] It is very much a myth that record companies were saying no, no, no to the Internet.

If that's true, what went wrong?

The principals of **Napster** claim they approached several major labels to get the rights to "distribute" music on their service. Their perception was that labels didn't pay royalties to artists and, being very pro-artist, Napster wanted to make sure that artists were paid royalties from their downloads (ironically).[6]

[4] Seagram's (previous owner of Universal) purchase of Poly-Gram was a major driving force for Edgar Bronfman in 1998. Bronfman claims to have embraced many aspects of Internet technology.

[5] Album format: Selling 12 or 14 songs as an album to the consumer for about $15.

But record companies faced these three obstacles in regard to licensing their catalog to online services in 1999:

- The lack of rights to distribute their catalog via digital/Internet.
- Desire to maintain control of the transition from the album format to singles so as not to upset the economics of the industry.
- Showing favoritism in the area of technology standardization.

These important factors were obviously lost on the aggressive Team Napster, whose average executive was barely 25 years old. Some execs had not even finished college. To them it seemed doubtful that these powerful labels, who could make or break careers, were claiming that they couldn't go boldly and quickly into something that seemed to them so very obvious. This series of meetings ended in a bloodbath.[7]

Leslie Zigel, former vice president of Business and Legal Affairs with **BMG's Latin American Regional Office**:

> *Leslie Zigel:* I think a little more humility [on Napster's part] could have allowed for some success. When I heard them speaking I thought these guys are a bunch of arrogant assholes that don't understand that they need certain rights [from the label] to do what they wanted.

Here's how the three obstacles broke down:

First Obstacle: Digital/Internet Rights Acquisitions

A fact glossed over by the media when criticizing record companies was that, in the mid 1990's, there was barely a single recording contract that granted the artist's rights for "digital distribution" to the major labels.[8] This was something labels did not tell the ISPs and other Internet-based companies for fear they would usurp them, which eventually some tried to do. (Napster, to name but one.) Artists were not willing to give these rights up so easily. Why? Years earlier record companies had approached artists for similar reasons to get the rights to re-release their music on the new compact disc format. Virtually every artist signed over these rights without receiving any upfront money. Why? They were told that they would be receiving higher back-end royalties because the CD would sell for about $12 (instead of the usual $7.99 in 1979–'80). But in the end, labels ended up charging the artist an additional "new technology deduction," lowering their penny rate[9] to equal the rate they were already getting for LPs. Many artists felt duped.

[6] See *All the Rave: The Rise and Fall of Shawn Fanning's Napster*, by Joseph Menn.

[7] Again, see *All the Rave*, by Joseph Menn, who was kind enough to quote me in his book.

[8] There were a couple of minor exceptions in the jazz area, which has generally catered to audiophiles, so the concept of "digital rights" was mentioned in their contracts.

[9] Penny rate: The actual amount an artist receives for the sale of one unit. For new artists, it's about $1.30 per CD album, for superstars it's about $2.50 per CD album. If you go to *www.MosesAvalon.com* and click on the Royalty Calculator, you'll see how the penny rate is calculated in major-label deals.

Now the labels wanted "Internet rights." Even though no one was sure exactly what those were, artists were not going to just bend over so easily. Thus, labels could not give Napster or any of the Internet-based companies the rights to distribute their catalog in 1998–2000, because they themselves didn't have all of it to license in this new way. [10]

Second Obstacle: Transition from Albums to Singles

Napster was a singles-driven format, something labels had worked hard over the past 20 years to get away from. Why start selling a new format when the old one (albums) is working just fine?

> *Leslie Zigel:* You have to remember at this time the record business was still fairly healthy. [Executives] were making their bonuses and felt as though they were doing everything right. Who was [Napster] to tell them that the business was about to change radically and people *really* wanted singles?

It was not just the record companies sitting stone-faced; songwriters felt the same way.

> *Jay Jay French:* Think about it, if album [sales] are no longer the means by which you quantify success, how are you going to get a publishing advance? What are you going to figure it against? Track by track?

Music publishing companies' advances were based on projected *album sales.* [11] Switching over to a singles-driven model may sound good from a consumer point of view, but a sudden change would have seriously affected the economics of just about every deal on the table.

Imagine you are an artist/writer and Sony Publishing is going to give you a $500,000 advance based on the fact that you are going to have an initial pressing of 300,000 albums with 14 songs that you wrote. When they hear that the labels are switching to a singles-driven model, things change. They are no longer going to issue 300,000 discs with 14 songs. They are going to post the name of a few tracks on a Web site and see how many downloads they get. Sort of an "on-demand" model with a rather unpredictable basis to forecast mechanicals. [12] What manager in 1998–2000 was going to let his artist/writer sign that deal? None.

[10] **Online catalogs:** Even though over time many eventually gave in, as of this writing (2005) rights for Metallica and Nirvana have not been fully negotiated, nor have Led Zeppelin, the Beatles, Bob Seger, or Garth Brooks.

[11] See Chapter 8 for why.

[12] **Mechanicals:** The royalties a songwriter makes each time a record is manufactured. A set rate (called a statutory rate) determines how much they are paid. Currently it's about 9.1 cents per record sold. In 1999 there was no established rate for Internet mechanicals. In fact, as of this writing (2005) there still isn't anything concrete established.

Third Obstacle: Digital Transmission Standardization

Due to antitrust concerns, there are limitations to the conversations that a major label can have with another major label or a tech company regarding a standard for digital transitions. In other words, if you, as a record company, make a deal with *one* company you could be required to make a deal with *all of them*. No one in 1999 was ready to do that. There were several companies competing for a "standard." If record companies sided with one company they could be slapped with an antitrust suit by the others.

> *Leslie Zigel:* If you look back to the Industrial Revolution when railroads came about, all the railroads were able to agree on one standard for track. Imagine how that could've worked if there could be one standard for digital downloading and one standard for wireless cellular technology. Today there is far more scrutiny.

If the antitrust climate that exists today were applied even less than 100 years ago, when one railroad company, Union Pacific, decided that they were going to create a transcontinental railroad with one type of track, every other train company that was trying to develop a standard would sue, claiming that they were bullying them into conforming to an inferior standard and not allowing them to compete.[13] We'd have railroads where you would have to change trains every 100 miles or so because train company A's trains won't run on train company B's tracks. Or, applying the same analogy to telecommunications, a telephone system where you could only call people within a certain territory because the New Jersey telephone company used a different dialing technology than the pulse-code standard, or a different type of cable than other phone systems adopted, or a network that used different encoding.

Here we had an already existing industry, well established in tradition and standards, being run by a successful old-school mentality. In order for real progress to happen, tech companies would need to work within the label's existing standards. They claim they tried.

> *Michael Ostroff:* I am not sure the tech companies were ever *really* "reaching toward us." They were interested in building a business on the back of ours *without* compensating us. [Universal was] trying to develop [Internet] business in a more controlled manner. I think that we didn't appreciate that all of that would come tumbling down.

[13] This is what got Bill Gates sued by the Justice Department in 1994 for allegedly trying to create a monopoly with Internet Explorer. Microsoft claimed that it was simply making Windows a better, more comprehensive product but settled with the Department of Justice.

[14] However, Grokster remains, as does Kazaa, two significant file-sharing entities that continue as of this writing to skirt the intent of the law.

[15] An interesting side note: The subject who gave this quote wanted to remain anonymous because he was concerned about a quote coming from a major-label source that Steve Jobs (owner of Apple Computers) wouldn't approve of. This is sort of like a major motion picture studio executive being afraid of offending the CEO of Blockbuster video. It's become clear who is now the slave and who is the plantation owner.

[16] Unfortunately, most artists start out as "one-hit wonders." At least that's the mentality a label will generally take until they prove otherwise. They will expect failure in the sophomore effort and become reflexively less enthusiastic about the artist's follow-up album. This will make it harder for new artists to "push through" and mature into superstars.

The rest is well documented elsewhere. Massive litigation and rewriting of copyright laws eventually closed down the free version of Napster.[14] More importantly, labels had drawn blood with ISPs and high-tech companies who simply did not understand their concerns or didn't care to, a wound that has not healed as of this writing. The music industry missed a chance (if they ever really had one) to partner up with the ISPs and now find themselves fighting for ground and air.

From Tactile to Ethereal

Major Label Senior VP: The future of music distribution is [definitely] moving toward the singles market again and *portable subscription.* People will pay 15 or 20 bucks a month and they will have all of the tunes, and will be able to take them everywhere.[15]

The future of music sales on a mass scale will certainly be through streams and downloads via some form of through-the-air (or net) transmission. The exact form may be in debate but not the concept. Aside from ringtones, the pervasive methods emerging are pay-per-download, where you own the file, and "subscription-based services," where you pay a flat fee per month for all the music you want. However, if the subscription lapses you will lose your record collection. Labels fought the rapid proliferation of this concept for years trying to assess how they would be compensated. Tech companies, on the other hand, saw this as the messiah.

Jay Frank, senior vice president of label relations for **Yahoo!**, was instrumental in liaising between reluctant record companies and the tech giant, and in creating the largest subscription-based model in the industry.

Jay Frank: Big artists should embrace the subscription model as they stand to get paid more over time. Take *The Eagles' Greatest Hits*, a must-own record. You pay for "Hotel California" once on the album and then maybe again when you buy the *Greatest Hits*, yet listen to it weekly. But in a subscription model, the **Eagles** will net more royalties monthly from that same user over a lifetime than they would from buying the album only once or twice. Not to mention the extra dollars from people who just "want to hear it today" who would never be buying it in the first place. However, the losers in this subscription-based model are those fly-by-night artists who have a brief hit but are forgotten in a matter of months. Only some might make more (the so-called turntable hits that are huge on radio and nobody ever buys).[16]

Leslie Zigel expands on Jay Frank's comments.

Leslie Zigel: I disagree with the notion that you make more on the full album [sale]. There are a lot of ways to make money on singles or even fractions of singles through ringtones… Figure **Beyoncé** sells half a million downloads of a 30-second ringtone, at two dollars and fifty cents, of which the labels get about 40 percent.

True. Minute for minute, both the label and the big artist make more money selling music both these ways than $12–14 for an entire album, which is about 60 minutes of music. Clearly this is the future, but this brings us to the fundamental problem. Music used to be a "tactile" sale. Meaning, you went into a store and you would touch the record and feel it in your hand, you would look at the album cover, and through the act of holding it, a desire to own it would geminate. Record companies facilitated the tactile sale by creating what I would call a mania around the music. Like starting a new religious cult, each new artist was a figurehead who was not only our guru du jour, but also an important reflection of our culture. To promote the "religion," labels relied on radio exposure, television, and in-store performances. These are all things that are mostly visual media, where the artist is being sold as much as the music itself.

In the future, aside from blanket licensing deals [17] (which I will speak to later), a personal record sale is going to go more like this: You are sitting in a restaurant and the cell phone at the next table rings. It has a cool loop on it and you say, "Where did you get that?" They reply, "myrings.com," or "YahooMusic.com." You go there. You browse through their catalog and pay three dollars (or perhaps it's already part of your monthly subscription) and now you've got that loop in your phone. Next month you'll replace it with something else.

The cell phone will become the new transistor radio, **iTunes** and **Yahoo!** the new music stores. This would make tech companies very, very happy. But all this means that the sale of music will no longer be in albums but in single-serving sales of one song, or, in the case of ringtones, a fraction of a song. This could of course mean a fraction of a royalty as well. [18] It will no longer come with interesting packaging that is an extension of the artist's message, or a lyric sheet so you can delve into the meaning of the song. You just get the snippet. Music becomes ethereal.

So what?

The significant factor, so far overlooked by many journalists and executives speculating about the future of music, is that when you go from *tactile* to *ethereal*

[17] Blanket licensing deals: Deals where a content company sells lots of recordings on a whole-sale basis for a flat fee or scaled fee. Like a record company licensing their entire catalog to Muzak for distribution in elevators.

[18] Unless artists' lawyers get smarter about the deals they've been doing lately.

you risk disembodying the music buyer from the artist. You make the music more disposable. You won't have personalized record collections any more, you just have this hard drive. This thing. This box. You can't clean pot on a computer screen. **Jay Frank** thinks artists have nothing to worry about in this regard:

> *Jay Frank:* If you're talking about the future of music, you do have to know that amongst teenagers and college students, the Web site has certainly replaced the album in the connection of fan to artist. And while they may not be able to hold it, the fact that they can regularly get updates (as opposed to the once-a-year re-lease) more than makes up for this. Where this is working best is Emo-punk "Warped Tour" bands who are regularly selling 250,000 to 500,000 per album with no radio and just touring and Internet promotion.

True if you're already a fan. But what if your sole introduction to the song is as a ten-second snip that you use in your cell phone? Also, even if you are already a casual fan of the artist before you download his song, if one forecasts that iPods over time will be lost, dropped, broken, and stolen, or that subscription services (which are based on a monthly credit card charge) lapse or are canceled, you could easily lose touch with them. This is no insignificant factor. You have your "record collection" backed up on your computer—the one that has the virus in it, or the one that you upgraded to a new OS and now it doesn't play half your songs—or you had to erase a bunch of them because you wanted new ones. Or, in the case of subscription services, you have a col-lection that you don't *own*. You only lease it at twice the price. This runs the serious risk that, emotionally, people could come to feel the same way about their music as they do about a leased car or apartment. When the lease is over, and you get a new car or move to a new apartment, your attachment to the old one fades rather quickly. Es-pecially with dozens of new products coming out daily to entice you.

> *Steve Addabbo:* That is a real seismic shift in how people use music and need music.... I think what is wrong with this business is the lost opportunity to train a new generation of record buyers. The fact is unavoidable. We are training tomor-row's record buyers to not care as much about the music as something that is per-sonal to their lives. It is merely a trendy commodity.

Okay. Still. So what? So music becomes a commodity. So there are fewer artists in the limelight. So we cut down advances because we're into a singles-driven model now. We'll survive. Right?

That depends on who "we" is. Here's the really interesting part. The part that's both sexy and frightening.

No Longer the Music Industry as We Know It

> *"It's not life as we know it, doctor."*
> — **Mr. Spock, *Star Trek*, 1967**

A little-talked-about fact of record business economics is that the record company doesn't make a great deal of money off the new artist the year of the first hit.

> *Leslie Zigel:* These days, between marketing and promotion costs, the [profit] margins are shrinking more and more.

If a new artist has a hit, the label gets their money back and makes some small profit. So if record companies don't make much off record sales, what pays for all the limos?

In the past, if you were going to start a record company, first you would buy a *catalog* of master recordings that had an existing revenue stream (retail sales and licensing). You would use this revenue stream to invest in future artists, which would become your future catalog.

Catalog is dependent upon one very important reality: a nostalgic appreciation of music. That is what creates *Greatest Hits of the New Nineties* and other compilations: the revenue generated from the master recordings (or composition) year after year, as an item of catalog—meaning, when the song has legs of its own and requires almost zero dollars to promote. A perfect example is "Wild Thing," a song that has been earning millions of dollars a year for both the record company that owns its master and the publisher who owns the composition's copyright. How much do they have to spend each year to promote "Wild Thing"? Little to nothing. Everybody knows the song even though it hasn't been sold as a single for about 40 years. It's been in hundreds of movies and makes it onto thousands of radio playlists around the world because it's part of our culture—part of the liquid tapestry, if you will.

In short, the entire economics of the music industry is based on catalog. Both publishing and master catalog.

If you pull the rug out from that model and train people to no longer have a nostalgic attachment to their music, then where is the engine that is driving the catalog-based model? It stalls for lack of fuel. Catalog becomes seriously devalued, as does the record company's assets as old records move into the public domain and new records have a very short shelf life due to lack of emotional attachment of record buyers. The record company, which once used catalog as a backbone revenue stream, now needs to find a new way to make money, a way in which revenue is not based on a personalized individual record sale and one that is stable enough to still attract investors.

Records and Reminiscence

The average record executive today is about 50 years of age. They entered a music industry that was about artistry and great three-minute songs. They listened to the **Rolling Stones** or **Grand Master Flash** when they lost their virginity. Cleaned their weed in the crease of a *Quadrophenia* LP. Now they find themselves locked into a business that is insisting that they chop up their product and sell it off in bits and pieces—sample licensing, ringtones, downloads—and with no consumer attachment whatsoever to the artists that created it.

As music becomes more liquid, as we sell pieces of songs, as the idea of sitting down and listening to music as a complete experience diminishes year by year, how many years will it be until we wake up one day and a record company president is saying publicly and without shame, "How valuable is the songwriter or the artist in the bigger picture?"

What will tomorrow's record company executive be nostalgic about when he is 40? "Remember that 30-second ringtone from the 2012 Nokia cell phone? Man, they don't make snips like that any more. Now they're only ten seconds at 12K." He'll sign on to a Web site called "Bob's Oldies," looking for the "full length" 30-second, 44.1K, 2008 iTunes MP4 file version of a song by an artist whose name he never even knew. Good thing he remembers the snip. He can search the "store" by humming the hook into his computer, which will do a *melody-match*. He really wants that 2008 version because when iTunes was bought out by Microsoft in 2010 they converted all the files over to a different format that no longer plays on all the older iPods made before 2005. "Man, those early iPods were cool," he reminisces. "My dad gave me his. You could share playlists with your friends."

This is the record industry of 2030.

⏵ Over the Next Thirty Years

Our productive lifespan (meaning the period wherein we make the biggest impact) is about 30 years. Many of us graduate from school between the ages of 18 and 25. Within 30 years we are between 48 and 55. Where will the business be during that time?

What I believe we will start to see in about five years is a sort of signing freeze on new song-oriented artists. What already has made it into the wallpaper's pattern will remain in full force. So the U2s of the world are safe. Things like *Classic Rock* will not go away. But new three-minute songs will find it harder and harder to find a slot to squeeze into the new media of music venues. (Read: Top 40 playlists.) After all, how many new classical composers have there been in the past 100 years who are as well known as Mozart? How many new baroque fugues that rival Bach? Or how many Renaissance paintings that are taking their places with Rembrandt?

In 50 to 100 years, all that will remain of the records we have today will be liquid ubiquitous wallpaper pattern consisting of about 5,000 masters that are as innocuous to a listener of that day as classical music is to an average 18-year-old today as he shops in a mall. It will be everywhere and nowhere at once. He'll know about the **Beatles** and will know the names **John, Paul, George,** and **Ringo**, but will only be able to identify a handful of specific songs as belonging to their catalog and "sniped" versions of their songs used as loops to create new snips and ringtones. Think it's farfetched? In the early 1800s, **Beethoven** was a "rock star" of the era. How many average music buyers under the age of 20 today can name his first concertos? (And don't say Beethoven's First Concerto, smartass.) How many know what sonata is being used in any one of a hundred car commercials?

What they *will* know, however, are the thousands of 10- and 30-second snips of "music" that bombard their PLD (personal listening device) and the music that came preloaded on their car stereo, computer, kitchen appliances, video games, "movets" (short movie-like programs that you can manipulate), and any other place that "record companies" can find to license their properties.

Terrestrial analog radio will certainly still exist and they will be playing lots of music since (in the US) terrestrial radio can play music without paying for master licenses.[19]

But satellite radio will eventually be merged with Internet radio and other broadband technology companies. They will not play as much music, however, due to skyrocketing music licensing fees that labels will be allowed to collect from them. Instead, this radio will be the realm of talk and sports shows. Look for "Classic Rock" (or "Classic Rap," for that matter) as an ever-widening format on the terrestrial radio dial and talk shows on satellite radio. The exception will be the satellite and Internet radio stations that are controlled by majors or their bigger artists. They will use these "stations" as platforms for selling new music. (I put "stations" in quotes because there will probably be no actual radio station, like today. It will all be done in home-sized recording studios and via podcast.)

[19] **Master licenses:** The fee for playing a record. US radio still has to pay for the use of the composition, but only in Europe do they pay for both the song and the recording of the song.

All this will create a kind of jigsaw puzzle of thousands of companies that make, sell, and license the music to all these entities and each other. That will become our new music industry: a web of thousands of production companies, each becoming their own distributor. You will not have major labels as we understand them today. They will become "rights aggregators." Mere brokers. There will be little need for large offices with hundreds of low-paid assistants and lawyers running around. The large advances for artist development will be very few and far between, as the lifespan of a hit master will be shorter, and you will only be dealing in singles or fractions of singles. In 2001 there were approximately 6,000 acts signed to US major labels and their affiliates. In 2005 there were fewer than 2,000. Expect that number to drop into the triple digits nationwide.

Meanwhile, the average artist making a living with his music will be more of an "author," combining hats of producer/writer and performer into one entity. He will not be signed to a major label. His most likely partner in crime will be his "aggregator." This may be an exclusive relationship, or it could be a non-exclusive relationship, where the aggregator has many clients and the author has many aggregators, one for each type of market. The same way that actors have several agents, some who specialize in TV, others in commercials, and others in endorsements and merchandising. He will have to join many PROs around the world and establish relations with as many of them as he can.

Those authors who show lateral success will probably not be signing record deals as we know them today. Since they are a commodity that stretches beyond music, these lucky 500 will be signing with agencies like **CAA, ICM, William Morris**,[20] or some such entity that can exploit their talent on many levels.[21]

PROs, Harry Fox, and Publishers

In approximately 15 years, after the adjustment to a liquid music environment and the complete collating of databases for every song and snippet of song and every master version of every song, the need for traditional publishers or performing rights organizations will be altered. This will not stop these billion-dollar entries from hanging around trying to convince authors that they should sign over valuable rights to them because they are necessary. As their usefulness deteriorates, count on seeing even bigger showcases and sponsored events by them designed, in part, to convince themselves, more so than the public, that they still have a job. In many cases they will succeed in this pitch for several more years. Eventually the terms PRO and publisher will come to mean something different than they do

[20] **The movie industry's three largest talent agencies.**

[21] **Record companies are legally prohibited from booking one of their artists in a movie in California, where many have corporate headquarters and most of these types of deals are made.**

today. So don't be fooled if there is still a company called ASCAP in 25 years. I'm not suggesting that there will not be. But their business model will be adjusted.

However, with the advent of the Internet, direct licensing and blanket licensing are inevitable through a "unified rights management" entity just as file sharing was an inevitability. Large PROs like ASCAP and BMI will have to downsize at some point (although it's hard to say exactly when) just to compete with the smaller unified entities that are more author- and community-based. An author (who is both a songwriter and creator/producer of the master) will not likely want to deal with multiple PROs and publishing entities. They will want entities that collect everything for both the song and the master. Right now that task is divvied up into record company for the master and, for the song, publishing companies and their main collection agents—the PROs. In the future it will probably merge into a single entity that collects for both, like a copyright management office.[22] The reason: ergonomics. The sweat of making vendors (movie companies, malls, advertisers) negotiate two licenses for the use of a snip will bottleneck the course of commerce and make licensing too complex. Ease of use will be the name of the game in the music business of 25 years from now. Those who can devise a model that "bundles" the rights of a snip in a quick, one-click purchase will seize the future.

Before this happens expect the opposite: new PROs designed to collect money strictly for the master recording will come of age. **SoundExchange** is currently the standard in the US, but this will be followed by a competitor, most probably a company called **Royalty Logic**. But even these will not satisfy the needs of the market in 15 years as authors will want "copyright manager companies" that specialize in different areas of distribution and licensing. Communities: for example, CMCs that specialize in pop songs on foreign television. CMCs that specialize in composers of instrumental music for movies. Starting a CMC may well be the most sought-after way to make money in this new industry. They will become the new record companies, and, like record companies of today, will likely be earning the same types of reputations and grievances that today's record companies must contend with. For this, expect new legislation and much resistance from broadcasters and live venues. They will fight tooth and nail to keep the number of entities they are required to negotiate with down to a minimum.

Product Placement and Cross-Marketing

In 2002, record companies were publicly complaining that they needed to find new ways to make money or they might perish. I asked this question of a Big Four

[22] The foundation for such things is already in existence: Bug Music, to name but one reference.

senior vice president: "Are record companies looking for more creative ways to make money via the music in *non-music-related things*?" For example, MTV represents 90 million viewers of the most desirable demographic: 13- to 35-year-olds with lots of disposable income. It seemed obvious to me that they should take a tip from their big brother—the movie industry—and start placing products in the videos for a fee.

The idea was met with ridicule. One marketing executive at a Big Four said that it would make no difference because "MTV doesn't even show videos anymore." While this is true of the network's cornerstone MTV, it's not as true of their myriad satellite stations who show almost *nothing but videos*: MTV2, MTVJ (rap), MTVS (Spanish), VH1C (country), VH1 (adult contemporary), VH1S (soul), MTV H, and CMTW. One must also consider the Web-streaming of videos on Yahoo! Music (or Y! Music), MSN, and the iTunes music store. Visual bundles of music are everywhere. So, why no active product placement?

> *Michael Ostroff:* Because the record company/artist relationship is really a two-way relationship. That said, I think that fewer and fewer artists are saying no to these kinds of tie-ups, and more and more artists are realizing that these are ways to break through the clutter. Whether it is sticking your song on advertisements or putting it in a movie or a television show, that is a way of differentiating yourself and that is what a lot of artists now *want* to do. There are some artists that still want to remain pure, and that is their right. I think that's a little unrealistic today given everything you've talked about. I think that the artists, record companies, and the world are growing more to accept the general concept of product placement and endorsements.

The word that has not yet been widely proliferated for this is *bundleability*.

In the eighties we had the word *signability*. It was code for *the artist is good-looking*. To sell an album you needed to make a video. If the artist was not attractive that would be a problem. (Just look at the career of some bands who were a bit tough on the eyes and where their careers went after the advent of MTV, if you think I'm exaggerating.) Much like the era of sound pictures ended the careers of silent actors who had funny voices, so too did video end the careers of many hopefuls who were extremely talented but did not possess the cheekbones. This has tapered off a bit in the new millennium, but not back to the point where it was in the 1970s.

And now, *bundleability*. In the immediate future, labels or agencies will be looking at how they can laterally integrate the artist's music into other products. For example, buying a computer and getting an entire catalog of songs preloaded into it, like software. Cross-marketing deals with soft drink companies to get a free download.

These are ideas that I wrote about in 2001 and that have all been unitized since. (See the sidebar, "Music Free? At What Price?")

To make this a reality, labels will have to look at how the artist's message fits into the message of other manufacturers. *Bundleability* will start to affect everything about the artist: the music, the video, the Web page, and the T-shirts.

The impulse is to see this as a bad thing. Thoughts like, "It's bad enough that artists already have to compromise their music and their image, now they will have to compromise their professional relationships." But there is a positive spin if we choose to embrace it. This can lead to an entirely new way for an artist to effectively send their message. For example, if you're a PETA fan, getting them to invest $100,000 in your video that will carry a pro-PETA message. Or for an extreme opposite, getting the army to throw you a few bucks for a pro-military message on your Web site. Or the NRA, for that matter, could package a Duel-Disk in with a membership or gun sale. There is no limit (except by one's imagination) as to how product placement (and politics) can and probably will play a role in artist development in the next decade. **Britney Spears** and **Pepsi** was only the beginning.[23]

[23] In fall 2003, Britney Spears did in fact put product placement in her video "Me Against the Music." It was for a car. The car company overtly paid for it and received a five-second shot at the beginning of the video.

Jam Bands and the Future of Touring

Recently I was partying with several music lawyers wherein a conversation evolved about how bands in the future would make money. One lawyer felt that the theories outlined above would ultimately mean that touring would be the focus of a band's income, since it was clear that making money from record sales would be relegated to snips or massive bundling deals that were the realm exclusively of a major agency's (labels). Think so?

First, a few facts to chew on. Since 2002, concert grosses have taken a nosedive. However, this is only the big labels' acts. Smaller acts and so-called "jam bands" were not affected economically. But predictions discussed in this chapter may change this.

Big acts rely on tour money to survive. As has been outlined exhaustively in *Confessions of a Record Producer*, the artist doesn't make any real money off record sales for some years. During that time they rely on touring to make up the difference.

With music becoming wallpaper I'm not very optimistic about that model holding up. Lack of personal connection to the artist will surely translate into less ticket sales. We've seen this happening already. To make up the difference, concert promoters have been raising the prices of tickets. The average ticket for a mid-level band is now $25. A marquee heritage act is easily over $100. Some are over $500.

MUSIC FREE? AT WHAT PRICE?

The following is an excerpt from the industry newsletter *Moses Supposes*, January 2001. Remember that this was written long before **U2** made it into iPods or before **Ray Charles** sold two million copies of a CD via a coffee chain.

Moses Supposes: *January 2001*

In the near future you may get to keep music free—most likely by digging for CDs in a box of Cap'n Crunch.

The key question perched on the lips of the entire industry is this: how, when the public's perception is that music should be free, do record companies create the perception that music should be paid for?

This is not a new problem. In fact, one can trace this exact phenomenon back to the controversy created by piano-rolls in the early 1900s. The Internet is just that—piano-rolls for the new millennium; just another manifestation of an industry dependent on control of distribution, fighting the public's conditioned incentive to get something for nothing.

Perhaps there is some young Stanford marketing-school graduate who can see a fresh angle here, but I see only two ways out for the majors:

1) Major labels will have to resort to the technique they've used many times in the past, whenever a new technology became overly accessible: they upgrade the standard to one that makes the old one sound absurd, cheap, and worthy of being free. The last time they used this strategy was the 1980s; most audiophiles would agree that CDs, when compared to LPs, didn't sound as full if heard on a high-quality stereo system. As part of marketing CDs, the parent companies of PolyGram and Sony (Philips Electronics and Sony International, respectively) who held the CD patent downgraded the quality of consumer listening systems: cheap boomboxes, integrated stereo systems for under $200, and other things that made listening to LPs "the right way" almost impossible. Left without a viable comparison, we are now a generation unable to fairly compare the quality of LPs to CDs. As a result "CD quality" became the sublime standard.

What to look for:

Special "audiophile" releases in 96-bit/60-kHz and players to support them. DVDs will incorporate albums that will include video footage and behind the scenes info. Also, record clubs with value-added things like concert tickets and contests for members who pay the monthly subscriber fees to Napster and the like.

2) If the above fails, record companies will have no choice, as I see it, but to go to the proverbial mattresses, tossing in CDs along with the sale of other items so that it seems free, much like the prize at the bottom of the cereal box. For example, buy a BMW and get the Beatles box set "free." A story published this month is the writing on the wall for this theory: ASCAP announced an alliance with Heineken to market a compilation CD. It will not be long before major labels and performing rights agencies begin exploiting this model and packaging new artists with products even before the record is released. Labels' decision-making process for whom to sign will begin to revolve around how they can package the artist with their affiliate/sponsors. (News flash: they already do, but now the volume will be turned way up.) Will artists go for this? They may have little choice if they want a major label deal. This gives the indies a new angle to sell. Go get 'em.

What to look for:

The telltale signs of this will likely be product placement in MTV videos before the end of 2002. Whereas before you might see **Britney Spears** doing a **Pepsi** commercial, now you will see a subtler, reverse version of this: Pepsi incorporated into the Britney video. No big stretch there, but how will this fit into the more subversive marketing campaign of, say, Limp Bizkit or Marilyn Manson? (Perhaps Marilyn's label can convince distributors of RU-486 to do a placement.) When record companies run out of condom and alcohol sponsors, what next? A&R: "Hey fellas, we see you doing the video where you have a dream that you're performing your hit for a room full of Metropolitan Life Insurance Company salesmen, and then out pops a chick, dressed like a Hershey's chocolate bar. Can you see it? Can you see it?

Have the costs of putting on a show gone up that much? No, but promoters have gotten older. Now looking towards retirement, they have a lot more personal overhead (mortgage, kids, and so on) and need to reap more booty in order to make it worth their while.

The good news is eventually they will retire. Then we can turn the clock back to the 1970s when most of the promoters were in their twenties and early thirties. They promoted first and foremost because of a love of music. If we get a slew of young Turks in place of the old regime the live-venue business stands a chance of revival.

In the meantime the small jam bands seem to be the only real money left in the live music space. True, most of them are cover bands, or tribute bands, but this lays the groundwork for the narrowing of the gateway of what will survive from the era of rock and rap as we design the wallpaper of tomorrow. Right now we have several **Grateful Dead** bands, as well as **Kiss** and **Led Zeppelin** bands. Count on more and more of these cropping up as the bands we know today become a thing of the past. Look for **U2, the Rolling Stones**, and **Pink Floyd** as prime new franchises. Count on these bands selling "tribute licenses" as they themselves get too old to tour. Or maybe there will still be one officially licensed "Rolling Stones" band that plays the arrangements with a different cast of characters, as the big bands of **Count Basie**, **Duke Ellington**, and **Glenn Miller** have done. Or how about the holographic version (*Pink Void?*) in which **David Gilmore** and **Roger Waters** images could perform while forever young.

⊘ Conclusion: Da Vinci on a Necktie (Requiem for an Industry)

For those of us who have been in the business since the 1980s, it would be easy to have a knee-jerk reaction to much of what has been said about the future of music. Many producers, writers, performers, and teachers were attracted to the music business for reasons that may no longer be relevant.

It's also entirely possible that the public has outgrown the need for pop gods and arena rock. Perhaps the twilight years of pop music are ahead of us. The years where it takes its place, with many other art forms, in the tapestry that has become *the life aesthetic*: Rembrandt on a postage stamp, Picasso wallpaper, da Vinci on a necktie. I have no doubt that there was a fine-art curator somewhere who publicly objected the first time he saw a print of the Sistine Chapel's ceiling as bathroom tile. No one listened. Commerce marched on. The only difference for pop music is that instead of irate art historians, we have major labels and their lobbying entity, the RIAA, fighting for air as their inventory slips into the public domain.

I start to wonder if the folks at **Disney** had the right idea. In 2004, Congress extended the length of a copyright to about double the lifespan of an average human.[24] Many thought it not in the spirit of the way copyrights are supposed to function: to allow the author a *limited* monopoly on his work and then when the copyright is over (in 15 or 20 years) for the author to release the work and let the public do what they will with it: cut it up, redesign it, do whatever. Perhaps the Disney people (who some sources claim financially backed the new law) knew something about art and the public domain that often forget. Just look at what the public generally does with great works when they don't have to acquire permission from their authors; the work takes on sillier and sillier forms until one day we see a XXX movie staring Mickey and Minnie. While our Constitution grants the right for such things, does this mean we as a society have to expedite the demand for it?

If we let go of pop music as an art form and let it too retire into the public domain, how long until we one day see an adult movie staring the characters and music from **KISS**?[25] Or how about a **Jim Morrison** lawn jockey that plays "Light My Fire"; a **Janis Joplin** anti-hangover pill; **Bono**'s Bartender Companion that helps you prepare favorite drinks of the Sinn Féin; a **Bob Dylan** calendar that each day has a thoughtful reminder *from a different religion*; and finally, **Steely Dan** condoms[26] that play "Go back, Jack, do it again".

For all these new music products we can thank companies that see pop music not as an art form, but as a commodity, like salt or soybeans. These are not companies run by musicians and certainly not run by people who have worked with musicians for the past four decades, financing their dreams, responding to their inspirations, and entering into business partnerships to market their hard work.

Record companies have taken quite a beating in the press since 2001. They've been accused of not understanding the needs of the market and thumbing their noses at the changing technology.[27] Of course, it's not as black-and-white as these critics would have us believe. I too have been openly critical of many record company practices, but recent events have allowed me to add some gray to my viewpoints. Record companies (as they existed then) were also fighting to preserve something wonderful about their product: its ability to play a role in our culture and its ability to create a stable economic base so that a music industry is even possible. Riding the media-stimulated anti-label zeitgeist also means resigning

[24] The Sonny Bono Copyright Extension Act made copyrights for some media "life of the author plus 75 years."

[25] For all I know, Gene Simmons already has this in the planning.

[26] If you get this joke, you are either born before 1965 or a real diehard 1970s music fan.

[27] Most of these criticisms have come from tech companies and their respective influence over the press.

ourselves to a possible future where the medium is reduced to cultural wallpaper, stripped of much of its artistry, its meaning, and its social consciousness. It also means a destabilization of industry economics. Perhaps in favor of a better one, but so far, the butcher's bill has been massive downsizing of both staff and label rosters by almost 50 percent, all this so that the public can give music away to each other without breaking the law. Is this worth the tradeoff?

So you have to ask yourself: Are the real enemies of music's future the record companies who are trying to retard this "progress," so that their product does not end up being the free toy at the bottom of a cereal box? Are they the *real* enemies?

If so, count me among them.

That's all for now.

⊗ Acknowledgments

Writing the acknowledgments is my favorite part of the book-making process for two reasons: first, it's the last thing I do and means that I can sit back and light up that Romeo y Julieta Churchill I've been saving. But the second reason is far more enlightening. It's where I get to take stock of everyone who helped make this book what it is. If you enjoyed *Million Dollar Mistakes* then take a minute to learn who is responsible.

First and foremost, those whose names are listed in the *Who We Are Hearing From* appendix should be acknowledged and acknowledged over and over. These are great people who really care about the business and the future. They gave their stories and their names to add credibility to this project. I am very grateful to each.

The same thanks go to the many who gave comments to this book only if I agreed to keep their names out of it. I would like to thank them, even though I cannot acknowledge them publicly. You know who you are.

Those who work to educate tomorrow's music business deserve our deepest gratitude: **Jim Porgris, Keith Hatschek, Catharine Moore, Jeff Weber**, and **Phil Burks**. Then there are a few lawyers I really like who have acted on an advisory capacity to me over the years: **Neville Johnson, Philip Lyons, Cheryl Hodgson, Ken Abdo, Leon Bass, Matt Greenberg, the Wolfeman, Darryl Cohen, Andy Tavel,** and **Don Passman**. Also I'd like to thank **Irving Azoff** for returning my emails so promptly—on Grammy night.

Some cool new friends, **Norman Chesky, John Lanac, Samm Brown, John Braheny, Don Sundstrom, Monica Wild**, and **Griff Morris** at **NARAS**, all of whom lent some form of help, tangible or otherwise. Also, two old friends, **Jay Frank** at **Yahoo!** and **Pat Cameron**, whose value to me cannot be easily quantified. Your contributions to music and the business are inspirational.

Tradition has it that you're supposed to thank your agent in this section, but I have none. However, I would like to thank all the literary agents who have rejected my work or jerked me around. You saved me 15 percent.

The entire crew at **Backbeat Books** all deserve mention: my editor, **Richard Johnston**, headhoncho **Matt Kelsey**, production editor **Amy Miller**, and those who work the sales end, **Nina Lesowitz** and **Kevin Becketti**. We've been through much together these years and have survived to both complain about the experience and enjoy the results.

Finally, my family, for putting up with mood swings that are common during deadline. Everything I do, I do for them. And my personal assistant, **Lisa**, who is efficient, sage, and a great asset to my organization.

Thank you all for making this project and my life a better place to spend my time.

—Moses Avalon

Who We Are Hearing From

In 50 years, most of the people interviewed in this book will probably be unavailable for comment. But through this book their wisdom and experience will always be accessible.

More than 50 people were interviewed for this project. But only half of them, in the end, wanted to have their names on the comments they contributed. (See the preface, *Skating on a Frozen Lake of Lies,* for how this process worked.) As a result many of the comments in the book are amalgamated from several quotes or simply attributed to an anonymous source. Below is a complete list of all those who speak on the record (and their credentials).

These people each deserve your thanks and appreciation for their candor and fortitude. If you ever have the chance, please give it to them. Organized first by category and then alphabetically, they are:

Producers, Managers, Engineers, and Others on the Creative Side of the Business

André Fischer	John (Jay Jay) French
Andy Wickett	John Luongo
Francis Buckley	Matt Forger
Geza X	Mervyn Warren
Jack Endino	Michael C. Ross
Jeff Weber	Paul Cooke
Joey Akles	Steve Addabbo

Attorneys, Executives (Present and Former), Educators and Others on the Business Side

Andrea Brauer	John Brodey
Barbara Graham	Leslie Zigel
Ben McLane	Mark Avsec
Bobby Borg	Michael Ostroff
Doug Breitbart	Moses Avalon
Gary Cable	Paul Menes
Jay Frank	Peter Spellman
Jerry Blair	Ritch Ezra
Jim Barber	Ron Gertz

❯ Producer, Managers, Engineers, and Others in the Creative Side of the Business

André Fischer

With 40 platinum and 25 gold albums, André Fischer is best known for his production, performing, and arrangement work on the legendary group **Rufus Featuring Chaka Khan**, and **Natalie Cole**'s *Unforgettable* (which earned seven Grammy awards). Additionally Mr. Fischer won three Grammy awards (including a Producer of the Year nomination in 1992), four American Music Awards, and numerous awards for songwriting, publishing, album/soundtrack sales, and f his cultural and fundraising efforts.

Mr. Fischer has held executive positions at various recorded music and film companies: senior vice president for **MCA/Universal Urban Music Dept.**, vice president of jazz A&R for **Quincy Jones, Qwest/Warner Bros.**, and vice president of publishing development at **20th Century Fox Records and Films**, to name a few.

Mr. Fischer is responsible for producing, executive producing, performing, and recording with many of the music industry's most gifted pop, R&B, rock, and jazz performers: **Patti LaBelle, Michael Franks, Natalie Cole, Tony Bennett**'s *Perfectly Frank* (which won a 1993 Grammy award for Best Traditional Pop Vocal), **James Ingram, B.B. King, Gladys Knight, Nina Simone, Frank Sinatra**, the **Pointer Sisters, Diane Schuur**, the **Temptations, Dusty Springfield, Brenda Russell, O.C. Smith**,

Dr. John, Laura Nyro, Lou Rawls, Jackie DeShannon, Nancy Wilson, Milt Jackson, Bruce Hornsby, Oscar Brown, Curtis Mayfield & The Impressions, Jerry Butler, the Rolling Stones tour, the Elton John tour, the Who tour, Etta James, Neil Diamond, Anita Baker, Janet Jackson, Vesta Williams, Leroy Hudson, Betty Wright, Phil Perry, Steve Khan, Tower of Power, Vanessa Rubin, Angela Winbush, James Moody, Ahmad Jamal, the Isley Brothers, Donny Hathaway, Richie Havens, Eddie Harris, Clark Terry, Randy Crawford, Ralph Tresvant, Jackie Lomax, Al Green, and Bobby Brown. Most recently Mr. Fischer has produced the new album by urban adult contemporary/smooth jazz/pop artist Eloise Laws.

Mr. Fischer is president of KSF Enterprises, providing all music production services—budget management and event planning, marketing, and lecturing—for a variety of entertainment and technology companies. He also serves on the advisory committee for the Arts and Humanities Council in Washington, DC, and is the former chapter president, governor, trustee, and outreach chairman for the Los Angeles Chapter of the National Academy of Recording Arts and Sciences. He has lectured at universities and professional schools such as UCLA, various California State Universities, and Full Sail University, Orlando, Florida.

Andy Wickett

Andy Wickett started his career in the '80s singing and playing in TV Eye, Duran Duran, the Xpertz & World Service, and supporting the Clash, U2, Culture Club, Duran Duran, Burning Spear, and Gregory Isaacs. Mr. Wickett has also produced and written albums with world renowned Asian artists Nusrat Fateh Ali Khan and DCS.

Following a degree in computer animation, Mr. Wickett worked as a freelance animation producer creating animated pop videos for broadcast on MTV and cable networks. These included videos for Asian artists Stereo Nation, Malkit Singh, and Nusrat Fateh Ali Khan. He has recently been working in collaboration with renowned cartoonist Hunt Emerson. He is currently producing his own "dark" version of "Girls on Film," which includes a video. A compilation CD is available on his website.

Francis Buckley

Grammy award–winning engineer/producer Francis Buckley has been making records for over 20 years. His experience ranges from the groundbreaking punk act Black Flag's first album *Damaged* in 1980, to winning the Engineering Grammy award in 1996 for *Q's Jook Joint* with Quincy Jones.

Mr. Buckley's contributions as engineer and mixer to such multi-platinum recordings as the Pointer Sisters' *Breakout,* Paula Abdul's *Forever Your Girl,* Wilson

Phillips's *Wilson Phillips,* **Alanis Morissette**'s *Jagged Little Pill,* and many others, have helped to sell over 50 million–plus records worldwide.

Mr. Buckley began producing while acting as chief engineer at **W.E. Studios** in Redondo Beach in 1979. In 1980, he became chief engineer for **Unicorn Records** and worked with many different acts, including Black Flag. In 1981, he moved to **MCA Music Publishing,** beginning a ten-year stand as director of recording services. It was at MCA that he met producer **Glen Ballard,** with whom he shared a 14-year partnership.

His numerous credits can be viewed at *www.francisbuckley.com/bio.htm.*

Geza X

Geza X cut his producing teeth on mariachi, funk, gospel, and disco. Although his legendary work with groups like **Germs, Black Flag, Dead Kennedys, Redd Kross,** and **Josey Cotton** helped create the face of American punk he is best known for his production of **Meredith Brooks**'s mega-hit song "Bitch," which stayed at No. 2 for an astounding six weeks, prompting *Billboard* to list him as one of 1997's top producers. Other productions include **Face to Face, 1000 Mona Lisas, Rimitti** (featuring **Robert Fripp** and **Flea**), **Magnapop, Ice-T, Charlie Wilson, Club Nouveau, Sir Jinx, Lighter Shade of Brown, Uzi Brothers, Keith Washington,** and **Rhyme Syndicate.**

Over the past few years, practically all of the records Geza worked with during punk's halcyon days have been reissued on CD, recapturing the raw and energetic sound that he helped create. The recent *Live from the Masque,* a three-CD set that marked the debut outing for **Year 1 Records** (co-owned by L.A. punk stalwart/former X vocalist **Exene Cervenka**) was the result of tapes Geza had mixed in his soundman days.

Jack Endino

As a Seattle-based record producer and engineer, Jack Endino has made more than 250 records in ten countries since 1985. He has also played in several bands, the best-known of which was **Skin Yard** (1985–1992, six albums). Much of his work could be described as "rock." His work with **Nirvana** in the early stages of their career is well known. His entire discography, too numerous to print here, can be viewed at *www.jackendino.com.*

Jeff Weber

Jeffrey Weber is a 27-year music industry professional. He has produced more than 145 CDs with releases on just about every major label as well as a host of independent labels. His projects have yielded two Grammys, seven Grammy nominations, at least seventeen Top Ten albums, two No. 1 albums, and an assortment of other honors.

Mr. Weber's discography includes work with **Nancy Wilson**, **Jackson Browne**, **Michael McDonald**, **Chick Corea**, **Stanley Clarke**, **Luther Vandross**, **David Crosby**, **Toni Tennille**, **Etta James**, **Linda Hopkins**, **Kenny Burrell**, **McCoy Tyner**, **Jackie McLean**, **David Benoit**, **Steve Lukather**, the **Utah Symphony**, **Marcus Miller**, **Bill Champlin**, **Gerald Albright**, **Tom Scott**, **Billy Sheehan (Mr. Big)**, **Cozy Powell**, the **Count Basie Orchestra**, **John Sebastian**, **Ronnie Dio**, **Ritchie Blackmore**, **Pat Boone**, **Buddy Miles**, **Billy Preston**, **Kenny Rankin**, **Dianne Reeves**, **Diane Schuur**, **Rita Coolidge**, **Simon Phillips**, **Jeff Porcaro**, and **Patrice Rushen**, among many others.

Because of their sonic excellence, his recordings have been repeatedly selected by major hardware manufacturers (**Sony**, **Toshiba**, **Tara Labs**, **Threshold**, **Boston Acoustics**, **Jeff Rowland**, **Martin-Logan**, and **Psion**, to name a few), to demonstrate their product lines.

Mr. Weber has founded, run, or participated in various label capacities from A&R, music supervision for film and TV, production, interactive programming, marketing, sales, international relations, business affairs, and art direction for independents as well as his own labels, **Weberworks** and **Stark Raving Records**. His productions have appeared on every major label including **MCA**, **Warner Bros.**, **Atlantic**, **BMG**, **Columbia**, **A&M**, and **Elektra** as well as **GRP**, **Hip-O**, **Sheffield**, **Concord**, **Bainbridge**, **Silver Eagle**, and **Zebra**, among countless others.

Mr. Weber is a former member of the Board of Governors of the **National Academy of Recording Arts and Sciences** (NARAS) as well as a former National Trustee and Chapter Vice President.

Joey Akles

Modern pop/rock songwriter and poet Joey Akles is best known as the co-author of the power-pop hit for the **Plimsouls** and **Goo Goo Dolls** "Million Miles Away." A native of New York, Mr. Akles has worked all over the figurative map in music. In addition to his songwriting accomplishments and industry positions, he has worked as a music journalist and a magazine editor, and was a published poet.

In the mid-'80s, Mr. Akles sang in the **Space Shot Orchestra**, a group produced by **Tin Machine**'s **Hunt Sales**. The band was the first to record "The Sphinx," a song he co-authored. The song was also recorded a year later by British bluesman **Alexis Korner**. He also co-wrote songs with **Jim Basnight** (of the **Moberlys**) and **Devin Payne**. As a manager, Mr. Akles worked with several acts, including **They Eat Their Own**.

Mr. Akles has co-authored a number of other songs, including the **Roadrunners**' "Haunted Forever," **Paul Collins & The Beat**'s "All Over the World," and "Talk to Me," recorded by **Phil Seymour**. He is presently the co-producer and co-leader of the avant-garde musical act **DJ Monkey**, with **Mick McMains**, onetime lead singer of **Earl Slick**'s **NYC**, and has played many parts in the music business, from label executive to vocalist to band manager.

John (Jay Jay) French

Jay Jay French was the founding member and lead guitar player for the 1980s rock sensation **Twisted Sister**, whose hits "We're Not Gonna Take It" and "I Wanna Rock" stayed in *Billboard*'s Top Ten for several months. Mr. French presently manages several groups.

John Luongo

John Luongo has been instrumental in mixing and producing songs that have benefited artists from **Aerosmith** and **ZZ Top** to **Jesus Jones** and **Bobby Brown**. Mr. Luongo mixed and broke many hit tracks such as **Don Henley**'s "All She Wants to Do Is Dance," **Dan Hartman**'s "Relight My Fire" and "Instant Replay," and **Huey Lewis**'s "I Want a New Drug" and "Power of Love," and remixes on artists such as the **Jacksons**, **Melba Moore**, **Brian Adams**, **Don Henley**, **Patti LaBelle**, **Gladys Knight**, **Dolly Parton**, **John Waite**, and **Cheap Trick**, to name a few.

He has taught the course "The Record Industry" at Northeastern University and has served a term as an elected member to the NARAS Board of Governors for the New York chapter. Mr. Luongo currently serves on the Producer and Membership Panels and is a voting member of the Grammys for over 15 years.

He became one of the youngest presidents of a CBS-associated label with his term at the helm of **Pavilion Records**, where he was responsible for discovering top R&B group **Fantasy**, which had a Top Five hit, as well as bringing talents such as **Patty Smyth** and **Full Force** to CBS's attention.

Matt Forger

Matt Forger has worked closely with **Michael Jackson** for over a decade, providing a technical foundation and an environment conducive to the artist's creative needs. Shortly after moving to Los Angeles, Mr. Forger secured a staff position at **Westlake Studios**, where he teamed up with producers **Quincy Jones**, **Rod Temperton**, and **Bruce Swedien**, working on albums that included Michael Jackson's *Thriller*.

His body of engineering and production work has allowed him to fuse technical prowess with an ear for hit music and intuition for bringing new and innovative styles and sounds together for commercial success. He has also worked with producers **Giorgio Moroder**, **Keith Forsey**, **Harold Faltermeyer**, and **George Duke** and on films for such esteemed award-winning film directors as **Steven Spielberg**, **John Landis**, **George Lucas**, and **Francis Ford Coppola**.

His production contributions stretch across the globe with 13 albums as recording engineer, mixer, and co-producer entering the *Billboard* chart at No. 1 and 2 and receiving Gold Disc Awards (Japan's Grammy equivalent). One such artist was Japanese pop superstar **Yumi (Yuming) Matsutoya**.

Mr. Forger's current involvement is helping artists achieve the success they desire by focusing the emotional content of their music and using technology to reach that goal.

Mervyn Warren

(Note: Mr. Warren's quote in the book was taken from a public speech he made in 2004 and was not part of a specific interview given for this book.)

Mervyn Warren, formerly of **Take 6**, is a five-time Grammy-winning and eleven-time Grammy-nominated composer, arranger, record producer, songwriter, and musician. His credits include the films *Living Out Loud, The Preacher's Wife*, and *Sister Act 2*, and he has worked with **Barbra Streisand**, **Whitney Houston**, **Chicago**, **Michael McDonald**, **Quincy Jones**, and **Boyz II Men**.

Michael C. Ross

In the last couple of years, Michael C. Ross has gone from being the recording industry's "best kept secret" to earning a Grammy nomination for his engineering of **Vanessa Carlton**'s smash single "A Thousand Miles." Over the years, Mr. Ross has compiled one of the most impressive discographies in the music industry; however, he is known for more than just recording and mixing records. Michael C. Ross's recording and mixing credits include **Christina Aguilera**, **Vanessa Carlton**, **Mick Jagger**, **Eric Clapton**, **Queen Latifah**, **J.C. Chasez,** and **Keith Richards**.

Since his Grammy nomination, Mr. Ross has received tremendous media coverage from industry publications such as *Billboard*, *Mix* magazine, *Recording* magazine, *Pro Sound Audio*, and *Music Connection*.

Paul Cooke

As a founder and member of the pop group **Sade**, Paul Cooke developed and played on the multi-platinum *Diamond Life* album, which included the hits "Smooth Operator" and "Your Love Is King," among others. He toured Europe with Sade and performed in the US, along with TV and radio performances on Britain's *Top of the Pops*, Channel 4, and BBC Radio One.

Mr. Cooke studied piano at the age of 7 and continued his musical education at Hornsea Secondary School, studying the euphonium, French horn, trumpet, and percussion. He finally ended up playing drums in the school orchestra at the age of 12. In 1980 Mr. Cooke moved to London and joined **Pride** with **Stuart Mathewman**.

After producing and collaborating with various artists in London throughout the late '80s, Mr. Cooke formed **Papa D**, fronted the band, and wrote and produced the music. Gigs at Moles Club and Ronnie Scott's ensued as well as various work for **Sony Records** and **Zomba Publishing**.

Mr. Cooke is currently a music director of Diamond Life Entertainment Ltd. and works in conjunction with **4M Records** in New York. All projects are distributed via **Caroline/EMI** in the US.

Steve Addabbo

Steve Addabbo is a renowned producer, recording engineer, and musician. He developed and produced **Suzanne Vega**'s first two albums and her Top Three hit, "Luka," and **Shawn Colvin**'s Grammy-winning debut album, *Steady On*. He has also worked alongside **Jesse Harris** and **Rebecca Martin**, folk legend **Eric Andersen**, **Jeff Buckley**, **Darden Smith**, **Dar Williams**, **Jane Olivor**, **Michael Brecker**, and new artists **Sonya Kitchell** (**Velour Records**) and **Ben Jelen** (**Maverick Records**). Currently, he owns **Shelter Island Sound** studio in midtown Manhattan, a vibrant part of the mixing and recording scene in New York for the past fifteen years. Mr. Addabbo remains active as a producer, writer, mixer, and musician.

⊛ Attorneys, Label Executives (Present and Former), and Educators

Andrea Brauer

Andrea Brauer has been in the music business for 25 years and has practiced entertainment law for 12 of these. A graduate of the University of Southern California Law School, she currently heads her own law firm in Los Angeles. A large part of her practice is devoted to independent music-business ventures and she currently represents numerous record labels, publishers, production companies, and managers as well as independent artists. Her specialties include trademarks, copyrights, and contract drafting/negotiations. Ms. Brauer is also a legal consultant to several music organizations in Los Angeles such as the **Songwriter's Guild** and **Los Angeles Women in Music**.

Barbara Graham

As an attorney with **Hart**, **Horwitz**, **Dillon & Graham**, **LLC**, Barbara Graham practices in the areas of entertainment law and domestic relations. Her clients and alliances include **Potzee**, **Starr 47**, **Louie V**, **Erika Johnson**, **COJC Music**, **Alkeisha Brown**, **Ambull Entertainment/Pure**, **Elijah**, **Dana Christian**, **Dr. Biggs**, **Gregg Haynes**, and **Untouchable Records' Steve Blast** (producer for **Nelly**).

A supporter of the St. Louis entertainment scene, Ms. Graham serves as chairman of **Performance Coordination/Artist Relations for the US Bank St. Louis Jazz Festival** and the **St. Louis Art Fair**, is a regular panelist for the **Inspired Music Entertainment Seminars** at the University of Missouri St. Louis, and was a member of the board of directors of **Streetwise Entertainment Inc.**

She was profiled as a "Woman on the Move" in *The Flipside Newszine*, October 2003, and served as co-executive producer on the Erika Johnson album *Erika Revealed*.

Ben McLane

Ben McLane is a Los Angeles–based lawyer who has worked for and with many top gold and platinum and Grammy-winning artists, as well as with up-and-coming artists. He's been presented with platinum and gold record awards for his involvement with the **Dixie Chicks, Tracy Byrd, Sparkle, Guns N' Roses, Afroman, 311, Cher, Mya**, the **Eagles, Khia, Big Bad Voodoo Daddy**, and the soundtracks for *Above the Rim* and *Swingers.*

Behind the scenes he's worked in legal and business affairs at **Rhino Records** and **Priority Records**, been head of business affairs/CFO for **JWP-USA/BMG Records** and a talent scout for **Sire Records**, and has participated in numerous and diverse projects involving, but not limited to, legendary artists such as **50 Cent**, the **Doors, Puff Daddy, No Doubt, Eric Clapton**, the **Rolling Stones, Tony Iommi, Bonnie Raitt, Cher**, the **Eagles, Jennifer Lopez, Phish, Roots, Shaggy, Yellowcard, Vladimir Horowitz, Willie Nelson, Ryan Adams, Ben Harper, Guns N' Roses, Jeff Beck, Flaming Lips, Sixpence None The Richer, Eva Cassidy, Rooney, Dashboard Confessional**, the **Black Eyed Peas**, the **Dixie Chicks**, the **Beau Brummels**, the **Beatles, Bobby Caldwell, Martina McBride**, the **Ozark Mountain Daredevils, Frank Zappa, Brewer & Shipley, Badfinger, Gloria Estefan, U2, Pearl Jam, Ritchie Valens, Bon Jovi, Diane Warren, Dio, Faith Hill, Madonna, Tim McGraw, Michael Jackson, Beyoncé, Little Steven, Kurtis Blow, Big Star, Gap Band, Big Daddy Kane, Tupac, Wilson Phillips, Alice Cooper, Yanni, Whitney Houston, Barry Manilow, Motorhead, Dr. John, Thelonious Monk, Mary J. Blige, Anita Baker, Naughty By Nature, Ying Yang Twins, Melissa Manchester, Chicago, Heart**, the **Bronx, Nancy Sinatra, Christina Milian, Boyz II Men, Dr. Dre, Knack, Jay Z, Frankie Avalon, Hank Ballard, Little Anthony, Nine Inch Nails, Stevie Wonder, Gloria Estefan, Bob Rock, Howard Benson, Henry Stone, Lifehouse**, and **Carson Daly.**

Bobby Borg

Bobby Borg is an international recording and touring musician with more than 25 years of experience in the music business. He has worked with a variety of artists at the major label, indie, and DIY capacity including the multi-platinum group **Warrant, Beggars & Thieves**, and his own band **Left for Dead**.

Mr. Borg is a music business and A&R consultant to music supervisors, labels, and producers, a prominent guest speaker at music industry events, a regular contributor to music business publications, and an instructor for UCLA Music Business Extension and the Musician's Institute Music Business program in Hollywood, California. He consults regularly with artists in Los Angeles.

Mr. Borg is a graduate of Berklee College of Music in Boston with a B.A. in Professional Music, and of the University of California Los Angeles (UCLA) Extension with a certificate in music business. He is also the author of the highly endorsed book *The Musician's Handbook: A Practical Guide to Understanding the Music Business* (published by Billboard Books). It can be found by asking any major bookseller or by visiting *www.bobbyborg.com.*

Doug Breitbart

Doug Breitbart is founder and CEO of **Broadbeard Productions**, **Inc.**, a successful entertainment concern involved with production, publishing, and management in the popular music industry. He has been a consultant and practiced law for over 20 years, predominantly in the areas of entertainment, intellectual property, contract, corporate, and technology-related transactions and ventures. He was responsible for the development and breaking of the career of **Debbie Gibson**.

Mr. Breitbart is founder and/or principal of several entities, including **Bedrock Ventures**, a venture accelerator that specializes in formulating and launching new businesses; COO of the **Institute for Music & Brain Science**, a leading Harvard- and MGH-affiliated research institute devoted to the study of music and the brain; COO of **Peter Pan Industries**, **Inc.**, a market-leading national manufacturer and distributor of audio, video, and printed products serving the children's and fitness markets; director of business development for **Silent Partner Consulting**, a firm specializing in the management of intellectual property rights and collections of fine art and culturally significant ephemera; CEO of **RightsCentral, Inc.**, an intellectual property rights enforcement services firm targeting protection of client intellectual properties on the Internet; COO for Internet start-up **UniverseONE Inc.**, a sports marketing firm engaged in the creation of virtual communities for professional sports franchises, where he oversaw the successful launch of the first site for the St. Louis Cardinals; and COO of **StorageONE**, a venture that developed a software platform enabling the creation of an unlimited-size media content server storage service providing real-time on-demand access to multimedia content for the entertainment and media industries. Before founding **Bedrock Ventures**, Mr. Breitbart was the founder and CEO of **Breiter Management Inc.**, a corporate, entertainment, and technology consulting practice.

Gary Cable

Gary Cable is one of Western Canada's leading entertainment lawyers. He teaches entertainment law and previously taught intellectual property law at the University of Alberta Faculty of Law. He has lectured extensively across Canada on numerous topics in the entertainment and intellectual property fields, and his views have been published in *Canadian Musician* magazine.

Mr. Cable has acted for **Stony Plain Records** (Canada's largest independent record company), **Tommy Banks Music**, **Keith Johnstone** (for MTV/Spike TV), **Purple Wolf Records** (music for *Party of Five*, Columbia/TriStar), **Corb Lund**, **Brad Johner** (**Louis O'Reilly Entertainment**), **Michael Carey** (with **Randy Bachman** and **Sony Nashville**), **Aaron Lines** (with **BMG Nashville**), **Cormel Music Publishing**, **Beanstalk Music Publishing**, **Allarcom** (ITV), and many other prominent recording and performing artists.

He has also been a professional musician for the past 30 years (pianist, keyboard player, singer, songwriter, producer, and arranger) and remains active in the Alberta professional music scene as a solo artist, bandleader, and producer.

Jay Frank

Jay Frank currently manages artist and label relations for **Yahoo! Music**, formerly **LAUNCH**, the music destination on Yahoo! Before the acquisition of LAUNCH Media, Inc. by Yahoo! in 2001, Mr. Frank was vice president of marketing and promotions, where he spearheaded all programming efforts for audio and video for LAUNCH. He has been responsible for procuring and managing the site's Live@LAUNCH calendar of live video and audio recordings for its Artist of the Month and Emerging Artist of the Month programs, which have boosted and launched some of the most well-received new artists and albums of the past years.

Currently, Mr. Frank manages and oversees all artist promotions with record labels and supervises Yahoo! Music's audio and video programming. He has developed key relationships with all the major record labels, as well as many independent labels improving Yahoo! Music's comprehensive music and music-related content, resulting in premieres and exclusives from artists such as **Madonna**, **Eminem**, the **Dixie Chicks**, **Nelly**, **Jason Mraz**, **Jet**, **Linkin Park**, **50 Cent**, **Faith Hill**, **Coldplay**, and many more.

Prior to joining Yahoo! Music, Mr. Frank was senior music director at **The Box Music Network**, managing all daily music activity on the music video network, and coordinated programming efforts that doubled Nielsen ratings during his tenure and resulted in the network's first Emmy award. He has also acted as marketing and A&R for Ignition Records, managed a live music venue, programmed broadcast radio stations, and created two local music video shows.

Jerry Blair

Having spent 11 years at **Columbia Records**, with the last five years serving as executive vice president, Jerry Blair has overseen the development of the careers of **Mariah Carey**, the **Fugees**, **Destiny's Child**, **Jessica Simpson**, and **Train**, and directed the campaigns that saw **Bruce Springsteen**, **Billy Joel**, and **Aerosmith**'s greatest triumphs. At **Sony Music**, Mr. Blair participated in the vision to devise and execute the strategy to introduce **Ricky Martin**, **Marc Anthony**, and **Shakira** to the general market, culminating in hundreds of millions of dollars in worldwide revenue.

At **Arista Records** he helped develop campaigns for **Non-Fronteras**, **Aterciopelados**, and **Santana**. As executive vice president of the label, Mr. Blair also directed the campaigns that broke **Usher**, **Outkast**, **Pink**, and **Dido**.

Jim Barber

Jim Barber is a producer and writer based in Los Angeles. His recent projects included **Ryan Adams**, **Courtney Love**, **Family Force 5**, and **Taylor Sorensen & The Trigger Code**. Over the course of a 20-year career, he's worked as an A&R executive at **Geffen Records** (**Girls Against Boys**, **Black Lab**, **Lisa Loeb**, **Hole**, **Aimee Mann**, **Guns N' Roses**), a manager (**drivin' n' cryin'**, **Adam Schmitt**, **Dumptruck,** and **Christmas**), a music publisher, radio DJ, and tour manager. His family is still waiting for him to get a real job.

John Brodey

John Brodey is a 25-year veteran of the music business. He has held many executive positions, including senior vice president of **Polygram Records**, vice president of promotion for **Mercury Records**, national director of promotion for **Geffen Records**, director of East Coast operations for **Casablanca Records**, general manager for **Giant Records and Films**, and, last but not least, a summer intern at the White House (true).

Mr. Brodey managed promotion and marketing campaigns that broke such artists as **Vanessa Williams**, **Tears for Fears**, **Tony! Toni! Toné!**, **Color Me Badd**, **Jade**, the **Eagles**, the *New Jack City* soundtrack, **Peter Gabriel**'s *So* album, **Whitesnake**, **Guns N' Roses**, **Cher**, **Def Leppard**, **John Mellencamp**, the **Scorpions**, **Bananarama**, and **Big Head Todd and the Monsters**.

He's also led marketing and sales campaigns that secured contracts with dominant radio stations in the top 50 markets of the country. He's worked with **Clear Channel**, **Emmis**, **Infinity**, and **ABC Broadcast** groups.

Leslie Zigel

Leslie José Zigel is an accomplished entertainment attorney whose practice focuses on counseling international entertainment-related clients. He is also a shareholder in **Greenberg Traurig**'s Miami office. Clients include **Kendra Todd** (winner on *The Apprentice 3*), **Nestor Torres**, **Raul DiBlasio**, and **Don Francisco**.

Prior to joining Greenberg Traurig, Mr. Zigel was vice president of business and legal affairs with **BMG**'s Latin American Regional Office and US Latin Operations. He was also a producer of music festivals and entertainment-related marketing initiatives for Fortune 500 companies before becoming an attorney. His diverse experience both on the creative and business sides coupled with his experience as an entertainment industry attorney gives him unique and pragmatic insight into the entertainment clients' needs.

Mr. Zigel has been a presenter or panelist at the **2003** *Billboard* **Latin Music Conference**, **2003 Copyright Society of the USA** mid-winter meeting, **2002 Entertainment & Sports Lawyer** annual meeting of the Florida Bar, and **2001 United States Copyright Office International Symposium on the Effect of Technology on Copyright and Related Rights**, and a featured speaker at his alma mater, the University of Miami. Mr. Zigel is also often quoted as an industry expert and has been featured in Spanish on CNN en Español's *Economia y Finanzas* program. He is an accomplished musician, having performed professionally on acoustic and electric bass.

Mark Avsec

Before becoming a music lawyer, Mark Avsec earned a living as a studio musician, producer, and songwriter, writing over 300 songs, and producing more than 25 sound recordings for, among other artists, **Bon Jovi** ("She Don't Know Me"), **Donnie Iris** ("Ah! Leah!" and "Love Is Like a Rock"), and **Wild Cherry** ("Play That Funky Music, White Boy"). He is an American Music Award winner and has been nominated for two Grammy awards.

Mr. Avsec practices in the Intellectual Property Practice Group of **Benesch, Friedlander, Coplan & Aronoff, LLP**, and has also practiced extensively with the Corporate and Securities Practice Group. A litigator and business attorney, he focuses his practice on entertainment, copyright, and trademark, particularly music industry and e-business matters, including private equity investments in music companies, copyright and trademark litigation, and other legal support with respect to various types of entertainment, Internet, media, and software companies.

Mr. Avsec serves as an Adjunct Law Professor at Case Western Reserve University School of Law, where he teaches "Law of the Music Industry." In 2004, he authored the following publications: "Nonconventional Musical Analysis and 'Disguised' Infringement: Clever Musical Tricks to Divide the Wealth of Tin Pan Alley," 52 Clev. St. L. Rev. 339 (2004–2005); and "*Bridgeport Music, Inc. v. Dimension Films LLC*: A New Standard as to What Constitutes Actionable Infringement of Sound Recordings in the Sixth Circuit," *New York State Bar Association Entertainment, Art and Sports Law Journal*, Vol. 15, No. 3 (Winter 2004).

Michael Ostroff

Michael Ostroff is executive vice president of business and legal affairs for the **Universal Music Group** (UMG). Mr. Ostroff serves as UMG's chief legal officer worldwide. He joined UMG's predecessor, **MCA Records, Inc.**, in 1984 as associate director of business and legal affairs. Mr. Ostroff was named to his current position in 1998, after **Seagram**'s acquisition of **Polygram Records**. From 1981–1984, before joining MCA Records, Mr. Ostroff was an associate at the Beverly Hills law firm of **Rosenfeld, Meyer & Susman**.

Moses Avalon

Moses Avalon began his career as a New York record producer and recording engineer. His combined work with Grammy-winning recording artists has earned him five RIAA platinum record awards. Today he is the founder and CEO of the **Moses Avalon Company**, a unique organization that functions in a duel capacity as both artist rights advocate and one of the nation's leading music business consulting services. He is the author of a best-selling music industry reference, *Confessions of a Record Producer*, and *Secrets of Negotiating a Record Contract*, which is required reading in the music business curriculum of over 25 schools, including UCLA, Loyola Law School, and NYU. Mr. Avalon has also acted in an advisory capacity to the **Senate Judiciary Committee** in their campaign to help legitimize areas of the music business. His award-winning Web site, which discusses controversial issues in the music business and his advocacy efforts, can be visited at *www.MosesAvalon.com*. His syndicated newsletter, *Moses Supposes*, which features informed editorials on the inner workings of the music business, reaches thousands of subscribers each month.

Paul Menes

Paul Menes is a partner and co-head of the entertainment law practice at **Tyre Kamins Katz Granof & Menes**, an AV-rated Westside boutique firm founded over 50 years ago. His practice focuses on entertainment and intellectual property–related matters and representation.

Mr. Menes has been a frequent speaker and writer on various entertainment matters, including **California Lawyers for the Arts**, the *Los Angeles Times*, the **UCLA and USC Music Business Seminars, Interactive 2000,** the **Music in the Digital Millennium** conference, **South by Southwest, Show Biz Expo, EAT'M,** the **International Association of Entertainment Lawyers,** and **North by Northwest,** among others. He has been profiled in several editions of *Who's Who in American Law.* Mr. Menes is also a member of the **National Academy of Recording Arts and Sciences, International Association of Entertainment Lawyers, National Association of Record Industry Professionals,** and various local and national bar and trade associations.

Peter Spellman

Peter Spellman is director of career development at **Berklee College of Music** in Boston and the author of several handbooks on the music business, including *The Self-Promoting Musician: Strategies for Independent Music Success* (2000, Berklee Press), *The Musician's Internet: Online Strategies for Success in the Music Industry* (2002, Berklee Press), and his latest, *Indie Power: A Business-Building Guide for Record Labels, Music Production Houses and Merchant Musicians* (2004, MBS Business Media).

Mr. Spellman has been a performer, arranger, producer, record label director, booking agent, artist manager, and music journalist. In addition, he teaches courses on entrepreneurship, music publishing, and music marketing at the University of Massachusetts–Lowell and offers a popular online course at *Berkleemusic.com.*

With over 20 years' experience as a performing and recording musician, Mr. Spellman started **Music Business Solutions** (*www.mbsolutions.com*) as a training ground for 21st-century music entrepreneurs. He performs regularly as percussionist with world music ensemble **Friend Planet**, and sings folk songs to his kids before bed.

Ritch Ezra

Ritch Ezra started out as a promotion coordinator for **A&M Records** in Los Angeles in 1980–1981. From 1981–1987, he was director of West Coast A&R for **Arista Records**. He signed the **Thompson Twins** and **Mara Getz**, a great pop singer. He also worked with **Whitney Houston, Aretha Franklin, Dionne Warwick, Melissa**

Manchester, **Tanya Tucker**, **Jennifer Warnes**, and **Jermaine Jackson**, and coordinated music for the *Ghostbusters* and *Perfect* soundtracks.

From 1987–1994, Mr. Ezra was an instructor at the **Trebas Institute of Recording Arts** in Los Angeles and UCLA. He was a member of the board of advisors for the Department of Performing Arts at UCLA, and initiated full-day seminars and discussion panels on the music business as well as created new course ideas and methods for expanding programs to keep students enrolled.

Since 1992, Ritch Ezra has been co-running the **Music Business Registry**, which includes the **A&R Registry**, the **Publisher Registry**, the **Music Business Attorney Registry** and the **Film and Television Music Guide**.

Ron Gertz

Ron Gertz is the president and CEO of **Music Reports, Inc.**, a company that represents broadcasters and other entities in their music licensing relationships with music publishers, composers, and the music performing rights organizations (ASCAP, BMI, and SESAC) as well as record labels and the recording industry (RIAA, SoundExchange) in the digital delivery of sound recordings.

Mr. Gertz specializes in both the private and governmental regulation of music licensing rights and royalty administration. He has been a participant in key legislative and regulatory initiatives to establish the ground rules for digital music licensing. He has also participated in significant rate-setting proceedings under both the ASCAP and BMI consent decrees and in Copyright Office arbitrations and rulemaking proceedings.

Mr. Gertz is a former chair of the Intellectual Property Section of the Los Angeles County Bar Association and a past president of the **California Copyright Conference**. He has been a director of the **National Academy of Songwriters** and a member of the **Interactive Multimedia Association's Intellectual Property Task Force**. He is currently on the board of directors of the **Broadcast Cable Financial Managers Association**.

Mr. Gertz was trained as a classical vocalist and guitarist, and has performed professionally in many rock tours.

A Million Dollars' Worth of Mistakes

The Top Reasons Why

Artists Fail

To begin research for this book I posted a survey on the Internet. It was taken by more than 100 music business professionals. Here are the results. They are broken down into what those on the creative side thought versus those on the business side. Sometimes there is overlap.

Creative Side

- Thinking that all it takes to be successful is talent. Waiting around to have your genius recognized.
- Assuming that things will be taken care of once you get signed.
- Not being naturally musical.
- Getting into the business for the money.
- Thinking that just because you have had some modicum of success, you deserve more.
- Not getting your own attorney, often using the same (not-so-ethical) attorney as the manager or label.
- Not adapting to the ever-changing technology.
- Leaving the business end to someone else.

- Believing that a major record deal with a major label is the holy grail.
- Believing the way the media portrays the music industry.
- Thinking that you have a future when you proceed in the old business model.
- Failing to understand that the business is 10 percent sexy and 90 percent mundane.
- Not being able to change with the times.
- Management giving too much power to the artist.
- Ignoring your fan base's requests.
- Management being so in love with the music and the personality as to not be able to stay objective and do the best job possible for the artist.
- Failing to register copyrights/trademarks, scrutinize accountings, and/or clear samples.
- Thinking your going to have the next big hit because "…there's nothing good on the radio," so the industry must be starving for talent.
- Overloading others with too much information, be it songs or insignificant details about your life.
- Thinking that the hype in *Rolling Stone* or on MTV is really the way artists behave, record, and perform.
- Telling people your age and all the bands you've been in or sessions you've done. This marks you as a loser.
- Thinking there's something wrong with you because everyone you know is already famous. They just kissed more ass or had better drugs or more powerful friends and didn't tell you.
- Thinking you can get by with a demo or, in layman's terms, a crappy-sounding recording.
- Burning bridges unless you have absolutely no other choice and only if you can justify your actions.
- Trusting a lawyer.
- Not understanding that no deal is infinitely better than a bad deal.
- The delicacy of a winning team that has produced success is hugely underrated by most established artists.
- In terms of writers, failing to learn the publishing business.

Business Side

- Taking on projects strictly for cash, projects that you don't believe in musically.
- Believing that just because you have a kind and generous heart, clients will flock to you.
- Spending a bunch of time and money on an artist prior to having a contract with them.
- Listening to people's demos while they are sitting there in your office.
- Getting cocky and trying to do management, lawyering, and more for artists, which leads to many conflicts of interest.
- Introducing a competitor to a client.
- Not having a good understanding of musicians/artists.
- Typecasting yourself by saying you only do one style of music.
- Believing that who you are makes a big difference in whether your artist is going to get signed to a major deal.
- Believing that a major record deal with a major label is the holy grail.
- Believing that the music business is about the business and not the music.
- Getting in way over your head with commitments (financial and otherwise) to artists, distributors, publicists, and so on.
- Not keeping up with the latest legal and business trends.
- Thinking that discovering a great act will make you rich and famous. It'll make somebody rich and famous, it just won't be you. In fact, it will probably get you fired after they take all the credit.
- Becoming arrogant or greedy.
- Taking a good artist and trying to push them into a style that may not be right for them.
- As a label executive, signing an artist who is extremely talented musically but does not have the drive and/or social skills to match.
- Not understanding that no deal is infinitely better than a bad deal.
- Spending your own money.

> About the Author

Who Is Moses Avalon and What Is the Moses Avalon Company?

Mr. Avalon began his career as a New York record producer and recording engineer. His combined work of producing and engineering with Grammy® award-winning recording artists has earned him several RIAA Gold & Platinum record awards. His soundtrack compositions have been used in films that went on to win outstanding achievement awards at Cannes, The New York Expo, and WorldFest. Today he is an artist's rights activist, author, educator, and consultant. Mr. Avalon has also acted in an advisory capacity to the **Senate Judiciary Committee in Sacramento**, the **Department of Justice**, and two **State Attorney Generals'** offices, in their campaign to help legitimize areas of the music business. His syndicated newsletter, *Moses Supposes*, which features satirical editorials on the inner workings of the music business, reaches thousands of subscribers each month. He is an active lecturer around the world and CEO of **The Moses Avalon Company**, a music business consulting firm and artist's rights advocacy organization. Through the Company Mr. Avalon and a team of advisors help and educate emerging artists about progressing their career and safeguarding their rights. The Moses Avalon Company also handles established artists for such things as expert witness testimony, contract analysis, and dispute resolution. His advocacy efforts can be reviewed at www.MosesAvalon.com.

Take the Confessions of a Record Producer Workshop

Now you can learn how the record business *really* works from one of the country's leading experts at the *Confessions of a Record Producer Workshop*. This acclaimed two-day workshop, attended by top industry pros, reveals tricks of the trade to help songwriters and artists protect their money and their rights. Learn what the most successful artists, managers, producers, and lawyers already know:

- How to get a six-figure advance.
- Protecting songs from copyright theft.

- Using digital distribution as an alternative to a major label.
- Getting out of bad contracts.
- The latest issues regarding artists' rights, the internet, and domain names.
- Revenue streams examined up close with *real dollar values.*

Hosted live by **Moses Avalon**, author of ***Million Dollar Mistakes:*** *Steering Your Music Career Clear of Lies, Cons, Catastrophes, and Landmines.*

"I was never quite able to decode the terms and cash flow of a record deal till I did the Confessions Workshop." —Geza X, **Producer**, Meredith Brooks, Dead Kennedys, **Los Angeles**

"Not one single music business workshop in the last ten years comes at a close second. It's worth ten times what you pay and it won't last forever." —Dave Paton, Booking Agent: **Van Halen**, **Tom Petty**, **Twisted Sister**

"The Confessions Workshop is an extremely valuable tool for the new artist who needs to be realistic about their first recording contract." —Philip K. Lyon, Attorney, Nashville, TN, whose firm represents **Kenny Rogers** and **David Allan Coe**

Don't sound like this in 10 years:

"Recording companies really, really do conspire against the artists."
—**Michael Jackson**

"Our record company, after selling 70 million [of our] records, still tells us we are unrecouped." —**Kevin Richardson, Backstreet Boys**

For information and calendar go to: **wwwMosesAvalon.com**

> Index

Record Plant studio, 12
recording engineers
    getting payment authorized, 14
    Hollywood vs. real music business, 34
    interviewed in this book, 214–220
    lies of, 10–13
    lies told by, 10–13
    tough choices of, 74–78
Recording Industry Association of
    America (RIAA), 174
Relativity Records, 61
release dates, Hollywood vs. real music
    business, 34
Rembrandt, 201
re-mixers, 99
renogotiation, 144–146
respect, 24–27
résumés, lies on, 2
Resurrection Boulevard, 26
Rhodes, Nick, 164–165
RIAA (Recording Industry Association of
    America), 174
Ricketts, David, 101
Righteous Babe records, 169–171
"rights aggregators," 202
"Rio" (Duran Duran), 164–165
Ripp, Artie, 157–159
"roll ups," 154–155
Rolling Stones, 42, 99
Ross, Michael C., 48, 219
Roth, David Lee, 110
royalties. *see also* copyrights
    black box accounts and, 175
    blanket licensing deals and, 197
    British vs. US law, 163–164
    rack jobbers controversy, 145
    record one, 136
    suspension and, 145
    using subscription model, 196
Royalty Calculator, 136, 193
Royalty Logic, 203
Ruffin, David, 147
Rufus, 160–161

S

SACEM, 173
Sade, 162–163
sample clearance, 148
Sanctuary, 138
satellite radio, 201
schmaltz, 19–20
Schwarzenegger, Arnold, 190
Seagram's Liquors, 166
sex, 111–114
Sex Pistols, 28
"She's Got a Way" (Joel), 157
shmearing, 124

signability, 204
Silent Partner Consulting, 223
singles
    making money on, 196–197
    Napster driven by, 194–195
    in next thirty years, 202
Skin Yard, 215
"Small Blue Thing" (Vega), 43
The Smiths, 164
"Smooth Operator" (Sade), 162–163
Snider, Dee, 163
"social face," 3
sociopaths, 15
Solitude Standing (Vega), 43
songs, Hollywood vs. real business of
    recording, 34
songwriters
    Billy Joel story, 157–159
    copyright mistakes of. *see* copyrights
    of Garry Glenn, 146–147
    money possibilities for, 29, 154
    politics and, 116
    withholding material, 159
Songwriters Guild, 132–133
Sonny Bono Copyright Extension Act,
    209
Sony, 168
SoundExchange, 203
South by Southwest (SXSW)
    symposium, 22
Space Shot Orchestra, 217
spammer, 182–183
Spears, Britney
    Debbie Gibson as precursor to, 140
    Joni Mitchell on, 129
    Mariah Carey vs., 110
    using product placement, 205
Spector, Phil, 36
Spellman, Peter, 22–24, 228
sport shows, 201
spouses, 177–185
    conclusion, 185
    family planning and, 181–184
    heritage acts, 179–181
    spousal abuse and, 177–179
"Stairway to Heaven" (Led Zeppelin),
    128
standards
    CD quality vs. LP, 206
    digital transmission, 195
Starkey, Richard, 162
Starr, Ringo, 162
statutory rates, 154
stealing
    morality of, 49–52
    music off Internet, 191
Steely Dan, 209